BUILDING A NEW YEMEN

BUILDING A NEW YEMEN

Recovery, Transition, and the International Community

Edited by
Amat Al Alim Alsoswa and Noel Brehony

I.B. TAURIS
LONDON • NEW YORK • OXFORD • NEW DELHI • SYDNEY

I.B. TAURIS
Bloomsbury Publishing Plc
50 Bedford Square, London, WC1B 3DP, UK
1385 Broadway, New York, NY 10018, USA
29 Earlsfort Terrace, Dublin 2, Ireland

BLOOMSBURY, I.B. TAURIS and the I.B. Tauris logo are trademarks of Bloomsbury
Publishing Plc

First published in Great Britain 2022
This paperback edition published 2023

Series design by Adriana Brioso
Cover image © Corbis News/Getty Images

A catalogue record for this book is available from the British Library.

A catalog record for this book is available from the Library of Congress.

ISBN: HB: 978-0-7556-4026-3
PB: 978-0-7556-4030-0
ePDF: 978-0-7556-4027-0
eBook: 978-0-7556-4028-7

Typeset by Deanta Global Publishing Services, Chennai, India

To find out more about our authors and books visit www.bloomsbury.com and
sign up for our newsletters.

CONTENTS

ACKNOWLEDGMENTS

We began recruiting authors for the book in late 2018 and we have had to adjust our thinking about the future of Yemen while the war continued and concentrate as far as possible on the issues that will be important no matter how the war ends, and Yemenis build their future. The editors are grateful for the patience and understanding of the authors over the length of the process. Sophie Rudland, our editor at Bloomsbury (I. B. Tauris), has been immensely helpful throughout, and we want to acknowledge the contribution of Sebastian Ballard to the maps.

CONTRIBUTORS

Rafat Ali Al-Akhali has been active in the field of youth development and youth political inclusion since 2004, and a peace building practitioner since 2015 focused on Yemen. Rafat is a fellow of practice at the Blavatnik School of Government, University of Oxford, where he is currently the Convenor of the Council on State Fragility; he previously managed the LSE-Oxford Commission on State Fragility, Growth and Development and the Pathways for Prosperity Commission on Technology and Inclusive Development. Rafat previously served as minister of youth and sports in the government of Yemen, and prior to that was leading the policy reforms team at the Executive Bureau for Acceleration of Aid Absorption and Support for Policy Reforms. Rafat earned his second master's degree in public policy (MPP) at the Blavatnik School of Government. His first master's degree was in business administration (MBA) from Ecole des Hautes Etudes Commerciales, Montréal, Canada.

Maysaa Shujaa Al-Deen is a Yemeni researcher and writer, who writes for several media outlets and research centers such as al-Monitor, Carnegie, Democracy Now, Atlantic Council, Al-Jazeera Studies, and Arab Reform Initiative Center. She is a non-resident fellow at the Sana´a Center for Strategic Studies. Maysaa holds a master's degree in Islamic studies from the American University in Cairo, on the subject "Radicalization of Zaydi Reform Attempts."

Amat Alsoswa served as Yemen's first woman minister for human rights, as Yemen's ambassador to the Netherlands, and as undersecretary and assistant deputy minister of information. For over six years she served as assistant secretary general, UNDP assistant administrator, and regional director of the Arab States Bureau, and has consulted with the World Bank for which she authored a number of reports. Between March 2013 and January 2014, she participated in Yemen's National Dialogue Conference (NDC) as a member of NDC's State Building Team and Chair of the Sub-Commission for Drafting the Criteria for, and Selection of Members of the Constitution Drafting Committee. In 2014/15 she was managing director of the Executive Bureau for the Acceleration of Aid Absorption and Support for Policy Reforms in Yemen. In this role she monitored and evaluated the set of reforms agreed upon by the government with regard to enhancing Yemen's energy sector, harmonizing the Public Investment Program with the country's public budget, improving the civil service Biometric Fingerprint System, adopting the International Monetary Fund (IMF) program on economic and monetary reforms, strengthening Public-Private Partnerships (PPP), adopting labour-intensive work projects for youth and women, and supporting the government's efforts to eradicate malnutrition and address humanitarian issues.

Sabria Mohammed Al-Thawr is a lecturer and researcher at Sana´a University, Gender Development Research and Studies Center (GDRSC). Her research expertise includes the topics of gender, development, conflict, and citizenship. Al-Thawr is working on her PhD in the field of international development, titled "Citizenship in Transition: Issues of Gender, Class, and Ethnicity" at Roskilde University, Denmark. Prior to this, she got her M.Ed. degree in Curriculum and Teaching Methodology in 1997. Ms. Al-Thawr has worked with various international development agencies such as various UN agencies, World Bank, GIZ, NDI, USAID, AED, ADRA, and Oxfam over the past fourteen years. Her main field of expertise includes conducting research and surveys, assessments, training and facilitation in education, and gender and conflict analysis in tribal areas. She has several publications related to various development, gender, and education issues in Yemen and the MENA region.

Hussein Alwaday is a communication expert and writer. He has written analyses and papers for several research centers and think tanks including Al-Jazeera Center for Studies, Yemen Policy Center, and Arab Reform Initiative, providing insight into understanding the roots and dynamics of the ongoing conflict in Yemen since the Arab Spring. He is an active Op-ed writer in several international and leading pan-Arab newspapers and websites including Al-Nahar newspaper, Daraj Media, Marayna, Irfa'a Sautak, and Huna Sautak. His writings cover a wide range of issues related to sectarianism, political Islam, terrorism waves, Islamic and Arabic thought, and the secularism debate in the Arab world. During the last decade he developed national communication and development strategies for prominent international organizations such as USAID, Oxfam, and UN.

Laurent Bonnefoy is a CNRS researcher at the Centre Français de Recherche de la Péninsule Arabique (CEFREPA) and an invited researcher at the Omani Studies Center of Sultan Qaboos University in Oman. He has written extensively on political, social, and religious dynamics in contemporary Yemen. Among many other publications, he is the author of *Salafism in Yemen: Transnationalism and Religious Identity* (Hurst, 2011) and *Yemen and the World: Beyond Insecurity* (Hurst, 2018).

Noel Brehony is an honorary vice president and former Chair of the British Yemeni Society. He has followed events in Yemen since the 1970s when he was a British diplomat serving in the Middle East, including Aden. He was later Middle East director for Rolls-Royce and Chair of Menas Associates. He is a former president of the British Society for Middle East Studies and former Chair of the Council for British Research in the Levant. He is the author of *Yemen Divided* (IB Tauris 2011), editor of *Hadhramaut and Its Diaspora* (IB Tauris 2017 and King Faisal Center 2018), co-editor of *Rebuilding Yemen* (Gerlach 2015 and King Faisal Center 2017), co-editor with Stephen Day of *Global, Regional, and Local Dynamics in the Yemen Crisis* (Palgrave Macmillan 2020), and co-editor of *Britain's Departure from Aden and South Arabia* (Gerlach 2020).

Joana Cook is an assistant professor of terrorism and political violence at Leiden University and a senior project manager at the International Center for Counter-Terrorism (ICCT, the Hague), as well as editor in chief of the ICCT journal. Joana is also an adjunct lecturer at Johns Hopkins University where she teaches on "Radicalization in Terrorist Networks." Her additional affiliations are as non-resident fellow on the Program on Extremism at George Washington University; research affiliate with the Canadian Network for Research on Terrorism, Security, and Society (TSAS); and digital fellow at the Montreal Institute for Genocide and Human Rights Studies (MIGS) at Concordia University. She has published extensively on the topics of women in terrorism and counterterrorism, and more recently on terrorist governance. She has presented her research to senior government and security audiences in a number of countries, and at institutions such as the UN Security Council, NATO, and the Parliamentary Assembly of the Council of Europe. She has been featured in media such as *Time*, the *Telegraph*, the *Washington Post*, the *New York Times*, and on *BBC World News, CNN, Sky News, BBC Radio*, the *National Post*, and *CBC*. In May 2019 she did her first TEDx talk on "women in security today." Her first book, *A Woman's Place: US Counterterrorism Since 9/11* was released in 2020 by Oxford University Press.

Stephen Day is adjunct professor of international affairs at Rollins College in Winter Park, FL, and former visiting assistant professor of Middle East Politics at St. Lawrence University and Stetson University. Between 2012 and 2014, he was designated a specialist in diplomacy, peace-making, and conflict resolution by the Fulbright scholarship organization. In addition to the numerous articles and book chapters he has published, he is the author of *Regionalism and Rebellion in Yemen: A Troubled National Union* (Cambridge UP 2012), and co-editor with Noel Brehony of Global, Regional and Local Dynamics in the Yemen Crisis (Palgrave Macmillan 2020).

Alia Eshaq is a Yemeni political analyst and entrepreneur. She is the co-founder and managing director of the Mashora Group, a public policy consultancy that focuses on the Middle East and Africa. Alia has a strong background in public policy with a focus on peace building and negotiations. She has worked for several years on the design and implementation of peace building projects. She has been a speaker at a number of international conferences and workshops focusing on the future of the Middle East. Alia worked for a few years in Yemen where she was closely involved with the National Dialogue Conference and the political transition process (2012–14). Following that, she was engaged in managing track 2 initiatives in Yemen focused on bringing key political stakeholders to dialogue (2014–18). Alia has a master's degree in public policy (St Hilda's, University of Oxford, 2014–15) and another in business administration (MBA, Hull International Business School, 2018–19).

James Firebrace graduated from Cambridge University with a BA and MA in social and political science, and later gained an MSc with distinction at the London Business School. His early career focused on the development challenges of the Middle East and Sahelian Africa, setting up, and running a number of consortia. A spell as director general of Consumers International led to extensive advisory work for the government and the private sector in the energy and water sectors. He set up James Firebrace Associates Ltd. in 1998, specializing in the analysis and management of longer-term strategic issues, particularly in relation to economic revitalization, energy, water security, sustainable livelihoods, innovation, and conflict prevention. He has published a range of analyses on Yemen's political, economic, and social challenges.

Helen Lackner is research associate at the School of Oriental and African Studies (SOAS), University of London, and visiting fellow at the European Council for Foreign Relations (ECFR). She worked as a consultant in social aspects of rural development for four decades in more than thirty countries of the Middle East, Asia, Africa, and Europe, including Yemen where she has spent more than fifteen years since the early 1970s. She writes extensively about the country's political economy as well as its social and economic issues, and is now focusing on trying to promote a commitment to equitable development and peace in Yemen. She is a regular contributor to *Open Democracy*, *Arab Digest*, and *Oxford Analytica*. Her first book, *A House Built on Sand: A Political Economy of Saudi Arabia (Ithaca Press)*, was published in 1978, and in 1985 she published *PDR Yemen: Outpost of Socialist Development in Arabia* (Ithaca Press). She has edited *Why Yemen Matters: A Society in Transition* (Saqi Books 2014), and co-edited *Yemen and the Gulf States: The Making of a Crisis* (Gerlach 2017), along with other books. Her latest book, *Yemen in Crisis: The Road to War*, was published in the United States by Verso in 2019.

Charles Schmitz is a professor of geography at Towson University in Baltimore, MD. He began his career as a Fulbright scholar in Lahej in the early 1990s. In the 2000s he worked for the American Institute for Yemeni Studies and was affiliated with the Middle East Institute in Washington. His current research interests are in religious change in Yemen, nationalism and regionalism, the geography of tribalism, and Yemen's political economy.

Bilkis Zabara worked as the director of the Gender Development Research and Studies Center (GDRSC), Sana´a University (SU), from 2011 to 2018 and acted as the manager of a master's program in international development and gender. Earlier she was the manager of a master's program in Integrated Water Resources Management at the Water and Environment Centre, SU. She holds a PhD in physical chemistry from SU (2004) and teaches chemistry at the Faculty of Science. Zabara tries to link gender issues with natural resources, conflict, development, and post-conflict reconstruction. Since 2005 she has worked on several academic and consultancy projects related to water, gender, and peace building with national, regional, and international partner research institutions and organizations. Among her publications are Al-Gawfi, Iman; Zabara Bilkis, Yadav Stacey (2020); The Role of Women in Peace building in Yemen (https://carpo-bonn.org/en/portfolio/ carpo-brief-14-the-role-of-women-in-peacebuilding-in-yemen/) Zabara, Bilkis and Ahmad, Abdulbari (2020). Biomass Waste in Yemen: Management and Challenges. (https://link.springer.com/chapter/10.1007/978-3-030-18350-9_160 .1007/978-3-030-18350-9_16.), Zabara, Bilkis (2018), Enhancing Women's Role in Water Management in Yemen. (https://carpo-bonn.org/wp-content/uploads/2018 /03/09_carpo_brief_final.pdf).

Notes on Transliteration

We have used the simplest method of transliterating Arabic into English. The only symbol used is representing ʿayn when it appears in the middle of words. Whilst trying to be as consistent as possible we have retained in references and quotations the transliterations used by the original authors.

INTRODUCTION

Writing and editing a book about post-conflict Yemen in early 2021, as the war continues, may seem a futile endeavor. Six years of conflict have damaged or destroyed Yemen's political, economic, and even social infrastructure. The cost in lives (possibly more than 230,000) and of war damage ($29 billion) is staggering, as is the number of men, women, and children who still live on the brink of famine (up to 16.2 million) six years into the world's worst humanitarian disaster. And these figures do not even reflect COVID-19's acute impact on Yemen. It raced through Yemeni society, lethal yet unremarkable, as overwhelmed public health officials and disinterested rulers lacked the means to measure its spread or disentangle it from the malnutrition and myriad other communicable diseases that have made death so common.

Though this damage far outpaces any grievances at the root of the current violence, the conflict's Yemeni and non-Yemeni participants say they want the war to end while making clear that they will not compromise to end it. Given this impasse, the editors and authors can only outline the problems faced by, and suggest policy fixes for, Yemen's post-war regime (or, just as likely, regimes), while hoping that exhausted domestic parties, regional neighbors wary of Yemen's large population and history of instability, and international concerns over al-Qaeda in the Arabian Peninsula's (AQAP) reemergence convince all involved that it is better to build a new Yemen than continue destroying the current one.

To focus their contributions, the authors graciously accepted three key requests: First, to be future-oriented without indulging in too much blue-sky thinking, while also having regard for Yemen's past without being imprisoned by it. No easy feat! In looking forward toward the problems that future regime(s) will address, they were asked to take account of current realities and to base their suggestions on what has and has not worked in Yemen in recent decades. Such a balancing act is tricky but essential for new thinking on post-conflict reconstruction. The occasional comparative perspective, as expanded in Firebrace and Eshaq's discussion and "futures thinking," and their knowledge of post-conflict recovery in Africa, was also welcome (Chapter 10).

Second, the authors were asked to write what they know. This volume is not intended to be a comprehensive study of the post-war situation, and by focusing on their areas of expertise, this collection of authors successfully detail key political, social, and economic concerns in focused, intelligent interventions. The first few chapters examine the political context with a special focus on the likely future structure of the state, including the role of women, and security issues and the remaining focus on the most significant sectors of Yemen's political economy.

Third, the editors wanted to assist the authors in avoiding the reproduction of prevailing conflict narratives so succinctly laid out by Laurent Bonnefoy in Chapter 1. The story of Yemen's conflict is not as straightforward as ratified by international powers in UN Security Council Resolution 2216, in which a Saudi-led coalition labors to uphold international law, restore an internationally recognized government, and wrest control of the country away from Iran-backed rebels. Nor is it one of unparalleled external aggression on Yemen's people, with the Saudis almost solely responsible for the country's grave humanitarian crisis. Adherence to these narratives has only clouded past interventions by policymakers and international organizations and would be sure to distort any fresh political analyses and resulting policy prescriptions.

For readers, however, the persistence of these narratives does pose a challenge: Is there a reasonable overview of Yemen's recent past and present political, economic, and social circumstances on which we can base, for the purpose of conversation, our future thinking? Mindful of our own fallibility, we will attempt to sketch such an overview in what follows.

War and Politics, Past and Present

Yemen has a long history, and it is no stranger to prosperity, on the one hand, and chaos, division, and famine, on the other. The Greeks and Romans knew it as *Arabia Felix* ("Happy Arabia"), and in medieval times, particularly under the Rasulids (1229 to 1454 C.E.), it was renowned for its wealth and cultural achievements.

The rise of the first Zaydi imamate in the tenth century established a loose pattern for present-day Yemen—an expansion-minded political/religious elite in the northwest, and fragmented polities in the south and east—through (at least) the founding of the Yemen Arab Republic in 1962. For centuries, Zaydi imams stitched together alliances among powerful but fractious and mostly Zaydi northern tribes to rule the northwest but were usually contained by powerful regimes based in the mainly Sunni-Shafi'i Lower Yemen, as outlined by Stephen Day in Chapter 2. Following the Ottoman occupation in the sixteenth century, the Qasimi Imams for a few decades were able to expand into Lower Yemen and the south. After the British arrived in Aden in 1839, they extended their influence into what is now south Yemen, signing protection agreements with the sultanates, emirates, and sheikdoms that had cast off rule by the Imam a century before.

The British and the Ottomans agreed to a border dividing north and south Yemen in 1905, without reference to the views of the Imam. The overthrow of the imamate in 1962 sparked an eight-year civil war that, like the current war, involved both Yemeni combatants and regional powers. Yemen recovered quickly, benefiting from more favorable economic circumstances than exist today: Yemen's population, now at thirty million, numbered only six million in 1970.

In the midst of the war, north Yemen provided a base that enabled revolutionaries to fight the British in the south and set up what became the Marxist People's Democratic Republic of Yemen (PDRY) in 1967. Civil war in the north ended in a negotiated solution, but government was unstable until the emergence of the regime of Ali Abdullah Saleh in 1978. Successive governments in both the YAR and the PDRY sought to unify Yemen, but each wanted to achieve unity on its own terms (Brehony 2011). The two Yemens were finally brought together in 1990 after internecine conflict in 1986, and the Soviet Union's patronage-sapping collapse in 1989 weakened the south. Flaws in the unity agreement led to a civil war in 1994 that saw the imposition of Saleh's rule over the whole country; in the 2000s, Saleh's marginalization of southern political and economic aspirations precipitated the resurgence of a southern nationalism now manifest in the separatist policies of the Southern Transition Council (STC).

Despite his recent death, the effects of Saleh's thirty-three-year regime remain. He—as had the Imams—built his political rule with the support of the major tribal confederations (Hashid and Bakil) of Upper Yemen whilst placing his own relatives and personal supporters in key positions in the military and national security bureaucracies. A boost in state revenues from oil exports after 1990, a major benefit of uniting with the relatively resource-rich south, sustained inclusive patronage networks which drew in politicians, military officers, tribal leaders, and businessmen; opponents of Saleh were excluded or marginalized. Saleh' s political party, the General People's Congress (GPC), proved an effective vehicle for mobilizing voters to win presidential and parliamentary elections.

To understand Saleh's longevity, one can reference the careers of figures like Sheikh Abdullah Hussein al-Ahmar, the head of the Hashid Tribal Confederation until his death in 2007. He shared Saleh's interest in maintaining patronage networks that benefited a privileged elite (Sarah Phillips, 2011). Sheikh Abdullah also headed the Yemeni Congregation for Reform—Islah—a conservative political party founded in 1990 which brought into a coalition Sheikh Abdullah's tribal elite, emerging business leaders, the Yemeni version of the Muslim Brotherhood, and even some Salafis.

While such a potent emerging coalition may have unnerved other authoritarian leaders, for Saleh, Islah, and Sheikh Abdullah it presented an opportunity. Within the relatively open, parliamentary system that governed Yemen post-unification, he used Islah to balance against the influence of the Yemeni Socialist Party (YSP), sprung from the PDRY and its allies in the YAR, and to maintain the superior position of the GPC. Saleh was mastering the strategy of "divide and rule"—what he once artfully described as "dancing on the heads of snakes"—to keep both allies and enemies off balance.

Where the utility of parliamentary politics ended, Saleh had no problem turning to strongmen to address his domestic concerns. Another close ally of Saleh was the current vice president of Yemen's internationally recognized government, Ali Mohsen al-Ahmar (no relation to Sheikh Abdullah), a military commander who played a conspicuous role in both defeating the southern army in 1994 and leading the domestic battles against the Huthis in the 2000s. A mostly behind-the-scenes figure until his dramatic break with Saleh during 2011's Arab Spring, he slotted well into an elite-driven political system that countenanced some disagreement while keeping the patronage widespread; al-Ahmar doubles as both a member of the GPC and a known supporter of Islah.

After oil revenues peaked in 2003, Yemen's elite increasingly competed for the diminishing resources, opening fissures within the regime. At the same time, Saleh's erstwhile allies—Sheikh Abdullah's sons and Ali Mohsen—fell out with Saleh and frustrated his plan to both extend his rule and to position his son Ahmad as his successor. These fissures manifested politically in the mid-2000s, when Islah united with the YSP and a set of smaller parties to form the Joint Meeting Parties (JMP), which sought to contest the GPC's parliamentary dominance. Then Sheikh Abdullah's death in December 2007 removed a restraining hand and intensified this rivalry.

During this period, Saleh began a dangerous encounter with the emerging Huthi movement, one which eventually led to his death in 2017. The Huthis, named after their founding figure Hussein Badr al-Din al-Huthi, emerged from a Zaydi revivalist movement in the 1980s and 1990s that spoke particularly (but not solely) to northern elites and former elites whose status (however local or relative) eroded after the imamate's overthrow. An influential subset of these elites were *sada* (also known as Hashemites), or those families claiming descent from the Prophet Muhammad through his grandsons Hassan and Hussein, a lineage celebrated in Zaydi belief (the al-Huthi family is itself Hashemite). These individuals and families, who felt cut out of the YAR's development policies and Saleh's patronage network, rallied around Hussein al-Huthi's blend of political populism, religious fundamentalism, and conspiracy-minded anti-imperialism. After tensions between the growing movement and an increasingly wary government came to a head in 2004, the first of the six "Sa'ada wars" ended in Hussein's killing and the advent of a durable martyrdom narrative (Brandt 2017).

Violent conflict only grew the Huthis' base and ambitions. During these wars, the Huthis, now led by Hussein's brother Abd al-Malik al-Huthi and their tribal allies acquired the fighting and organizational skills that helped them to take control of Sana'a in September 2014 and to fight the Saudi-led coalition through to the present day. Yet even as leading general Ali Mohsen al-Ahmar bitterly fought the Huthis, Saleh continued his divide-and-rule tactics through occasional, discreet support that kept the Zaydi group strong enough to balance against the Sunni-oriented Islah party and the more militant Salafist elements in the north; Saleh's policies were also a factor in exacerbating longer-term weakening of the influence of local tribal sheikhs that the Huthis were able to exploit (Chapter 3). Meanwhile, southerners disenchanted by Saleh's policies in the south backed Hirak, a movement formed in 2007 that sought to restore an independent south (Chapter 2). The longer-term effects of this divide-and-rule game continue to plague Yemen as do the corruption and other ills of the Saleh period.

The Arab Spring's 2011 arrival fatally fractured the regime. In June and September 2011, civil conflict seemed likely between Saleh on one side and Ali Mohsen and the sons of the late Sheikh Abdullah on the other, this latter camp splitting from Saleh and nominally adopting the protesters' demands for a new government. Eager to shuffle Saleh off the scene, regional and global powers intervened to negotiate the "Gulf Cooperation Council Initiative." Saudi Arabia and other wealthy Gulf neighbors of Yemen, supported by the United States and major western powers, negotiated a deal for Saleh's resignation in February 2012 in exchange for immunity for himself and his family. Out of this deal, Yemenis got the stage-managed election of President Abdo Rabbuh Mansour Hadi, Saleh's longtime vice president, in 2012, alongside a coalition government of the GPC and Islah-dominated JMP. A key part of the transition was an inclusive National Dialogue Conference (NDC) which eventually produced the recommendations that provided the basis for drafting a new constitution at the end of 2014.

The GCC Initiative could not survive its flaws. It permitted Saleh to stay in Yemen as head of the GPC, and he used his influence to undermine President Hadi and the transitional government, undeterred by UN sanctions. Hadi, a southerner who had fled to Sana'a in 1986, may have been head of state, but he lacked a strong power base in the north and antagonized parts of the northern elite by appearing to favor politicians from Abyan, his home governorate. An essential restructuring of the military and security organizations to remove the influence of Saleh's networks was only partially implemented. Ordinary people, who had been promised a better life by the international community, saw living standards fall. There is now a consensus that too much emphasis was placed on the political process at the expense of economic growth and service delivery during the transition.

The Huthis initially cooperated with the GCC deal through their political party, Ansar Allah; at the same time, their militias and tribal networks extended Huthi influence outside the movement's Sa'ada homeland. Saleh, still commanding the loyalty of many civilian and military officials, secretly allied himself with the Huthis. This was a Faustian pact. After a months-long, coercive campaign through the northwest, the Huthis entered Sana'a in September 2014. Military forces loyal to Saleh stood aside as Huthi militants seized government buildings and confronted units led by Ali Mohsen and associated with Islah. Through UN mediation, the Huthi/Saleh forces entered the Peace and National Partnership Agreement (PNPA) with Hadi's government.

Hadi's position deteriorated through January 2015, when the delivery of the new constitution, which included an arrangement for a federal Yemen that did not satisfy Huthi or southern interests, set in motion the events that led to his resignation, the Huthi assumption of power in February 2015, and the Saudi-led intervention of March 26, 2015. The UN Security Council passed Resolution 2216 the following month, which supported the intervention, demanded the restoration of President Hadi, and imposed conditions that the Huthis, having taken the military initiative, were (and remain) loathe to accept.

Saudi Arabia, which had maintained interests in Yemeni politics since the 1930s and grew alarmed at evident Huthi ties to Iran, took charge of the war in the north and trained, equipped, and paid remnants of the Yemeni army supplemented by newly recruited soldiers to undertake ground fighting supported by Saudi air power. Saudi land forces defended their southern border from Huthi incursions. Southern Yemen and the west coast became the responsibility of the UAE, which trained, equipped, and mentored Yemenis to fight the Huthis. Many were drawn from southern nationalists who might support President Hadi's internationally recognized government against the Huthis but who ultimately sought independence for the south.

In the thicket of Yemeni politics, Saudi and Emirati interests diverged. In the north, Saudi Arabia needed the support of Islah because of its influence within the Hadi regime and its aligned fighting forces. In the south, the UAE refused to work with Islah, in keeping with Abu Dhabi's policy of seeking to eliminate movements with ties to the Muslim Brotherhood. These divisions, and the general incoherence of the anti-Huthi coalition ostensibly fighting for Hadi, has all but ruled out Hadi's clean restoration in Sana'a, and superior Saudi weapons and airpower have contained the Huthis only at the cost of thousands of civilian casualties. The internationalization of Yemen's conflict in 2015 clearly exacerbated the country's fragmentation. (Chapter 2)

Though the war has taken a number of twists and turns since March 2015, its defining feature has been stalemate: the Huthis are not strong enough to take over all of Yemen, and the Hadi government, even with Saudi support, is too weak to prevent them from solidifying their control of the northwest. Notable developments that will have long-lasting reverberations for Yemeni politics, such as the Huthis' 2017 murder of Saleh after his attempted break with the movement, or the UAE's formal withdrawal from the conflict, cannot shift this stalemate.

At the time of writing (January 2021), the two *de facto* regimes—the Internationally Recognized Government (IRG) and the Huthi Supreme Political Council (SPC), through which the Huthis rule—are not prepared to make the compromises necessary for peace. The Huthis continue to fight for territory, and still threaten Marib, the Hadi government's last major stronghold in the north. The IRG, in response, has been able to use UN-sanctioned legal, administrative, and financial devices that, along with the coalition-imposed blockades of air and sea ports, exacerbate the financial stresses faced by the Huthis. On the other hand, the Huthi SPC's government is doing what no recent regime has been able to achieve: it balances its budget (Chapter 6) even if the means of raising income are questionable.

Throughout the conflict, peace talks have been much discussed but seldom engaged in good faith, and multiple rounds in Switzerland and Kuwait were unsuccessful. A breakthrough seemed to occur with the signing of the Stockholm Agreement in December 2018, which averted a Saudi-led coalition offensive on the port city of Hodeida, due to its likely humanitarian fallout; the agreement, however, has floundered, and violence persists in the regions surrounding this Huthi-controlled city. Successive UN Special Envoys have attempted to organize mediation processes that adhere to "the three references": the GCC transition deal, the outcomes of the NDC, and UNSCR 2216. All are thus potentially relevant to the likely structure of the post-war settlement. UNSCR 2216 no longer reflects the political and military reality after six years of conflict and will require substantial amendment or replacement, as will the GCC deal. The NDC and draft constitution may be acceptable to President Hadi, the GPC and Islah, and some smaller parties, but not to the Huthis and the southerners, who remain resolutely opposed to the draft constitution's federal structure of six regions, four in the north and two in the south, albeit for different reasons. Thus, these references are no longer valid and will have to be amended or renegotiated and based much more closely on the reality of the situation on the ground.

The Current Political Map

Map 1 shows the various parties' main areas of control in early 2021. The UN Panel of Experts estimates that up to 80 percent of Yemenis live in these areas (UNPoE, 2021) although we assess that it is around 65–70 percent. The two sides to the war are quite different in structure. In Chapter 3, Hussein Alwaday and Maysaa Shujaa al-Deen demonstrate that the Huthis relied on tribal militias to take power and were able to mobilize the tribesmen to fight. They seem strong enough to maintain rule of much of Upper Yemen, where the pre-conflict power structure that revolves around a central command is still dominant. The Huthis have only reinforced this structure by deploying a raft of supervisors to oversee governing institutions at the national, governorate, and local levels. These supervisors keep the extant bureaucracy, much of which was responsive to Saleh before his killing, in line with the desires of paramount leader Abd al-Malik al-Huthi and his close circle of family members and advisers (Chapters 1 and 3). Using their networks, knowledge of tribal politics, and the families of the *sada,* they have consolidated their control. Their grip could eventually slip as resentment grows over some of their policies: their privileging of the *sada,* the imposition of taxes, repression of critics, their harsh treatment of tribal opponents such as the Hajour (Chapters 1, 3, and 6) and rivalries within the leadership, and financial abuses (UNPoE 2021). They have few regional or international allies except for Iran (and its associates), although this support has not been insignificant; Iranian weaponry and technical advice underlies Huthi ballistic missile and drone attacks on Saudi Arabia. Designation of the Huthis as a terrorist organization by the Trump administration on January 19, 2021 was reversed by President Biden but, even so, it seems likely that they will face increasing economic and financial problems, leading to greater dissatisfaction with their rule. These long-term trends will not affect their ability to remain in control in the short to medium term. The Huthis have been successful at portraying the war as one of foreign aggression against Yemen (Chapter 1) and use the war "to justify their extreme austerity, heavy taxation, and manipulation of markets" (Chapter 6).

The IRG was seemingly coherent in 2015 but has fragmented and is not in actual control of all Yemeni regions notionally loyal to President Hadi (Chapters 1, 2, 6, and 10). It suffers from weak leadership and its reputation is undermined by the actions of some of its leading figures ((UNPoE (2021)). Its one success story— Marib, a once marginalized governorate that has thrived throughout most of the conflict—owes much of its progress to a powerful local governor that holds the

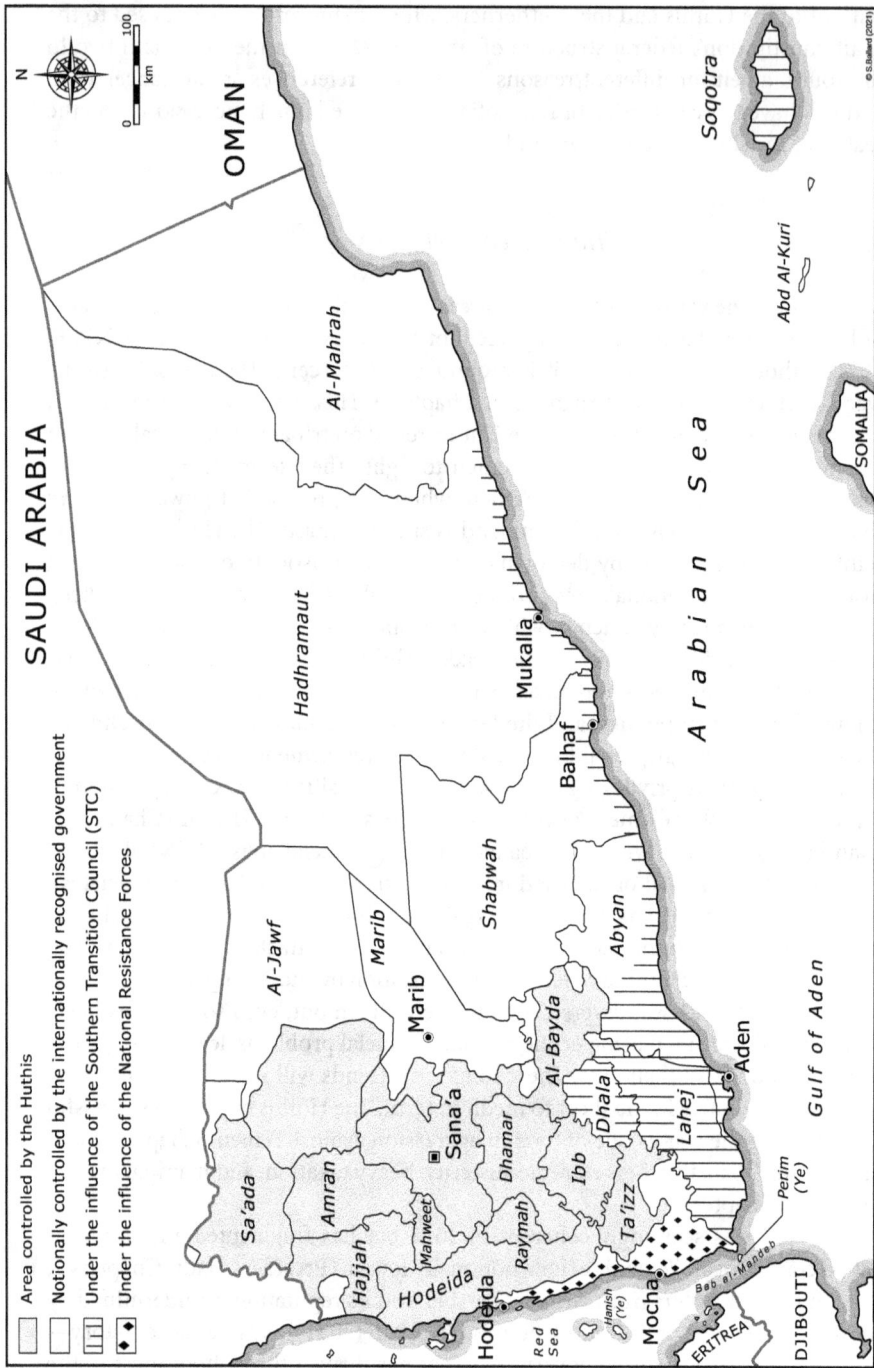

Map 1 Approximate areas of control in early 2021.

Legend:
- Area controlled by the Huthis
- Notionally controlled by the internationally recognised government
- Under the influence of the Southern Transition Council (STC)
- Under the influence of the National Resistance Forces

SAUDI ARABIA

OMAN

N

0 100 km

Al-Mahrah

Hadhramaut

Mukalla

Balhaf

Al-Jawf

Marib

Marib

Shabwah

Sa'ada

Amran

Sana'a

Al-Bayda

Abyan

Hajjah

Mahweet

Dhamar

Ibb

Dhala

Aden

Raymah

Ta'izz

Lahej

Hodeida

Hodeida

Red
Sea

Hanish
(Ye)

Mocha

Perim
(Ye)

Bab al-Mandeb

Gulf of Aden

Arabian Sea

Soqotra

Abd Al-Kuri

SOMALIA

ERITREA

DJIBOUTI

© S.Ballard (2021)

Hadi government at arm's length (Chapters 6 and 10). The governorate is virtually self-governing and has been able to benefit from the war economy, although recent Huthi advances threaten its state of semi-autonomy. Islah has significant support in Marib and in the IRG-controlled parts of Ta'izz.

The STC commands a substantial power base among the Security Belt, Elite Forces, and other militias created and supported by the UAE. These militias are particularly strong around Aden, which the STC controls, but weaker in the eastern parts of the former south, such as in Shabwah and Hadhramaut, where newly empowered local groups want greater self-government rather than a return to the prewar status quo when control of their affairs was in Sana'a (or Aden in the PDRY). The STC has considerable support in coastal areas, but the northern areas of these governorates are in the hands of military units allied with Ali Mohsen and Islah, which can be reinforced from Marib.

Clashes between the STC and forces loyal to Hadi in the summer of 2019 led to Saudi intervention (the UAE withdrew most of its forces from Yemen in 2019 though it continued to finance the STC and some related militias) and the signing of the Riyadh Agreement, designed to prevent further infighting among anti-Huthi coalition members. It had only been partially implemented at the time of writing, and the ultimate aims of the IRG and the STC do not seem to be reconcilable. The National Resistance Forces, led by Tariq Saleh, a nephew of the late president who has the support of the UAE, is a significant influence in the Tihama region along the west coast, but it is itself a messy coalition of former northern Yemeni military units and leaders, militias from south Yemen, and local Tihama resistance fighters determined to repel any Huthi incursions. All these various local or regional groups command fighters and lucrative local war economies, which give them the power to demand that their interests are met in any peace deal and post-conflict structure—and the ability to sabotage anything that they disagree with.

State building will be complicated by the way that the war has exacerbated the sectarianism which has been growing in Yemen since the 1970s, and this is explored in Chapter 3. The rise of the Huthi movement was in part provoked by the spread of the Muslim Brotherhood via Islah and of the Salafism first encouraged by the Saleh regime to counter Marxist currents in the 1970s, but the actions of the Huthis and the war have strengthened extremism as well as generating the intolerance and hatreds that all wars inspire.

Further complicating matters, most fighting has focused on the control of resources, ports, and key sources of potential income, whether this involved the war between the IRG and the Huthis or the many local conflicts that have flared up alongside it. The two sides also fight an economic war: for example, the IRG has used its control of the internationally recognized Central Bank to put economic pressure on the Huthis, while the Huthis have developed a separate currency to delink northwest Yemen from the rest of the country. As Charles Schmitz writes:

> The logic of Yemen's political economy subjugates the long-term interests of the economy to the short term interests of the many competing political factions. Today Yemen is at war, and logically the economy serves as a tool in the war,

but unfortunately subordination of the economy to political aims is the norm in times of peace as well as war. Rather than staking their political careers on mobilizing Yemen's social and physical resources to achieve economic growth, policy makers in Yemen use the economy for short-term political interests. (Chapter 6)

The UN Panel of Experts reported in January 2021 that "The pattern of conflicts shifted toward widespread economic profiteering perpetrated by networks of commanders, businessmen, politicians and local leaders" (UNPoE, 2021). That applied to all sides.

Potential Future Scenarios

In the face of a stalemated conflict, the situation is so uncertain that attempts to create possible scenarios for future state structure must engage in much speculation.

It is likely that, when the war finally ends, there will be two main political entities: the Huthis in most of what was north Yemen and the IRG in the center and south. As part of a peace deal, it is probable that they will agree to share power in a federal arrangement that enables Yemen to have a government functional enough to manage relief, reconstruction, the restoration of public services, and redevelopment. At best, this government might provide a means for cooperation that, over time, builds sufficient confidence between the SPC and the IRG to enable a gradual expansion of its powers. At worst, it could become little more than an extended cease-fire that at least allows the delivery of humanitarian support and a degree of economic cooperation over access to ports of entry and major roads.

The SPC and IRG will exercise political power in their separately administered areas. They could become separate states. The SPC (that is the Huthis and their allies from the old northern establishment) will seek to impose control of the north by force and negotiation; there could possibly be some limited decentralization where, for example, the populous areas of Lower Yemen under SPC control may be given more freedom on how they govern themselves. That would require a degree of pragmatism that the Huthi leadership has not yet shown. Despite the current (intermittent) fighting in and around Ta´izz, there is some cooperation between opposing groups to assure the delivery of food and basic services, and such local action could become a permanent feature and extend to other contested areas. (Writing in Chapter 5, Bilkis Zabara and Sabria Al-Thawr give examples of local initiatives, often led by women, to foster local reconciliation and cooperation.) Within a federal Yemen, Ta´izz and Ibb might become a separate region: al-Janad, as envisioned in the 2014 constitution.

The IRG seems too fragmented to enable the return of a strong central ruling group and will need to build a decentralized or federal arrangement that enables regions or governorates to have the power to govern themselves. Given the strength of the STC, it is possible that the southern governorates might try to restore an independent southern state (it would itself need to be federal, which the STC accepts) with the current IRG restricted to Marib and Al-Jawf. However, it is possible that Hadhramaut, Al-Mahrah, and Shabwah could have separate arrangements—they remain contested by the IRG and STC, and many of their leaders prefer much more self-government to being linked to the IRG or STC-dominated Aden, Lahej, and Abyan (such a division of the south is in the 2014 Constitution).

It is probable that after the war the regions in the IRG will come under external pressure to stay together at least for a few years to focus on rebuilding infrastructure and services. The 2014 constitution (as discussed in Chapters 7 and 10) does address how revenues derived from oil fields and economic assets should be apportioned between central, regional, and governorate/district levels and could be a useful starting point for building new arrangements.

Previous authoritarian regimes based in Sana'a and the northern highlands (and in Aden in the days of the PDRY) failed to overcome—and may have exacerbated—regional divisions. The logic of Yemen's geography, the distribution of its key resources, and present political fragmentation strongly suggest that a federal state is likely to be the most stable outcome despite the failure of previous attempts to develop an acceptable federal system (Chapter 2). Such an arrangement would not necessarily portend tranquility. The history of the YAR and PDRY demonstrates that if there are two—let alone more—regimes in the same country, they will compete for resources and each will seek to impose its political system on the other (Halliday 1990). In 2021, local groups throughout Yemen, flush with weapons and cash derived from local war economies, have the means to disrupt governing arrangements that do not take account of their interests. It should not be forgotten that one reason for the rise of the Huthis was the perception that their Sa'ada homeland was marginalized more than other Yemeni regions after 1970 and that the crisis in 2015 was precipitated in part by a proposed federal arrangement that left Sa'ada in a federal region lacking sufficient resources (Chapter 2). Thus any federal arrangement will need to be carefully negotiated and ensure that all Yemenis benefit from it.

Security and Terrorism

It is now widely recognized, and reflected in several chapters of this book, that security and economics are interlinked in post-conflict situations. Progress in one area must go hand in hand with progress in others. One of the key concerns of external powers is the threat posed to them by AQAP and, to a lesser extent, by the Islamic State of Yemen (ISY).

While outside powers have dithered in assisting Yemen's economy or incentivizing good governance, they have acted decisively (and at times, arguably, single-mindedly) to address terrorist threats emanating from Yemen. After September 11, 2001, the United States took the lead in trying to empower the Saleh and Hadi governments to fight terrorism by enhancing Yemen's security services whilst also using drone and air strikes to degrade these terrorist organizations. Only on the cusp of the Arab Spring did this securitized approach get a rethink. The Friends of Yemen, co-chaired by the United Kingdom and set up in 2010 in the aftermath of a failed AQAP attempt to bring down a US airliner, was a belated international effort to go beyond dealing with the symptoms of terrorism and to start addressing the political, economic, and social ills that allowed AQAP to flourish.

Since emerging in early 2009 as the merger between al-Qaeda in Saudi Arabia and Yemen, AQAP has pursued ambitious global and local agendas. It organized attacks against international targets, including, in August 2009, the attempted assassination of the head of Saudi Arabia's counterterrorism organization. The Yemeni-American citizen Anwar al-Awlaki helped pioneer what was called "auto-jihad" by exploiting the internet to foment lone wolf attacks in the West.

In Chapter 4, Joana Cook recounts how AQAP has used the war to gain new recruits, sources of finance, and weapons, adopting a variety of strategies. In central Yemen, it presented itself as a defender of Sunni Islam against Zaydi Shi´a revivalists. In Abyan and Shabwah it set up "Islamic emirates." In Mukalla, which AQAP occupied for a few months in 2015/16, it operated as the "Sons of Hadhramaut" and worked with existing authorities to provide services that the state had failed to deliver. These achievements fell well short of the group's professed goals and were not to last.

In early 2021, AQAP is at the weakest it has been for many years as a result of counterterrorist missions conducted by UAE-trained Yemeni forces and US drone attacks on key leaders. However, AQAP is far from eliminated and remains ready to exploit the opportunities that a chaotic post-war situation might create. It has not lost its ambition to be a global as well as Yemeni force. Whilst the campaign against AQAP must continue, government or governments in post-war Yemen will need to do much more to address the issues that enable AQAP to win recruits. Policies are needed to improve the lives of Yemenis and give the people a strong stake in supporting the government. Cook refers to this as full-spectrum counterterrorism which includes both "hard" or "direct" and "soft" or "indirect" lines of effort that must work together cohesively.

Role of Women

Of the many issues that Yemenis will need to tackle in building a new state, few are more important than the status of women. In 2018, Yemen was ranked last out of 162 countries in the Gender Inequality Index, mostly reflecting the pre-2011 situation—though in the PDRY, women's guaranteed rights were well in advance of most other Arab states. During the 2011 uprising and the following transition, women played an increasingly influential role, making up 30 percent of the participants in the NDC, albeit nowhere near 50 percent, and leading some of the conference's deliberations. The resulting 2014 draft constitution granted stronger protections for women's rights. These have been eroded by the war, but

"Yemeni women have demonstrated levels of resilience in finding new roles, often as the main breadwinner for their family (while continuing their domestic tasks) and in maintaining the resilience of the society during the humanitarian crisis" (Chapter 8).

Any conclusions about the role of women need to be qualified, as there are immense regional variations and significant differences between women of different social strata, and generalizations can be misleading. Many women are prominent in organizing humanitarian relief programs, creating economic opportunities in their local communities, and even enrolling in the security forces of state and non-state actors. But as a recent study has indicated, "contributions by women to the social requisites of peace far outweigh their role as participants in the war and thus highlights their capacity to contribute to durable solutions to Yemen's most pressing problems" (al-Gawfi, Zabara, and Yadav, 2020).

Women must be brought into the peace-making process so that they have a voice in the final conflict settlement and its implementation. At a minimum, women should be guaranteed the 30 percent participation rate in state institutions agreed at the NDC. In post-war Yemen, women are likely to want to play a greater role in the workplace and the economy using the experience and skills they have gained in the war years. There will be resistance and it will take time, but an impatient younger generation will increasingly demand such changes, a point made in several chapters, notably Chapter 5.

Economic Recovery

We have suggested that the most likely outcome of the war is a weak national government obliged to work with politically powerful regional forces that can disrupt policies perceived as undermining their interests. There could also be two—and possibly more—states. Several book chapters address the issues that any government or governments will face as they struggle to bring relief, stabilize the state(s), and start building a new Yemen.

Charles Schmitz ends Chapter 6 by saying, "Yemen's post war prospects 'appear to be very bleak indeed.'" Yemen has at different times come to depend on remittances, foreign financial support, and hydrocarbon revenues. All are in irreversible decline, but all are still important, putting policymakers in a tough spot. Oil and gas remain a significant source of foreign exchange;[1] remittances are a lifeline for many Yemeni families, even if opportunities for emigration are currently reduced; and the vested interest of Yemen's neighbors in providing enough support to prevent region-undermining instability. All will have to be crutches for a recovering patient.

A major dilemma in post-conflict situations is how much attention should be devoted to economic policies relative to the security priorities and political arrangements of the post-conflict period. Ideally, an integrated approach is needed since investment cannot take place without an enabling political environment and security. It must start with the restoration of functioning service delivery capacity such as health, education, water, sanitation, and electricity whilst in parallel focusing on macroeconomic stabilization through efficient fiscal and monetary policy implementation. Government institutions will remain fragile for some considerable time and will need support to deliver services and rebuild infrastructure. National institutions will need to be reconstituted so that they can mediate between private, public, and informal sectors as well as respond to the diverse needs of Yemeni citizens, thereby helping create a sense of common identity and purpose (Chapter 8). Without rapid investment, research shows that the typical post-conflict country faces a 40 percent risk of reversion to conflict during the first decade. An integrated approach is essential and there will need to be much more realistic time lines for implementation than were put forth in the transition deal of 2011.

Yemen faces the most formidable challenges, not least from water shortages and the uncertain impact of climate change (both examined in Chapters 9 and 10). It will have to find ways of generating the income it needs for investment to pay for the 90 percent of staples it imports for a population likely to reach forty-five to fifty million by 2050. Rafat al-Akhali (Chapter 7) proposes that Yemen focus on export potential, as domestic demand is likely to be weak for some years; he shares ideas on ways to begin this shift that chime well with recommendations made by Firebrace and Eshaq (Chapter 10) and the analysis of Schmitz (Chapter 6).

One key area to deal with is what Chapter 7 describes as the chaotic, *de facto* decentralized authorities at governorate level. Key pillars of development are "empowered local authorities capable of leading the development process and the delivery of basic services at the governorate level effectively." Any new government will probably face the task of restoring "national coherence and coordination across the different governorates, while providing them with the resources and capacity to take a leading role in the development process and service delivery in their areas" (Chapter 7). Interestingly, Firebrace and Eshaq, (Chapter 10) while agreeing on this, suggest that the reality of fragmentation or regionalization can be used in a positive way so that regions are enabled to develop as viable economic entities managed by well-resourced regional administrations (Chapter 10).

Some estimates indicate that during the first post-war year alone, the development aid needed will be as high as $14 billion (Bayoumy, 2016). An ever-present danger is that following the cessation of hostilities, regional powers with a continuing interest in influencing Yemen's affairs will attach unwanted strings to development aid. Another major problem will be Yemen's ability to absorb this vast amount of development aid and coordinate its effective use in all sectors post-conflict.

A future for Yemen dictated from the top-down, with undue influence by external actors, will fail, as recent experience in Yemen has shown: "The reform policy of the past formulated by donors and external players were short term and piecemeal, failing to address the need for systemic, comprehensive reform" (Chapter 8). As Chapter 1 warns, an inadequate understanding of Yemen has led to flawed interventions in recent history. What is needed now is a social contract that establishes a system based on respect for the constitution, law and order, the peaceful transfer of power through elections, and equal citizenship for all. It is necessary to broaden political participation and protect the rights and culture of local communities—a very tall order.

One essential need is for the involvement of Yemenis on the ground—those directly affected by what happens—to ensure that their needs are met and that there is effective coordination to prevent unwelcome and unforeseen implications. The NDC outcomes remain on the table and are a testament to what Yemenis can achieve when working together. That gain must not be allowed to crumble, but should be reinforced, implemented, and then further developed. The role of women in this respect must be part of the process.

Drawing on her personal experience during the post-2011 transition, Amat Alsoswa argues that prewar problems will also need addressing. These were summarized in the Executive Bureau's 2015 Final Report's commentary on the difficulties of government absorption of donor pledges: "Those challenges are primarily caused by the government's continuation in pursuing old and ineffective practices and mechanisms of dealing with the donors, the unstable political and security situation, the poor capacity of government's cadres in charge of absorption practices, and the complex procedures and excessive bureaucracy that accompany the implementation process of donor-funded projects" (Chapter 8).

After the first post-war years, Yemen will not be able to rely on foreign aid and will need to look at internal means of raising revenues and encouraging investment by the private sector—domestic, diaspora, and foreign—to provide jobs and a base for taxation. Saudi Arabia and the GCC, which are likely to provide the largest source of external assistance, can help by allowing Yemeni workers access to GCC labor markets in the early stages of post-conflict recovery, which will sustain the flow of remittances. Today, Yemenis are thought to make up less than 10 percent of the fourteen million expatriates working in the GCC. There are political difficulties for the GCC countries in allowing more Yemenis to enter the labor market at a time when they are trying to nationalize their labor force, but this has to be offset against the risks to their security of instability and poverty in Yemen.

A Greater Role for the Private Sector

The private sector will have to play a decisive role in building a new Yemen. The state sector can no longer provide jobs on the scale of the past. Post-conflict, the government will have to reconceptualize the traditional role and modus operandi of previous governments and look to the private sector to produce jobs, and to the local governments to lead the delivery of basic services. Development strategies must focus on increasing employment, earnings, and investment across all sectors, particularly those that can create new jobs. Yemen needs a capable state that has the resources to help develop the economy and can provide a sense of security that allows Yemenis to feel secure in investing in their future (Chapter 6). Broad growth across all sectors creates a more diversified economy more immune from the vicissitudes of commodity fluctuations, and one which distributes income more evenly (Chapter 7).

The country is not well endowed with natural resources and therefore needs to exploit its greatest resource: its people. That requires investment to raise skill levels and produce jobs, a daunting challenge for a country that in 2015 needed to create 150,000 jobs a year just to keep pace with population growth (ILO 2015). It also will make it easier for Yemenis to find jobs abroad and contribute to remittances. A very important area for development will be the manufacturing and service industries linked to the urban economy, which had enjoyed steady growth in the prewar period. What that sector now needs is investment in improved infrastructure and reliable sources of energy.

Firebrace and Eshaq (Chapter 10) agree but warn that there may not be much foreign direct investment in the early years, so the "Yemeni private sector will have a particular responsibility to spearhead the immense task of rebuilding the Yemeni economy." They point out that "An enabling business environment is needed to allow the private sector to deliver its full potential. A minimal level of security and judicial reform, such as over enforceability of contracts, will be required to provide the guarantees needed for external investors. This will also help in time create the conditions for a rise in entrepreneurship and SMEs [small and medium-sized enterprises] across Yemen."

Investors will want to see in place a fair legal system, transparent decision-making processes, and a financial structure that will encourage investment. If these are absent, Yemeni businessmen will look outside the country for places to invest or will invest in relatively safe, liquid sectors such as commerce and transportation; only investors with political protection will invest in Yemen, and even these investors will keep one foot outside of Yemen (Chapters 6 and 7). If Yemenis feel confident enough to themselves invest, then foreign direct investment will follow. Yemen's established businesses are well placed to make major contributions to reconstruction efforts, whether undertaken as sole ventures or through Public Private Partnerships with donors. Yemen's large diaspora could play a crucial role in providing some of the capital and skills needed by the private sector, but the government will need to create the conditions to incentivize them to do so—in addition to setting up mechanisms to deter corruption (Chapter 10).

The Enduring Importance of Agriculture

Given the size of the agricultural sector and the number of people dependent on it (Chapter 9), investment will be needed to support techniques and develop innovative solutions (drawing on the experience of other post-conflict economies) to enable the sector to improve its low productivity, increase exports (only 11 percent at the moment), and reduce dependency on imported staples. It is vital to switch, as far as possible, from irrigated to rain-fed agriculture, both to reduce dependence on depleting aquifers and to enable poverty reduction. There are opportunities for coffee and other cash crop growth, but these will compete with *qat* for water and land use; ways will have to be found to persuade farmers to switch from *qat*. Policies need to be put in place and enforced to limit the sinking of new tube wells and extracting water for *qat* crops, which is currently assumed to account for up to 40 percent of irrigation use in Yemen.

Yemen has a long tradition of successful dry farming, utilizing crops with low water requirements and sustainable water collection systems of small dams and cisterns that have been in place for up to three millennia. Conducting research on and then disseminating drought-resistant and fast-maturing varieties of traditional cereal crops are important first steps, particularly given the preference of Yemenis for local cereals for which, income permitting, they are willing to pay higher prices. In addition to this, which would also contribute to reducing the need for imports, households living in rain-fed areas also need cash crops, therefore research and dissemination of new high-value rain-fed crops must also be top priorities (Chapter 9). Innovative approaches will be needed to enhance productivity, raise standards, and make the best use of modern technology and sustainable methods of the past.

Water and Climate Change

Laurent Bonnefoy (Chapter 1) highlights water depletion as an object of profound (if not existential) concern for Yemenis themselves as well as for the world. Addressing this depletion will need to be at the core of all development plans in the years to come if Yemen is to have a future, as a state and as a society. Helen Lackner (Chapter 9) provides an authoritative analysis of the great challenges presented by water shortages, not just to the agricultural sector but also to Yemen's urban population: "Yemen suffers from extreme water scarcity: it has been using annually one third more water than its renewable supply." Chapter 10 augments Lackner's arguments. The main cause for this is high population growth exacerbated by the use of diesel-operated pumps and deep-well drilling technology that has enabled extraction of water significantly above recharge levels, thus causing depletion of the aquifers, and the loss of topsoil due mostly to neglect of terraces used in rain-fed cultivation.

Lackner argues that

> unless strong policies are rapidly enforced to shift water usage from agriculture to domestic supplies, the most densely populated parts of the country are likely to become uninhabitable within less than a generation. There will be significant migration to urban areas as well as rural locations with better aquifers. The larger urban populations will need more water, most of which will come from rural aquifers, except on the coast where desalination will have to be a major contributor.

Yemen may not be suited for the type of desalinization projects in other states of the Arabian Peninsula, but Firebrace and Eshaq point out that technological innovation is reducing costs.

Chapters 9 and 10 refer to threats from climate change, although there are always uncertainties about how much local areas will be affected. Yemen is likely to become more arid overall even as rainfall could increase in certain regions of the country (though not to the point of recharging major aquifers). It is likely that there will be an increase in drastic weather conditions, especially damaging flooding due to stronger storms from the Gulf of Aden. Aden is vulnerable to forecasts of rising sea levels.

A Vision for New Yemen

We conclude the book with a more positive vision for Yemen's future provided by Firebrace and Eshaq in Chapter 10, albeit grounded in the practicalities of dealing with the issues highlighted in other parts of this volume. It is easy to describe Yemen in increasingly apocalyptic terms: as a failed state, facing political, economic, and environmental collapse, massive food insecurity, and the severe impoverishment of its population. But it is vital to look at the potential not only to recover but also, in time, to generate significant and widespread prosperity. The authors provide examples of potentially new sources of revenue and Yemen's unrealized potential. Clearly, Yemen needs a government that can provide the environment in which the private sector, Yemeni and external, can realize those opportunities.

Longer-term thinking is needed to see the opportunities and threats ahead more clearly and to allow better more farsighted decision-making. As al-Akhali notes in Chapter 7, the traditional approach to post-conflict recovery tends to follow a phased sequence: relief and humanitarian assistance, then reintegration of fighters, refugees, and internally displaced persons, followed by rebuilding of physical infrastructure, and finally interventions geared to facilitate economic growth. Firebrace and Eshaq show how futures thinking can help in conceptualizing a vision of what Yemen could achieve and help guide planning in the short and medium term.

When sooner or later Yemenis negotiate a peace settlement and the structure of a new Yemen, they will face the enormous problems outlined in this book. But as they start work, they should keep in mind the vision outlined by Firebrace and Eshaq. If people can see that a new Yemen can be a reality, they can be motivated to achieve it. The self-interest of the international and regional states points toward a stable and prosperous Yemen, and they can help Yemenis build a new state by working with them as partners and learn from the misunderstandings of the past. Yemenis need to reach a historical reconciliation that can sustain peace and then with the support of its regional neighbors and the international community to start building a new Yemen.

Note

1   There may be possibilities to incentivize oil exploration to ensure that Yemen gets the maximum it can from this resource (and from its potential mineral wealth). China, for example, has not been deterred by Yemen's political problems in seeking to explore Yemen's natural resources.

References

al-Gawfi, I., B. Zabara, and S.P. Yadav (2020), The Role of Women in Peacebuilding in
  Yemen, CARPO—Center for Applied Research in Partnership with the Orient, Bonn.
Bayoumy, Y. (2016), "Exclusive: Civil War Costs Yemen $14 Billion in Damage and
  Economic Losses." Reuters. August 17, 2016. Available online: https://www.reuters.com
  /article/us-yemen-security-damages/exclusive-civil-war-costs-yemen-14-billion-in
  -damage-and-economic-losses-report-idUSKCN10R2B7 (accessed April 17, 2020).
Brandt, Marieke (2017), *Tribes and Politics in Yemen: A History of the Houthi Conflict*. New
  York: Oxford University Press.
Brehony, N. (2011), *Yemen Divided: The Story of a Failed State in South Arabia*. London :
  IB Tauris.
Halliday, F. (1990), *Revolution and Foreign Policy: The Case of South Yemen, 1967–1987*.
  Cambridge: Cambridge University Press.
International Labour Organization (ILO 2015), *Yemen Labour Force Survey 2013–14*.
  Beirut: International Labour Organization, 7.
International Rescue Committee, Failure to end civil war in Yemen could cost $29 billion,
  Sanaa.2 December 2019. Available online: https://www.rescue.org/press-release/failure
  -end-civil-war-yemen-could-cost-29-billion (accessed April 17, 2020).
Phillips, S. (2011), *Yemen and the Politics of Permanent Crisis*. New York: Routledge.
UNPoE (2021), *Final Report of the Panel of Experts on Yemen* (S/2021/79) January 22. New
  York. January 22.

Chapter 1

YEMEN AND THE INTERNATIONAL COMMUNITY

FRAGMENTED APPROACHES

Laurent Bonnefoy

Contemporary Yemen holds a paradoxical place in the imagination and policies of the international community. While often being depicted as a strategic country located at the crossroads of continents and commercial routes, or as a source of quasi-existential threat when contemporary jihadi groups are mentioned, its habitants remain marginalized. The strategies of the world's great or regional powers focusing on Yemen have thus generally lacked coherence, continuity, and relevance. Dominant interest for Yemen among foreign decision makers and experts has for long appeared to be structured around a set of selective obsessions (Bonnefoy, 2018). These rarely had much to do with Yemen itself and more often than not let its inhabitants appear as pawns of wider dynamics. Consequently, it comes as no surprise that the conflict which began in the wake of the "Yemeni Spring" of 2011 often remained poorly framed by international actors, when it was not bluntly ignored (Lackner, 2017).

Historically, one could state that concern for the political future of the country was constructed around issues that, to a large extent, alienated Yemenis. From the nineteenth century onward, its geographic position had made it a prey for colonial empires (Willis, 2012). Between the 1960s and 1990s, with Yemen divided, this territory was a playground for conflicting regional and global powers in the context of the Cold War (Brehony, 2011; al-Madhhagi, 1994; al-Uqab, 1998). Only in the early 1990s did interest in Yemen appear to be somewhat linked to internal dynamics, then concerned with its unification and democratization processes. However, the parenthesis was short-lived, first due to the failure of these processes, and then because of the "global war on terror" (Carapico, 2013). Counterterrorism became the matrix through which Yemen was invited to interact with the world during the first years of the new millennium (Burgat, 2006). Internal dynamics were thus neglected, amongst which were the Zaydi revivalist issue (Brandt, 2017) and the Southern question (Augustin, 2018; Day, 2012). The "Yemeni Spring" of 2011 rapidly became a golden parenthesis full of promises (Bonnefoy and Poirier, 2012). However, even then, counter-terrorism loomed high on the agenda of the international community (Longley Alley, 2013 ; al-Salahi (ed.), 2012). From 2015 onward and ever since the current war, new narratives emerged and blurred much of the way Yemen was perceived by the international community at large, meaning world leaders, but also international organizations, NGOs, and the international press. Fragmentation and division became the dominant features of the way the various incarnations of the international community engaged with the conflict.

Rather than depicting Yemen's interdependent relationship with the international community as a collection of rational interactions and perceptions, this chapter intends to develop an opposite stance, showing how policies on Yemen by the so-called international community highlight a fragmentation, and a number of inconsistencies. More than ever, perceptions of Yemen at war by international actors have become structured around competing narratives and visions. This holds true even within the same entities. For that matter, states are not necessarily to be seen as unitary actors which share a common understanding of Yemeni affairs. Ministries may well act differently from one another and agencies of the United Nations do not all frame issues and solutions in the same way, in part due to specific institutional subcultures.

Such diversity, in turn, generates diverging or even incoherent policies and interventions that explain much of the current chaos, as well as the inability of foreign actors to actually solve the crisis in Yemen. Fragmentation is only more profound as Yemeni institutions themselves are divided and the object of fierce competition at all levels, economic (al-Muslimi, 2019; al-Akhali, 2016), political, tribal (al-Dawsari, 2012), and military (al-Shargabi, 2018). These conflicting narratives and interactions will likely need to start converging and to take into consideration the livelihoods and aspirations of Yemenis if peace and reconstruction are to be achieved. The future of Yemen very much depends on it.

The World Competing to Make Sense of the War

Early on, the way the war in Yemen was framed and depicted became an object of controversy at the international level (Clausen, 2015). To put it in overly simplistic terms, it was either seen as a conflict between local elites that developed a regional dimension, or as one based on a foreign aggression. For example, determining the date of its very beginning sparked disputes, not only between Yemeni actors themselves, but also among external ones. Many outside the country, in particular in the media, considered that the armed conflict began on March 26, 2015, when the Arab coalition, led by the Saudi military, dropped its first bombs on the capital city. Others, who generally opposed Huthi rule, stated that the war had in reality started when the rebels took military control of the capital on September 21, 2014, put pressure on the legitimate government, held President Abdo Rabbuh Mansur Hadi under house arrest, expanded their control toward the south of the country with alleged Iranian benevolence and support, and used military planes to bomb positions of their adversaries in Aden. Without any proper declaration of war, the situation was left open to interpretation. No doubt, historians will end up determining what chronology is the most relevant.

By all standards, this dispute is far from neutral. It questions the root causes of the conflict and, as such, the legitimacy of foreign meddling. These perceptions are meaningful since they all advocate different forms of intervention by the international community and regional actors. From the onset, numerous players competed to impose their narratives, generating another layer of complexity and blurring the perceptions of the general public. With no clear dominant narrative, the conflict remained hidden to many or was simply ignored. The near absence of foreign journalists on the ground in Yemen also contributed to a lack of knowledge of what was happening. Coverage and interest at the international level changed over the course of the third year of war with growing concern over the deterioration of the humanitarian situation. However, such diplomatic and public concern later receded, with Yemen almost disappearing from the radar as it entered a new crisis: confronting the Covid-19 pandemic in a tremendously fragile state.

Beyond the belligerents, who all had their own media arms (in particular al-Masira on the one side, al-Arabiyya and Suhayl TV, on the other) and were trying hard to gather the support of the wider public outside of Yemen, international NGOs, foreign journalists, diplomats, think tanks and researchers had a say in pushing one particular narrative over the others. The polarization of the expert and academic fields in the West did not reach the depth witnessed during the Syrian war. However, debates on the Yemeni conflict were harsh and many (in particular, supporters of the Southern movement) believed that a biased "pro-Huthi" perspective had become dominant in the international public sphere. Others often put the blame on the Arab coalition, generating some frustration, in particular among segments of the Yemeni diaspora who felt marginalized and incapable of imposing a frame that would stick with their own political views or that would add nuance to them (Aboueldahab, 2019). Initiatives like DeepRoot Consulting as well as the Sanaʿa Center for Strategic Studies and the Yemen Policy Center, however, contributed by gathering significant data and fostering fascinating analysis that would, for instance, emphasize the role of the economy in peace building.

Nevertheless, three competing narratives have to a large extent continued to structure the understanding of the war within the international community at large. Describing these narratives must consequently be at the core of any analysis of the way international actors have been dealing with the conflict in Yemen and of how they will position themselves once the fighting is over.

The dominant approach taken by international institutions and Western powers focused on the issue of constitutional legitimacy and its restoration. This "institutional narrative" was the one that structured the United Nations Security Council's (UNSC) different statements and resolutions. It framed the conflict mainly as a confrontation between competing political groups within Yemen and depicted the Arab coalition's military intervention in March 2015 as a legitimate response to a call by the Yemeni president.

The adoption of international sanctions before that date and the focus on the preservation of the legitimate and constitutional political process showed how concern for Yemen had not, per se, been triggered by the Arab coalition's intervention. Additions to resolution 2140 (initially adopted in February 2014 to establish targeted sanctions against specific individuals who were accused of compromising the political transition after the fall of Ali Abdullah Saleh) were made, including new names of spoilers. Resolution 2201 adopted in January 2015 also showed how the rationale of the international community was to a large extent focused on the defence of the legal framework. Efforts by then UN Special Envoy Jamal Benomar to build a consensus between conflicting parties thus exemplified the significance of this approach even before bombs started falling on the country. The aim of the international community in Yemen was mostly, prior to the war, to preserve the constitutional legitimacy of the government and preserve the political transition.

After the launch of operation "Decisive Storm" (Asifat al-hazm) by the Saudi-led coalition, Resolution 2216 of the UNSC, voted on April 14, 2015, reasserted the depiction of the war as a matter of legitimacy. The vast majority of countries closed down their diplomatic representation in Sana'a, with the exception of a few Arab states and Russia. The founding rationale for intervention was thus to restore President Hadi to power. However, the legal framing appeared shaky according to different legal analysts (Ruys and Ferro, 2016): President Hadi's two-year term which began in February 2012, and its one-year extension by the National Dialogue Conference, had ended before the launch of the war. The Yemeni state's institutions could then be understood as evolving in a constitutional vacuum. Over the years, the UNSC's maintained assertion that Hadi remained the legitimate ruler of Yemen (unless he resigned, would die, or new elections would be organized) would become a handicap for many. Various members of the UNSC pushed in 2018 to have a new resolution that would open the way for alternatives, but all international actors were bound by the legal fiction of aiming to restore Hadi to power, something that in reality not many wished, or even considered any longer feasible after the years of war and his exile in Riyadh.

This narrative, built on international legality, is thus one that gradually lost political and practical relevance, but nevertheless still remained central in determining the way significant players of the international community officially interacted with Yemen. Allies of Hadi consequently projected themselves as able to defend their legitimacy as the sole representatives of the Yemeni government and of the state. Such a situation generated much complexity as the Yemeni state was in reality fragmented. The Central Bank, whose independence while being in Sana'a and refusal to side with Hadi became in late 2016 unacceptable to Hadi and his allies, became the ironic symbol of the emphasis put on formal legitimacy over political and economic efficiency. Indeed, the complex transfer of the Central Bank from Sana'a to Aden left many civil servants without salary for months and further disorganized the economy and the currency, the Yemeni riyal.

The second international narrative (often made compatible with the previous one) has described the conflict in Yemen as a proxy war between regional powers, namely Iran and Saudi Arabia. It has been central in particular among belligerents within Yemen but also among Saudi decision makers who have persistently constructed the war as one against Iranian encroachment in the

Arabian Peninsula. In justifying Saudi involvement in Yemen, Saudi Crown Prince Muhammad bin Salman would go as far as to compare Iranian expansion to the Nazi one: "He [i.e., Ayatollah Khamenei] wants to create his own project in the Middle East very much like Hitler who wanted to expand at the time."[1] On May 16, 2019, his brother, Khalid bin Salman, Saudi vice-minister of defence, claimed on his Twitter account that the drone strikes carried out by the Yemeni rebel group on Saudi territory were "terrorist attacks ordered by the regime in Tehran and carried out by the Huthis." Such a way of framing the conflict in Yemen would never be challenged by the Western powers and even be increasingly supported by the American administration. In January 2021, the "eleventh hour" attempt by the Donald Trump administration to classify the Huthis as a "Foreign Terrorist Organization"—a move that was criticized by many, including the incoming Joe Biden administration, since it put humanitarian efforts in jeopardy—exemplified the remnants of a principled approach that lacked nuance, and saw Yemeni political actors as pawns in a wider game.

While at times more implicit (and then concealed by the legitimacy-based narrative), the portrayal of the Huthis as agents of the Islamic Republic of Iran, and as a group alien to Yemeni culture, gave the conflict ideological and sectarian dimensions. Segments of the Saudi media would be particularly active in pushing forward such a framing of the conflict, in particular through the discourse of certain religious actors such as Aidh al-Qirni or Abdulaziz Al al-Shaykh who often focus on the unorthodoxy of the Zaydi's religious discourse. Publications hostile to Zaydism and to Hashemites (descendants of Prophet Muhammad, of which the Huthi family is a member) further served as a way of delegitimizing the Huthis. Their religious practice would become associated with Twelver Shi′ism while all *sada*, due to their specific genealogy, would easily be portrayed as foreign intruders. Such would for instance, be the ideological background of *Ghagha*, a famous Yemeni Ramadan television show hosted by Muhammad al-Adhra′i, shot in Riyadh, and broadcast in Yemen on Suhayl television.[2] Figures of the Huthi movement would themselves feed such a narrative by also engaging in sectarian discrimination.

Focus by the Arab coalition on the need to enforce the arms embargo highlighted the significance of the proxy-war narrative, giving high importance to the issue of Iranian support to the Huthis. Debate over the origin of certain weapons used by the Huthis, in particular missiles and drones able to target Saudi or Emirati territory, became a central question in the reports of the international panel of experts who monitored the diverse sanctions adopted by the UNSC. Should their Iranian origin be proven, and should they have been delivered after 2015, then the international resolutions would have been violated, putting Iran under increased pressure. The strategy to gain control over the port of Hodeida and accusations of potential collaboration of neighboring countries in importing Iranian-made weapons to Yemen showed the centrality of such an interpretation. Experts in international relations and Yemeni politics, however, were generally skeptical about this narrative that placed Iran at the core of the rationale, stressing that Iranian encroachment in Yemen, although existent and likely to be increasing, was in reality limited (Juneau, 2016 ; Kendall, 2017).

The third narrative is one that has become more and more commonly heard as the war has raged on. First of all, broadcast by the Huthis themselves, the aggression narrative has to a large extent become dominant among the international media and NGOs. With a focus on Saudi Arabia's intervention, the war in Yemen has consequently been increasingly depicted as a war on Yemen, waged with questionable objectives. The humanitarian crisis, massive destruction of infrastructure, and the many civilian casualties in the bombardments by the coalition, in addition to the manifest stalemate on the military side, have generated increased criticism, including in early 2021 coming from the recently sworn-in Joe Biden administration in the United States.

Competition in the international media to impose this aggression narrative, or to nuance and deny it became fierce. Media reports were often biased, and some appeared to be politically loaded. Media coverage by Qatari-owned Al-Jazeera is a case in point. As tensions between Doha and its Gulf neighbors mounted in June 2017 and its army left the Arab coalition, Qatar media's reports suddenly became outwardly critical of Saudi Arabia and of the United Arab Emirates. Al-Jazeera developed an editorial line that was sharply different from the benevolent one it had until then broadcast before coming back to a less critical approach in January 2021 as tensions with Qatar's neighbors eased, even bringing certain documentaries such as one on Emirati policies in Soqotra to a halt. While it was less biased, focus by Western journalists from other mainstream media on the humanitarian crisis also reinforced the narrative of an unjustifiable war. Humanitarian agencies of the United Nations had since the beginning of fighting raised the alarm over possible famine and the fragility of Yemen and were consequently inclined, through the data they gathered, to feed the aggression narrative. Such was also the case of aid agencies of the United Kingdom, Germany, and France, but also of significant numbers of members of parliaments who developed critiques of the coalition that diplomats and ministers from these countries could hardly contest in public. Put under pressure, the UNSC and High Commission on Human Rights triggered enquiries in 2017 on rights violations and potential war crimes by the warring parties. A committee headed by Tunisian activist and former minister, Kamel Jendoubi, launched its investigations but faced resistance from all parties when requesting access to the field.

Despite some initial reluctance by various governments, including France and the United Kingdom (who claimed a discrete form of critique was a more efficient tactic to engage members of the Arab coalition), this third narrative has put Saudi political and military inconsistencies in the spotlight. It became significant among a variety of governments, in particular at an early stage the Netherlands, following media coverage of the war and opinion polls that highlighted condemnation of bombardments by the general public. Attempts by Saudi decision makers to invert such an image by highlighting the fact that the Huthis were launching missiles inside Saudi territory and thus acting as aggressors had little effect.

This narrative was often seen by the Huthis' opponents as unfair as it largely ignored alleged crimes of the rebels against civilians, in particular the issue of internationally banned anti-personnel landmines. Nevertheless, the third narrative gradually became dominant within Western countries, whose governments were accused of complicity in the war. Arms trade and contracts signed with the Gulf monarchies' military faced serious criticism in Europe and North America. Critiques, coming from a wide range of parties, generally saw these contracts as problematic and claimed imposing an arms embargo could be a possible lever to help impose peace, or at least halt bombing by the coalition. Votes in the parliaments in the United Kingdom and the United States (Postel, 2018), as well as by the European institutions, sought to exercise stricter control and transparency, but in reality, never had much effect. They nevertheless put Western decision makers under pressure through public as well as legal scrutiny. A number of these countries such as Germany, Sweden, and Spain ended up imposing a *de facto* embargo on arms trade with Saudi Arabia. Popular mobilizations against arms deliveries, such as in May 2019 in the ports of à Le Havre (France) and Genoa (Italy) exemplified the significance of the aggression narrative.

The Kingdom clearly had an image problem at the international level. While the United Arab Emirates was also playing a central role in the Arab coalition, that government's policies were not subject to much public scrutiny, concealed as they were by the focus on the leading Saudi role and the UAE's efficient public relations. However, gradually accusations regarding the existence of illegal prisons managed by the UAE as well as alliances with Salafi militias began to feed this third narrative, which although partial, had generated increased (albeit certainly nonlinear) concern for the situation in Yemen. That context likely influenced the Emirati decision in August 2019 to recall most of its troops positioned in Yemen and opt for a lighter footprint. Nevertheless, its alliance with the Southern Movement and its encroachment in Soqotra generated significant criticism from within Yemen.

Fragmented Interventions

Considering the gap between each of these conflicting narratives, it is not surprising that they generated fragmented interventions on the part of the international community. While a certain consensus had prevailed in the context of the "Yemeni Spring" of 2011 to support the political transition as defined by the "Gulf agreement" (al-mubadara al-khalijiyya) (Poirier, 2012; Girke, 2015; Muhammad and Sahabi, 2016) sponsored by Saudi Arabia and the "Friends of Yemen" group of donors, the subsequent war generated chaotic responses.

Beyond the apparently strict rationale of the military operations of the Saudi-led coalition, and the more or less direct support of the Huthis by the Islamic Republic of Iran, one finds that the international community's actions have lacked coherence and seemed chaotic. Since its various incarnations did not have a common understanding of the root causes of the war, and at times were incapable of choosing between the aforedescribed competing narratives (due to the absence of precise information, but also in order to preserve commercial interests linked to hydrocarbons and weapons), diplomatic strategies seemed lost.

Contrary to a dominant assessment that presupposes the existence of a clear agenda for Saudi Arabia and the UAE in Yemen (Hokayem and Roberts, 2016), it may well have been the absence of fixed objectives and policies that explains the failure of operation "Decisive Storm" (Partrick, 2018). From the onset, the coalition itself, in which the roles of each country were never fully clarified, exemplified such limits. Mobilization of foreign mercenaries, allegedly coming from Columbia, or of Sudanese soldiers could only impede the capacity of the coalition to engage on a terrain that its forces did not master. The fact that Qatar in 2017 and Morocco in 2019 quit the coalition, hesitations by Pakistan whose Parliament voted against participation in 2015 before its new prime minister finally sent a limited number of troops in 2018, and controversies surrounding possible participation of Senegalese soldiers in the spring of 2015 weakened the coalition's position both militarily and politically. Inside Yemen, fragmentation was only emphasized by the diversity of interests of the anti-Huthi camp which involves actors as diverse as Salafi militias, Southern secessionists, leaders of the Islah Party, liberals, and heirs of the Saleh clan from late 2017 onward. Considering the depth of enmity between each of these, it is hard to believe that any coordination could be achieved on a daily basis or in terms of long-term objectives.

Regional players within the coalition also appeared to develop diverging strategies as they were each pushing forward and repressing different actors. Beyond a shared opposition to the Huthis, allies and foes of the UAE and Saudi Arabia had different objectives on the ground. Abu Dhabi's military and diplomats were focusing on establishing an alliance with the Southern Movement but at the same time on preserving their country's relationship with the clan of former president Ali Abdallah Saleh many of whom had important financial interests in Dubai and the federation's capital. At the same time, the UAE was putting tremendous pressure on the Islah Party, associated with the Muslim Brotherhood which it regionally saw as its arch enemy, while neglecting (if not slandering) the legitimate government of Hadi. It even supported a move to oust Prime Minister Ahmed Bin Dagher in Aden in January 2018. For its part, Saudi decision makers were apparently keen on maintaining Hadi in place and on supporting unity of the country, and gradually reestablished significant relations with al-Islah as it became clear that they needed its support in various regions, in particular Ta'izz and Marib.

Rather than presuming that decision-making is centralized in these two states (in particular around the two specific princes—Muhammad bin Salman in Riyadh and Muhammad bin Zayed in Abu Dhabi—as many reports do), it may be relevant to claim that the war in Yemen has also been waged by the coalition in a fragmented manner, generating confusion and improvisation on the field. Further research on the day-to-day functioning of Saudi foreign policy, intelligence, and military institutions (and for that matter, of Emirati ones) is needed but there is no reason to consider that the Gulf States would be more unified and centralized than those of others. Political sociology has amply stressed the significance of bureaucratic fragmentation and institutional pluralism. These blur public policies, including diplomacy. Steffen Hertog's work (Hertog, 2010) on the functioning of the oil rent in Saudi Arabia gives a relevant insight into such realities, even in absolute monarchies. Such is also the case of the cultural policies of the smaller monarchies, as shown by Alexandre Kazerouni in his work on the development of museums in Qatar and the UAE (Kazerouni, 2017).

In the specific context of the conflict in Yemen, this fact may have been forgotten due to the illusion of control granted by apparently unlimited military budgets. However, non-trustworthy information coming from Yemeni allies impeded the capacity to implement decisions taken from above in an efficient manner. Ministries of foreign affairs of the UAE and Saudi Arabia, humanitarian agencies, the military, local clients and patrons, tribal leaders, all claimed to be acting in coordination. They were, in fact, operating separately, developing interventions and plans according to their own institutional subculture. The evolving tactics on the ground as much as the changing shape of the coalition implied a rather pragmatic approach, although one that could be depicted as poorly efficient.

Pragmatism did not generate coherence. Internal public policies such as the "Saudization" of the job market and the consequent deportation of many foreigners, in particular over 100,000 Yemenis, could hardly be seen as making a positive contribution to the military or the humanitarian situation. The loss of remittances sent by workers to Yemen as much as the forced expulsion of expatriates who would now resent Saudi policies and join the Huthis evidently clashed with the objective of reducing popular support for this group and solving the humanitarian crisis (Al-Awlaqi and others, 2019). Contradictions were thus manifest with the position of Saudi Arabia as the main financial contributor to the international humanitarian response organized by the UN agencies. The institutional subculture of the King Salman Humanitarian Center, a para-state organization, with a recognized capacity to answer parts of the basic needs of the Yemeni population, involving—by all accounts—aid workers who believed in helping civilians and in acting in the name of the higher interests of Saudi Arabia somehow controverted the mindset, actions, and policies of other actors. This was in particular the case for the military, which too claimed to be intervening in the name of Saudi Arabia, of the Arab coalition, and of the international community. It is these contradictions, which surely exist within all state structures, however centralized they may appear, that are often overlooked despite the fact that they explain much of the mess of world politics.

Despite these realities, many Yemenis, critical of the coalition's strategy, as well as many Western decision makers and analysts continuously assumed the existence of a consistent Yemeni strategy of the coalition or of each member of it. Conspiracy theories claiming to reveal the higher motives of UAE involvement in the south of Yemen are popular but should not be taken for granted, much like claims that Saudi Arabia is voluntarily destroying Yemeni heritage or aiming to kill as many civilians as possible. These happen largely out of deeply rooted contempt and disdain for Yemenis, but also out of limited competence and understanding. Grand strategies and coherent master plans may exist in the minds of decision makers and their advisers, but they can hardly be implemented due to lack of manpower, experience, knowledge, or trustworthy local relays. Large budgets are only a part of the solution. Implementation is more important than so-called visions.

However, despite its evident weaknesses, the myth of consistent strategies and of centralized policies before and during the war in Yemen has had a performative dimension. It is also because of this perception that the United States along with the European Union largely followed the agenda set by Saudi Arabia and the UAE in 2015. At the time, debates within the White House under the Barack Obama administration highlight an initial reluctance to support foreign military intervention in Yemen. Nevertheless, Western governments accepted the idea that they could play secondary roles. Their obsession with the fight against terror implied that they had lost track of other meaningful political dynamics in Yemen: the Huthis' rise to power, Iranian encroachment, Saleh resilience, and inter-Sunni Islamist competition. Implicitly acknowledging that they were themselves incapable of solving these issues, if not even of understanding what was unfolding in the country, they thereby left Saudi Arabia in the frontline. Saudi leaders were to a large extent perceived as knowledgeable and experienced enough to intervene and it was taken for granted that a plan existed and could be implemented. While trust in the Yemeni policies of Saudi Arabia and the UAE has evidently eroded in European capitals and in Washington over the years of war, Western diplomats have been unable to develop alternatives. Nor are they forecasting effectively what reconstruction of Yemen will actually imply for themselves as much as for regional powers. Such lack of planning is likely to come at a high cost for Yemenis.

Indeed, world powers, namely the five permanent members of the UNSC, can hardly be seen as having developed clear Yemen policies of their own or to have presented unified ones. The United States, United Kingdom, and France, albeit sticking to the first legal narrative and voting for the resolutions that structure it, more or less overtly implemented other options on the side. Military support to the coalition remained something decision makers were rarely willing to brag about and yet pursued, causing much democratic debates in parliaments, among parties, and in the media. In parallel, funding of humanitarian aid by these powers as well as majority votes by parliaments requesting to end support for the war expressed the kind of aforementioned fragmentation that states experience as they carry out foreign policies.

Furthermore, the fight against al-Qaeda remained an important determinant, but Western governments appeared to have trouble connecting it with the rationale of the war and its consequences. Between 2015 and 2018, American drone strikes continued to be used as a principal lever, managing to eliminate certain leaders of al-Qaeda in the Arabian Peninsula, yet generating further grievances amongst the population (Phillips, 2019). The collapse of the Yemeni state, in particular as the Huthis were largely in control of the intelligence apparatus that had previously interacted with other foreign services, at first benefited jihadi groups who managed to exercise control over large pieces of territory and important cities like Mukalla. Changes in policies on the ground by the coalition, tribes, and the military turned the tide and put pressure on jihadi groups from 2016 onward. However, Western powers did not manage to set a clear priority between the fight against two diverging enemies. In May 2019, declarations by French minister of foreign affairs, Jean-Yves Le Drian, regarding the context of the war in Yemen and the reasons why France was continuing to support the Arab coalition, highlighted how his government either misunderstood realities in Yemen or was willing to consider that the Huthis were a terrorist group responsible for exporting violence in a way comparable to al-Qaeda.[3]

For their part, China and Russia, although often willing to appear as political alternatives to the other three permanent members of the UNSC, never really accepted the need to transform the Yemeni issue into a factor of international polarization. Resolution 2216 was adopted by all except Russia which abstained. Only once did this country threaten, in 2018, to use its veto power on a draft resolution that would have condemned Iran for violating the arms embargo on Yemen based on the information collected by a panel of experts who monitor the sanctions regime. Russia had also allegedly pressured the experts to weaken their accusations against Iran.[4] Beyond that, and despite the capacity of its government to maintain a diplomatic presence in Sana'a and be able to speak with all parties, it remained at the back of the stage.

Parallel to each of these policies, a significant axis of intervention on the part of the international community rapidly became mediation as a means to achieve peace. Three successive special envoys of the United Nations secretary general received a mandate to help find a solution to the conflict, but their actions were constrained by the legal framework of resolution 2216, as well as by the warring parties. Talks were held in Switzerland twice (2015), then in Kuwait (2016) and in Sweden (2018), but little was achieved. British mediator Jamal Ben Omar had been active in the framework of the "Gulf Initiative," supporting the transition process. He resigned weeks after the beginning of the war after being seen by each of the parties as biased in favor of its opponents. His successor from April 2015, Mauritanian diplomat Ismail Ould Cheikh Ahmed, would rapidly face similar accusations, unable, for example, to engage with the Huthis in Sana'a for over a year. In February 2018, the nomination of Martin Griffiths, yet again a British special envoy, was intended to open a new chapter, benefiting for example from the support of Oman as a facilitator as well as his experience as a leading figure of international mediation, in particular through the Geneva-based Centre for Humanitarian Dialogue. Yet, apart from a September 2020 agreement to exchange over 1,000 prisoners, tangible results of his commitment remained scarce.

The framing of the negotiations on Yemen as ones between two competing legitimacies—the one of the Huthis versus the Hadi government generated inefficiency as it excluded local actors from talks and commitments, in particular the Southern movement, as well as regional ones. The latter could thus continue to act unilaterally, deciding on their own whether to increase humanitarian aid, fund militias, or exercise new military pressure. It has been impossible to acknowledge fully the regional dimensions of the war so that parties like Iran are excluded from the negotiations, thus adding to the complexities of finding a solution.

Confronted with such deadlocks, initiatives by organizations more or less independent of their governments to support "track 2" diplomacy were illustrative of a certain pragmatism. They were intended to circumvent the legitimate Yemeni government which suffered from poor popular backing, as well as UN agencies. At the same time, they also highlighted a certain form of competition between Western countries to take the leadership, including between European Union members. Projects by the Berghof foundation of Germany or by French association Promediation exemplified such attempts but unfortunately never had the capacity to produce game-changing processes. The support they received from the authorities of their own country also highlighted the unease of these Western governments toward the policies favored by the Arab coalition and largely endorsed by the United Nations Security Council. Attempts to foster negotiations at the sub-state level lacked efficiency due to the fragmentation of the political field in Yemen as much as the will of the Hadi government to preserve its position as the sole legitimate interlocutor of the international community.

The issue of humanitarian aid encountered similar limitations and also became a lever that the international community would use on various occasions to try to foster a shift in regional policies. Such was the case with the humanitarian conference held in Paris in June 2018.[5] In the weeks after the beginning of the war, the various bodies of the United Nations had almost instantly raised the alarm and referred to the crisis in Yemen as the "most important in the world," if not potentially of "the last fifty years" as Mark Lowcock, the head of the UN office for the Coordination of Humanitarian Affairs (OCHA), would state in January 2018. However, the figure of casualties produced by the United Nations was stuck between mid-2016 and mid-2018 at 10,000 deaths. The figure was a gross understatement that had little coherence with the way actors within the UN were depicting the situation on the ground. The important cholera epidemic of mid-2017 served as a means to mobilize the international community and the media. Pictures of dying children and the threat of a large-scale famine aimed to reorient the policies of world and regional powers by generating popular pressure on decision makers in democracies. However, some international humanitarian NGOs like Médecins sans Frontières were uneasy with the instrumentation of the Yemeni humanitarian crisis by all parties and the persistent depiction of the war in Yemen as one that was "hidden" or "ignored." In reality, international involvement was very significant, albeit poorly calibrated. International aid, much like in other situations, generated corruption and served the development of a war economy (International Crisis Group, 2018). The existence of certain safety nets, in particular remittances and humanitarian aid deliveries, had actually prevented the catastrophe from reaching the level official bodies of the UN had predicted. This was certainly not to deny the existence of a humanitarian catastrophe but to understand the ways through which many Yemenis had, to a certain extent, managed to survive despite the crumbling economy, if only to ensure that these nets could be maintained throughout the war or reinvented, as was the case with the Central Bank. The Covid-19 pandemic in 2020 raised similar questions regarding resilience of the society, with many Yemenis ending up considering that the virus was a scam (al-Rubaidi and al-Absi, 2020), and consequently generating few dedicated public policies on the part of the authorities. Nevertheless, the period coincided with a shrinking of funding for aid programs in Yemen.

Conclusion

The story of the international community's involvement in the Yemen war since 2015 is one of missed opportunities and unexplored alternatives. Trapped by a legal framework and narrative that gradually lost its relevance, regional as much as world powers have, contrary to a dominant assessment, projected chaotic policies. The military option did have prevalence for some but was also implemented along with other options and interventions, with little if any long-term vision. Such a statement does not imply that if one option had been chosen over all others, it would have entailed more efficiency. Coherence is not always equivalent to success. Consequently, the depiction of such fragmentation of the international community's interactions with the Yemen war should not be seen as prescriptive. It is merely an assessment of the diversity of the international community and of interventions at the sublevel of states and institutions.

However, this chapter also suggests that the different diagnoses (or narratives) regarding the root causes of the war and of how to bring stability to Yemen may appear altogether problematic. They remain too focused on short-term issues, neglecting to look at what Yemen may look like in the next decade. Understanding of the history of Yemen and of the country's various challenges in reality remain partial. Water depletion (Weiss, 2015), demographic growth, economics, and identity politics are bound to become objects of profound (if not existential) concern for Yemenis themselves as well as for the world. These issues, however, hardly appear in the representations of the international community. They are yet fundamental and will need to be at the core of all interactions in the years to come if Yemen is to have a future, as a state and as a society. Due to the interdependent nature of regional dynamics, let it be clear that the fate of its neighbors is also to a large extent contingent on the international actors finally clarifying their narratives, policies, and priorities when it comes to Yemen.

Notes

1   "60 Minutes," CBS News, March 19, 2018.
2   Khaled Al-Khaled and Laurent Bonnefoy, "La télévision yéménite en temps de ramadan : Un miroir de la guerre," *Orient XXI*, May 24, 2019.
3   http://videos.assemblee-nationale.fr/video.7711088_5ced54a495504.commission-des -affaires-etrangeres--m-jean-yves-le-drian-ministre-de-l-europe-et-des-affaires-etr-28 -mai-2019. Comments on Yemen by Jean-Yves Le Drian start after 1h 24 minutes.
4   https://www.politico.com/magazine/story/2018/07/19/russia-got-me-fired-from-the -un-219019
5   Pierre Bernin, "Le Yémen, la guerre et la France," *Orient XXI*, July 2, 2018. https:// orientxxi.info/magazine/le-yemen-la-guerre-et-la-france,2537

References

Aboueldahab, N. (2019), "Reclaiming Yemen: The Role of the Yemeni Professional Diaspora," *Brookings Institute*, Doha Center paper 26, Available online: https://www .brookings.edu/wp-content/uploads/2019/04/Reclaiming-Yemen-The-role-of-the -Yemeni-professional-diaspora_English_Web.pdf (accessed April 17, 2020).

al-Akhali, R. (2016), "Yemen Transition 2.0. M-Floos: A Game Changer?," *DeepRoot Consulting*. Available online: https://www.deeproot.consulting/single-post/2016/06/09/ Yemen-Transition-20-MFloos-A-Game-Changer (accessed April 17, 2020).

Al-Awlaqi W. and others (2019), "Yemen's Expatriate Workforce Under Threat: The Essential Role of Remittances in Mitigating Economic Collapse," *Sanaa Center for Strategic Studies, Rethinking Yemen's Economy Papers*, p. 39. Available online: http:// sanaacenter.org/files/Rethinking_Yemens_Economy_No5.pdf (accessed April 17, 2020).

al-Dawsari, N. (2012), "Tribal Governance and Stability in Yemen," *Carnegie Middle East Papers*, 26 p. Available online: https://carnegieendowment.org/2012/04/24/tribal -governance-and-stability-in-yemen-pub-47838

al-Madhagi, A.(1994), *Yemen and the USA: A Study of a Small State and Super-Power Relationship (1962–1994)*, London: IB Tauris, p. 244.

al-Muslimi F. (2019), "Revitalizing Yemen's Banking Sector," *Sanaa Center for Strategic Studies*, p. 18.

al-Rubaidi, A. and K. al-Absi (2020), "Religious Discourses on Coronavirus in Yemen," Konrad Adenauer Stiftung Polities Reports, 6 p. Available online: https://www.kas.de/ en/web/rpg/detail/-/content/religious-discussions-on-coronavirus-in-yemen (accessed March 16, 2021).

al-Salahi F., ed. (2012), *Al-thawra al-yamaniyya. Al-khalfiyya wal-afaq*, Beirut: Arab Center for Research and Policy Studies, 494p.

al-Shargabi A., (2018), "The Restructuring of the Yemeni Army," *AlMuntaqa*, 1 (1): 38–50.

al-Uqab A. (1998), *Tatawur al-ilaqat al-yamaniyya al-sa'udiyya*, Aden: Dar Jami'at, Adan, p. 361.

Alley A. L. (2013), "Yemen Changes Everything… and Nothing," *Journal of Democracy*, 24 (4): 74–85.

Augustin, A-l. (2018), "Generational and Political Change in Southern Yemen: 'The Generation of Unity' Envisions its Southern State," in Marie-Christine Heinze (ed.), *Yemen and the Search for Stability: Power, Politics and Society after the Arab Spring*, London: IB Tauris, pp. 93–114.

Bonnefoy, L. (2018), *Yemen and the World: Beyond Insecurity*, London: Hurst, p. 234.

Bonnefoy, L. and M. Poirier (2012), "The Structuration of the Yemeni Revolution: Exploring a Process in Motion," *Revue française de science politique*, 62 (5): 895–913.

Brandt, M. (2017), *Tribes and Politics in Yemen: A History of the Houthi Conflict*, London: Hurst, p. 480.

Brehony, N. (2011), *Yemen Divided: The Story of a Failed State in South Arabia*, London: IB Tauris, p. 304.

Burgat, F. (2006), "Le Yémen après le 11 septembre 2001 : entre construction de l'État et rétrécissement du champ politique," » *Critique internationale*, 32, pp. 9–21.

Carapico, S. (2013), *Political Aid and Arab Activism: Democracy Promotion, Justice, and Representation*, Cambridge: Cambridge University Press, p. 261.

Clausen, M. -L. (2015), "Understanding the Crisis in Yemen: Evaluating Competing Narratives," *The International Spectator*, 50 (3): 16–29.

Day, S. (2012), *Regionalism and Rebellion in Yemen:; A Troubled National Union*, Cambridge: Cambridge University Press, p. 369.

Girke, N. (2015), "A Matter of Balance: The European Union as a Mediator in Yemen," *European Security*, 24 (4): 509–24.

Hertog, S. (2010), *Princes, Brokers, and Bureaucrats. Oil and the State in Saudi Arabia*, London: Cornell University Press.

Hokayem, E. and D. Roberts (2016), "The War in Yemen," *Survival*, 58 (6): 157–86.

International Crisis Group (2018), *How to Halt Yemen's Slide into Famine*, Middle East and North Africa Reports, 193, 31 p. Available online: https://www.crisisgroup.org/middle -east-north-africa/gulf-and-arabian-peninsula/yemen/193-how-halt-yemens-slide -famine (accessed April 17, 2020).

Juneau, T. (2016), "Iran's Policy towards the Houthis in Yemen: A Limited Return on a Modest Investment," *International Affairs*, 92 (3): 647–63.

Kazerouni, A. (2017), *Le miroir des cheikhs: Musée et politique dans les principautés du golfe Persique*, Paris: Presses Universitaires de France.

Kendall, E. (2017), "Iran's Fingerprints in Yemen: Real or Imagined?" *Atlantic Council Issue Brief*, 14 p. Available online: https://www.atlanticcouncil.org/images/Irans _Fingerprints_in_Yemen_web_1019.pdf (accessed April 17, 2020).

Lackner, H.(2017), *Yemen in Crisis: Autocracy, Neo-Liberalism and the Disintegration of a State*, London: Saqi, p. 400.

Muhammad, F. and N. Sahabi (2016), "al-quwa al-iqlimiyya al-muathira bi amn wa istiqrar al yaman. Al-mamlaka al-arabiyya al-sa'udiyya namudhajan lil-muda 1990– 2015," *Majalah al-adab*, 116: 443–74. Available online: https://www.iasj.net/iasj?func =article&aId=114893 (accessed April 17, 2020).

Partrick, N., ed. (2018), *Saudi Arabian Foreign Policy :Conflict and Cooperation*, London: IB Tauris, p. 416.

Phillips, S. (2019), "Making al-Qa'ida Legible: Counter-terrorism and the Reproduction of Terrorism," *European Journal of International Relations*, 25(4), 1132–56.

Poirier, M. (2012), « L'initiative du Golfe et le processus institutionnel de transition », in L. Bonnefoy, F. Mermier, and M. Poirier (eds.), *Yémen: Le tournant révolutionnaire*, Paris: Karthala – CEFAS, pp. 167–72.

Postel, D. (2018), "Progressive Surge Propels Turning Point in US Policy on Yemen," MERIP, n°289, Available online: https://merip.org/2019/03/progressive-surge-propels -turning-point-in-us-policy-on-yemen/

Ruys, T. and L. Ferro (2016), "Weathering the Storm: Legality and Legal Implications of the Saudi-led Military Intervention in Yemen," *International and Comparative Law Quarterly*, 65 (1): 61–98.

Weiss, M. (2015), "A Perfect Storm: The Causes and Consequences of Severe Water Scarcity, Institutional Breakdown and Conflict in Yemen," *Water International*, 40 (2): 251–72.

Willis, J. (2012), *Unmaking North and South: Cartographies of the Yemeni Past*, London: Hurst, p. 276.

Chapter 2

THE FUTURE STRUCTURE OF THE YEMENI STATE

Stephen Day

When Yemen's transitional government collapsed months before international warfare commenced on March 26, 2015, a plan existed in the capital, Sana´a, to restructure the state along federal lines. The plan was based on outcomes of a UN-sponsored National Dialogue Conference (NDC) held between March 2013 and January 2014. The most momentous and controversial decision taken at the NDC was to devolve powers of government decision-making to elected authorities in multiple regions around the country. While all delegates consented in principle to a federal devolution of power, they could not agree on the number of new federal regions and their boundaries. As a result, the final decision was left to a special executive committee appointed by President Abdo Rabbuh Mansour Hadi (Day, 2014).

Meeting in February 2014, the committee on federal regions was tasked to choose between two options: one, a two-region state defined primarily by the country's pre-1990 north-south boundary line; and the other, a six-region state dividing the more populous northern half of the country into four regions and the southern half into two regions, all based on the boundaries of existing provinces. After the committee opted for the six-region option, a new constitution was prepared by the end of 2014 with subsequent plans calling for a popular referendum in 2015 prior to national elections and formation of a new government. But in January 2015, Huthi rebel leaders acted in league with former president Ali Abdullah Saleh to block adoption of the constitution, kidnapping Hadi's chief of staff, Ahmed Bin Mubarak, and placing the president and prime minister under house arrest. This precipitated armed conflicts across the country several weeks before Saudi Arabia intervened at the head of an international military coalition (Day, 2015). In short, the NDC federal constitution was one of the main reasons for the country's descent toward violence.

The question of Yemen's state structure is at the heart of political problems in the country that extend back decades before its national unification in 1990. Prior to 1990, separate northern and southern states existed on opposite sides of a line drawn originally by imperial Ottoman and British authorities in the decade prior to the First World War. The old north-south border was always artificial because it largely served foreign imperial interests rather than interests of the wider population on the ground. Following the collapse of the Ottoman Empire, the border remained in place largely due to Britain's colonial interests in Aden, which it began using as a coaling station along the sea route to India in the 1830s. The city later served as a British base and major shipping port on global trade routes. Shortly after Britain withdrew from Aden in the late 1960s, Cold War politics injected new life into Yemen's north-south border when a Soviet-allied regime came to power in Aden, while Western and Saudi interests sought to keep Sana'a outside the orbit of the USSR.

The heightened political relevance of Yemen's north-south division during later decades of the Cold War was ironic because a boundary line drawn decades prior to actual Cold War divisions of the world, such as Germany, Korea, and Vietnam, masked multiple divisions of far greater importance. It is essential to bear in mind that Yemen's north-south division was not a creation of the Cold War, unlike the divisions in Germany, Korea, and Vietnam. When north and south Yemen united in 1990 just months before formal German unification, observers wanted to believe that Yemen's internal divisions were fully resolved by the fortuitous ending of Cold War rivalries. But the erasure of Yemen's north-south border unmasked multiple divisions of greater relevance in the country's history. Today, these multiple divisions are at the root of Yemen's domestic problems, and they will remain at the root of problems concerning the future structure of the state.

Yemen's centuries-old internal divisions are shaped and defined by tribal, sectarian, and other sociocultural differences within the population that primarily correspond to distinct features of the country's remarkable landscape, including towering mountains, deep valleys and canyons, and a broad interior desert. Differences of dialect, dress, and other customs distinguish communities in separate regions, including the highland plateau in the west extending from Ibb's al-Samara pass in the south to Sa'ada on the border with Saudi Arabia in the north; the Tihama coastal plain that stretches along the Red Sea; Ta'izz and the fertile "midlands" north of Aden; the city of Aden and its hinterland; Bayhan, Marib, and Al-Jawf on the edge of the interior desert; and the relatively separate Hadhramaut and Al-Mahrah, near the eastern border with Oman (Day, 2012, pp. 44–53).

Prior to the end of Yemen's Zaydi imamate in 1962, the vast highland plateau around the capital Sana'a served as the Zaydi seat of power for roughly one thousand years. Zaydi imams ruled this mountainous northern region as a heterodox branch of Shi'a Islam with none of the sectarian grudges of Shi'a in northern Arab countries like Iraq, Syria, and Lebanon. Yemen's Zaydi generally sought accommodation with local Sunni populations. Yet, dynastic Ayyubid rulers of Tihama along the Red Sea coast and Rasulid rulers of Ta'izz fought wars with Zaydi imams, seizing control of Sana'a at different times between the twelfth and fifteenth centuries. Historically speaking, the Zaydi of Yemen lacked social, cultural, political, and economic roots in coastal, southern, and eastern regions, each of which tended to be ruled by separate authorities. Before the Islamic era, similar divisions existed between separate regional authorities because Yemen's rugged landscape rarely allowed unification under a single ruler. In other words, topographical features clearly defined Yemen as a mosaic political culture over millennia. Across Islamic history, the Tihama and Ta'izz were home to chief rivals of the Zaydi imamate. Populations in these areas are not Zaydi, subscribing, instead, to one of four orthodox Sunni schools, the Shafiʿi. The 1962 revolution which unseated the last Zaydi imam gained momentum from political activism in Shafiʿi areas around Taʿizz.

The old sectarian contest over state power was revived when Huthi rebels seized power in Sanaʿa during 2014 and 2015. They descended upon the national capital from the traditional seat of Zaydi authority in Saʿada to the north, where the Huthi family launched Zaydi revival in the 1990s. Former president Saleh fought six wars against Huthi rebels in the 2000s, yet after being removed as head of state in 2011, he enabled the rebels to seize control by forging new alliances within two powerful tribal confederations: Hashid and Bakil. Huthi alliances with Hashid and Bakil mirrored a centuries-old pattern on Yemen's highland plateau, where imams rose to power on wings of the same two tribal confederations in keeping with Zaydi traditions. Today, the effect of the Huthis' rise to power destroyed what little remained of national unity in Yemen because it sharpened opposition among Shafiʿis in Taʿizz and the Tihama, as well as southern and eastern regions of the country, while importing highly contentious politics of Shiʿa in northern Arab countries, particularly through contact with Iranian-backed Hezbollah in Lebanon (see Chapter 3).

Yemeni politics typically reflect politics elsewhere in the Muslim world. Due to its strategic location on the Arabian Peninsula at the Bab al-Mandab entrance to the Red Sea, it invites outside interference. But the country is notoriously difficult for foreigners to conquer. Saudi Arabia's military campaign in alliance with the UAE confirmed lessons learned by King Abdulaziz in the 1930s, which were learned before and after him by Ottomans and Egyptians, respectively. The impact of Saudi-Emirati actions also contributed to Sunni-Shiʿa rivalry in Yemen because they justified their actions as Sunni Arab resistance to the spread of Iranian Shiʿa politics. As Huthi leaders sought closer ties to Iran and its Hezbollah allies in Lebanon in order to arm themselves against Saudi-Emirati attacks, it made Saudi Arabia and the UAE more vulnerable to counter-attack by Huthi forces using Iranian/Hezbollah-supplied military technology.

Internationalization of Yemen's conflict in 2015 clearly exacerbated the country's fragmentation. This was especially true in the south where Saudi and Emirati forces provided aid and support to rival factions. As a result, it became more difficult to address the domestic causes of Yemen's problems. The latter is the only way forward to rebuild the country, and it requires revisiting outcomes of the UN-sponsored National Dialogue Conference (NDC). Can the six-region plan be adapted as the basis of a unified federal state, perhaps along other lines with a different number of regions? Or will the plan inevitably be abandoned, resulting in the creation of two or more independent states, perhaps linked in a weak confederation with each other?

Historical Background

There are four episodes in modern history when the option of federalism arose during discussions of state structure in Yemen: first, during the late 1950s and 1960s when Britain proposed federation in the south at the end of the colonial period; second, during the late 1980s and 1990s when confederation was briefly discussed at the time of Yemen's national unification; third, the middle 1990s when federalism was proposed by southern politicians on the eve of a 1994 civil war, followed by Saleh's plans of political decentralization after the war; and fourth, the planned six-region federal state after the NDC in 2013/2014 once Saleh's rule ended amid the "Arab Spring" revolutions of 2011. Lessons from all four episodes apply to Yemen's current predicament, so they are worth reviewing before considering future options.

The idea of federalism was first introduced by British colonial leaders who proposed a Federation of South Arabia in 1959. Ever since, the concept has been associated with foreign interests, which local nationalists believe conspired to keep Yemen divided. This was one of the main problems with the six-region plan in 2014 because the UN-sponsored NDC was backed by GCC and Western diplomats. There is a repeated pattern of ambitious leaders of hegemonic groups in Yemen accusing foreigners of seeking to weaken the state by dividing it into parts. When Huthi leaders overthrew the transitional government in 2014/2015, it was a prime example. They opposed the post-NDC six-region federal plan, using nationalist rhetoric about foreign enemies to justify their seizure of power in Sana'a. Regardless of how appropriate federalism is to Yemen's future political and economic development, the effort to implement it will undoubtedly be challenged by hegemonic actors like the Huthis.

During the late 1950s, when the British government in London prepared to depart Aden, it attempted to transfer power to a federal council of more than twenty local emirs, sultans, and sheikhs. The latter previously helped rule separate areas of south Yemen under a British "protectorate" system that was generally administered in eastern and western zones. Local sultans in the eastern protectorate adamantly refused to unite with rulers of the Western protectorate. Plans to rotate the presidency were hindered by rivalries and distrust among those who agreed to join the federation. Meanwhile, two popular national liberation movements, one of which received support from Egyptian commanders aiding Republican forces in north Yemen, mobilized the population against the federal plan, using violence to pursue their agenda. Leaders of one liberation movement came to power when Britain departed at the end of November 1967. They scrapped the federal plan and sought to centralize government authority in Aden.

Across the 1960s, Yemeni nationalist sentiments surged across the north and south following revolutionary events in both halves. Republicans in the north who overthrew the last Zaydi imamate sympathized with southern resistance fighters who opposed the British federal plan. Revolutionaries on both sides embraced the idea that all Yemenis should unite as one nation, something which remained a strong aspiration of the two revolutionary governments. Over the following decades, the concept of federalism was buried because popular sentiments in both halves of the country associated it with former British rule. Thus, when national unity talks began in the 1970s, leading to the drafting of a single constitution, the possible value of federalism was never considered because participants favored a centralized state.

When north and south Yemeni officials met in 1989 to negotiate national unity, a proposal of confederation was briefly raised by both sides. Delegates suggested that domestic and economic policies should be left in the hands of leaders in Sana'a and Aden, while the two sides merged their foreign and national security policies. But southern leader Ali Salem al-Bidh favored an immediate, complete merger of the two governments, and northern president Ali Abdullah Saleh accepted his proposal. The unity agreement was based on a power-sharing formula that granted Saleh the title of president and al-Bidh the title of vice president on a five-member presidential council with three members from the north and two from the south. Southerners were allowed to hold the positions of prime minister and speaker of parliament, and the first cabinet was evenly divided on a 50:50 basis.

Shortly after Yemen's unification on May 22, 1990, the country's long history of civil strife and political assassinations returned as the unity agreement proved paper-thin. The new state experienced major problems, forcing a postponement of the first scheduled parliamentary election from the fall of 1992 to the spring of 1993. When voting did not result in majority party rule, it forced negotiations during the summer of 1993 to form a coalition government. This led to political stalemate as sentiments of "buyer's remorse" spread among southerners who were outnumbered more than four to one by northerners. It was at this moment that southern leaders of the Yemeni Socialist Party (YSP), which was placed third behind Saleh's ruling General People's Congress party (GPC) and a conservative Islamist party called Islah ("Reform"), revived discussions of federalism, demanding decentralization of government in two regions. Northern politicians suspected talk of federalism was part of a southern plot to secede, so they accused YSP leaders and their supporters of treason.

During the winter of 1993/94, an early series of national dialogue conferences prefigured work of the NDC in 2013/14. The majority of participants from all regions favored decentralizing power to locally elected governors and mayors at provincial, district, and municipal levels. This became the key element of an agreement signed by northern and southern politicians, including President Saleh and leaders of the YSP and Islah Party, at a February 1994 meeting held under the auspices of King Hussein in Amman, Jordan. Ink on the agreement, known as the Document of Pledge and Accord (DPA), was barely dry when Saleh ordered his military to launch an attack on a southern army camp. Soon afterward, the country descended into civil war in late April. Northern troops gradually overran southern lands, and by early July YSP leaders fled into exile. Thereafter, most southerners felt they lived under northern occupation because President Saleh instituted centralized military rule.

The prewar DPA did not amount to a full federal plan in Yemen. It merely suggested government decentralization as a way to avoid military conflict. If Yemeni politicians had unified the country in 1990 on the basis of federation or confederation, it is possible the 1994 war and much of the preceding troubles could have been avoided. This is true because the incentive to compete for post-electoral control over the central government would have been dramatically reduced. Saleh clearly sought to use the civil war to consolidate and preserve his powers over the central government in Sana'a. Before the fighting ended, however, he made a commitment to decentralize government by allowing elections of local governors and mayors, as promised when he signed the DPA in Amman. At this point, following intervention by Egyptian President Hosni Mubarak and UN diplomats who negotiated a cessation of hostilities after northern victory was assured, Saleh recommitted himself to the DPA principles.

UN officials and Arab leaders in Egypt and Jordan recognized that the DPA offered a potential way to reconcile political differences in Yemen and avoid further alienating marginalized populations. The problem was that President Saleh did not take the need to decentralize government seriously. Through the remainder of the 1990s, he postponed implementation of DPA principles calling for local elections. During the long delay, Saleh and members of his ruling party continued treating public calls for decentralization as a sign of treason against the nation. Proponents of full federalism were regularly intimidated and harassed by agents of the state, especially in southern and eastern regions. What little remained of national unionist sentiment quickly disappeared under a regime that amounted to military dictatorship with corrupt politicians exploiting national resources for their own benefit.

President Saleh finally advanced legislation defining Yemen's "local authorities" in February 2000. The law allowed elected "advisory councils" at provincial and district levels, but these were poorly funded and tasked merely with providing advice to governors who remained appointed by the president (Day 2012, 186–9). In short, Saleh intended to keep tight control of all decision-making in Sana'a. Two years earlier, the president had forced tens of thousands of southern civil servants and military officers into retirement. By cutting employment and offering no effective means of democratic representation, Saleh created deep disillusionment among southerners, including close allies who helped him maintain the pretense of north-south unity after 1994. At the end of 2001, some southern allies organized a group called "Sons of Southern and Eastern Provinces." They sent Saleh a letter demanding a greater share of political, social, and economic opportunities. When Saleh ignored them, they went public with their demands (Day, 2012, pp. 191–3). At this point, it became inevitable that Saleh would face mass protests.

The significance of internal dynamics in Yemen driving mass opposition in the 2000s is how these dynamics reflected regional divisions that undermined national unity, thus making it necessary to decentralize government, whether via federalism or other means, once Saleh resigned in 2011. There were three primary sources of mass opposition: first, and most importantly, the armed Huthi rebellion which started in 2004 along the border with Saudi Arabia in Sa'ada province; second, the 2006 formation of a broad coalition of opposition parties, known as the Joint Meeting Parties (JMP), which ran a viable opposition candidate for president during the same year; and third, the southern Hirak movement that began in 2007. Two of these three centered on specific regions. Only the JMP represented a national constituency with potential to unseat Saleh while maintaining a single governing authority, yet the JMP failed to inspire passions comparable to Huthi rebels and Hirak street protesters.

Throughout President Saleh's thirty-three-year rule, he played a dangerous political game by constantly shifting alliances to keep domestic rivals off balance. He called the game "dancing on the heads of snakes." In the early 1990s, Saleh relied upon conservatives of the Islah Party, whether members of the Muslim Brotherhood or allies of Wahhabi clerics in Saudi Arabia, to defeat the southern YSP. Then, shortly after the 1994 civil war, he broke relations with Islah and tried to govern solely through his GPC party, while attempting to create a family dynasty with his sons and nephews serving as top commanders of the national armed forces. Saleh's gamesmanship eventually aided Huthi and Hirak because they, too, considered Islah an enemy. If Saleh had continued his alliance with Islah, a relatively strong national unionist government was possible. But the effect of his political maneuvers compelled Islah to join the YSP and other opposition parties in the JMP coalition. Amid ongoing warfare with Huthi rebels in the north and repression of Hirak protesters in the south, the JMP forced a total shutdown of politics when it organized a nationwide boycott of Yemen's fourth parliamentary elections in 2009.

Two full years before the "Arab Spring," Saleh appeared extremely weak in the face of strong opposition. This made Yemen unique among revolutionary "Arab Spring" states because the regime's pending downfall was widely expected, in contrast to others like Tunisia, Egypt, Libya, and Syria. For decades, analysts of Yemen foresaw a combination of economic, social, and environmental crises leading to a total collapse of the state (Lackner, 2014). Indeed, its 2011 revolution occurred at a time when Yemen was on the verge of becoming a "failed state."

During the momentous year of Arab revolutions, nothing less than Yemen's short-lived, historic unification was at stake. For this reason, the subsequent transition period with the National Dialogue Conference as its centerpiece served primarily as an attempt to salvage national unity. When the NDC opened in Sana´a during the spring of 2013, the grievances of Huthi rebels were addressed inside a working group called the "Sa´ada matter," while Hirak's grievances were addressed in a separate working group called the "Southern matter." These forums were unique at the NDC because they were the only ones dealing with regionally based opposition. Another one of eleven total working groups, entitled "State structure," advanced discussions on federalism.

Despite the similarities of how the NDC dealt with Huthi and Hirak grievances, the two groups held different interests and motives. Although Hirak never formed a unified leadership, the heads of its most active factions favored full southern independence. They chose to boycott the NDC in Sana´a because they refused any and all associations with the north, federal or otherwise. Meanwhile, Huthi leaders opposed federalism because they held hegemonic interests to exercise power through the central government, essentially aspiring to inherit Saleh's position while reviving Zaydi power and authority. Nonetheless, they went along with the NDC because they were glad simply to have a seat at the table.

Due to Hirak's boycott of the NDC, President Hadi was forced to recruit southern delegates to act in the group's name. Leaders of the delegation preferred a two-region federal state, north and south, yet President Hadi and many northern delegates feared a two-region state would revert to the pre-1990 division. Hadi was originally from the south, and he feared a two-region state would allow his main southern rivals to return to power, especially former southern leader al-Bid and his allies directly north of Aden. Northern delegates from the Tihama coast, midland provinces of Ta'izz and Al-Bayda, and interior provinces of Marib and Al-Jawf agreed with Hadi's rejection of a unified southern region, but they also refused to continue living under the influence of traditionally dominant tribes on the highland plateau around Sana'a. For the latter reason, northern delegates from outside the highland region preferred dividing northern lands along multiple lines. This was the main reason why the NDC ended in disagreement on the number of federal regions, requiring President Hadi to appoint a special committee that chose the six-region plan. Hadi was strongly criticized for arranging the special committee outside the NDC process, and he was accused of "rigging" the outcome, yet few critics had a viable alternative plan given the country's many divisions.

Huthi delegates went along with the NDC consensus in early 2014, but by the end of the year their leadership became the strongest critic of the six-region federal plan. They mainly complained that the plan deprived their homeland in Sa'ada of access to a port on the Red Sea. For the sake of convenience, the post-NDC committee on federalism defined the six regions along boundary lines of existing provinces, and Sa'ada previously lacked access to the Red Sea. Once the new federal map was published, citizens in many areas complained about the artificial nature of provincial boundary lines. Hadi's government received numerous suggestions of better ways to create the six regions. But the president and his staff preferred to negotiate after a new government was established in 2015. In other words, Hadi never denied Huthi leaders access to a Red Sea port. He simply wanted to postpone redrawing regional boundary lines (Bin Mubarak, personal interview, 2019). Nonetheless, Huthi leaders staged their September 2014 coup in alliance with former president Saleh to block implementation of the six-region federal constitution in early 2015.

Evaluating Yemen's Future Prospects

Following six years of highly destructive and deadly warfare, it is difficult to imagine Yemen being reconstructed in the 2020s with a draft constitution prepared at a time of relative peace in 2014. The joint coup by Huthi leaders and former president Saleh destroyed what little potential existed for the NDC-derived federal constitution. In September 2014, just prior to the coup in Sana'a, President Hadi's chief of staff Bin Mubarak traveled to Sa'ada province with UN Special Envoy Jamal Benomar in order to meet Huthi leaders and try to persuade them to support outcomes of the NDC. According to Bin Mubarak, Abd al-Malik al-Huthi raised his right hand while claiming ownership of all northern lands in pre-1990 Yemen (Bin Mubarak, personal interview, 2019). In other words, the Huthis rejected the federal constitution not simply because their homeland in Sa'ada province lacked port access on the Red Sea. Instead, they sought complete control of the central government in Sana'a.

Political dynamics of the 2014/2015 coup by joint Huthi-Saleh forces derive from the tendency of powerful actors on the highland plateau to seek hegemony over the entire country. Zaydi imams who ruled in alliance with sheikhs of the dominant highland tribes, Hashid and Bakil, had done the same for centuries. People of Tihama and southern and eastern provinces, including Ta'izz, Marib, and others beyond them, opposed the historic ruling alliance between Zaydi leaders and highland tribes. Thus, the coup revived an age-old pattern in Yemen, as Huthi leaders relied primarily upon the same support systems of the Zaydi imamate. Before and after the coup, Huthis proved highly effective at winning the loyalty of leading sheikhs of Hashid and Bakil, undermining not only Saleh's base of power, but also the power of former ruling sheikhs of Hashid who led the Sunni Islamist party, Islah.

This is the first significant point arising from events in Yemen: namely, the revival of Zaydism. Saleh played a crucial role because his survival instincts and desire for revenge against Islah leaders led him to support Huthi leaders during and after the 2014/2015 coup. Earlier in the 1990s, elements of Saleh's ruling circle aided the Huthi family when the latter initiated Zaydi revival among the youth of Sa'ada province, despite the fact that Saleh supported Salafi groups at other times as part of his customary divide-and-rule strategy. Those who sympathized with Huthis viewed Zaydism as a means of weakening the influence of Salafis and other Sunni Islamists who gained influence with Saudi assistance between the 1970s and 2000s, especially those within the Islah Party. But Zaydism was bound to inflame intercommunal conflicts that proved destructive of national unity, while antagonizing Saudi Arabia. The importation of Saudi-Iranian rivalry and the resulting Sunni-Shi'a religious tensions are entirely new phenomena in Yemen, complicating any effort to reconstruct the country along federal or non-federal lines.

The second significant point also reflects historical patterns, although limited to the modern era when ambitious leaders of hegemonic groups opposed federal decentralization. Similar to the rhetoric of leaders of southern national liberation in the 1960s, Huthi leaders accused foreigners of conspiring to use federalism to divide and weaken the state. It was largely on this basis that they mobilized against the six-region federal constitution in early 2015. They claimed President Hadi conspired with UN diplomats and other foreigners, especially US and Gulf Arab diplomats, to destroy Yemeni national unity by advancing the NDC-derived constitution. It is worth appreciating that this aspect of the Huthi position reverses historical patterns. Back in the 1960s, it was the traditional Zaydi clerics of Sa'ada province who allied with Saudi Arabia and Western governments, while the latter faced opposition from anti-federalist leaders of southern liberation movements.

In early 2015, when Huthi leaders used the rhetoric of Yemeni unity to rally national support for their cause, they faced strong opposition after launching their military campaign outside the highland plateau. This was true prior to the start of international warfare in late March 2015. For instance, opposition arose south of Ibb's Samara pass in the "midland" province of Ta'izz. The same occurred in Hodeida province to the west, and Al-Bayda and Marib provinces to the east, as well as the former southern half of the country. People in these regions generally distrusted Huthi leaders, whom they perceived as opportunists pursuing a self-serving agenda. Huthi leaders gained some degree of sympathy once they came under attack by the Saudi-led coalition, yet foreign intervention reversed the momentum of their military campaign, compelling them to retreat and leaving most territory beyond their control.

Throughout 2016, a stalemate existed on all battlefronts. Pockets of territory fell under control of different authorities, including southern Abyan and eastern Hadhramaut provinces where al-Qaeda on the Arabian Peninsula (AQAP) governed under the name "Ansar al-Sharia" (see Chapter-4). Huthi leaders held the highland plateau and Tihama coast in the west. President Hadi and Saudi-allied forces of the Yemeni army primarily operated from the interior desert province of Marib, home to one of Yemen's main oil fields and an important electricity plant. Militia forces linked to Hirak took control of Aden and southern coastal regions with the help of the UAE's army. Before 2016 ended, UAE forces removed AQAP as a governing authority in Abyan and Hadhramaut. Nonetheless, due to the wide array of forces on the ground, Yemen was badly fractured. The central government in Sana'a lost its influence when the Central Bank moved to Aden. The reach of Yemen's central government was always limited, including inside Hashid and Bakil areas around Sana'a. But multiple rival authorities now arose in different regions under Huthi, Saudi, and Emirati control.

The main problem of reviving plans to create a federal state is that the longer the war continued, the more vested interests were created among powerful actors in different regions of the country (Salisbury, 2017). In other words, the problem is not simply that Huthi leaders in Sana'a opposed the original NDC-derived six-region constitution. Other regional actors, especially south and east of Sana'a, are far less likely to sacrifice control of their own affairs by resubmitting to central government authority. This is particularly true in Marib and Hadhramaut to the east, as well as Aden, Lahej, and Dhala to the south. Beginning in 2017, Emirati control of the south allowed former Hirak leaders to create a governing body called the Southern Transitional Council (STC), which clashed with President Hadi's guards in Aden. In August 2019, STC forces drove Hadi's guards from Aden, seizing power with hopes of reuniting all former southern lands in an independent state (Rasmussen and al-Batati, 2019). Sizable percentages of populations in Shabwah, Hadhramaut, and Al-Mahrah in the east oppose being controlled by a future Adeni government. In short, Yemen's multiple divisions were magnified by war, so the country's future political order may resemble a loose confederation, if not four or five entirely independent states.

There is no escaping the fact that government decentralization along federal or confederal lines must be addressed to end Yemen's war and bring peace to a suffering population. For the sake of national unity under a relatively strong central government, federalism offers the best solution. External interests in a stable Yemen are more likely to favor this outcome, yet the federal option will prolong the war because internal interests will continue fighting for the sake of greater local autonomy via confederation or total independence. During the NDC in 2013, there was an indication that Huthi delegates collaborated with members of Hirak around the idea of a north-south redivision of the country. This was especially true of Hirak leaders who refused to participate in the NDC: namely, the faction linked to exiled southern leader al-Bid who lived at the time in Beirut, Lebanon. But it was also true of Hirak delegates at the NDC who were linked to exiled southern leader Ali Nasser Muhammad. The possibility exists for Huthi leaders to seek north-south confederation with former elements of Hirak.

A sticking point in negotiations to end Yemen's war is the continued presence of foreign powers in the country: namely, Saudi Arabia and the UAE, each of which maintains armed forces on the ground. The presence of Saudi and Emirati forces gives them the ability to shape the path forward. Saudi Arabia is unlikely to favor an outcome that empowers Huthi leaders along with leaders of Hirak who have allies in Beirut. Modern history shows Yemen is highly susceptible to foreign interference because it is one of the world's poorest countries in a highly strategic location. Wealthy foreigners with geostrategic interests in Yemen have long been able to shape its internal politics, and influential local actors are adept at manipulating foreigners with deep pockets. As a result, Yemen's political dynamics are a complex mix of internal and external forces, reflecting foreign and domestic rivalries (Day and Brehony, 2020).

Conclusion

When President Saleh resigned after mass protests in 2011, Yemen had a mere two decades of experience as a national union. During a brief time period, Saleh failed to advance policies that could establish state legitimacy across the territory. Prior to unification in 1990, this was a perennial problem in each half of the country due to multiple divisions within the population. Unification did not alleviate the problem. Instead, it made matters worse by increasing not only the size of territory that the government in Sana'a claimed to rule, but also the number of rival groups vying for a share of public goods.

Once Saleh resigned in late 2011, the country's political, economic, and social troubles necessitated holding broad dialogue on how best to reform the state. By January 2014, the UN-sponsored NDC reached consensus that federalism was the best option, but the trouble was in the details of the six-region plan. Today, the array of fighting forces and governing authorities in Yemen is highly complex. As a result, it is difficult to know what the end game is, and how the state will eventually be reconstituted. Yemen is not like Syria where a long-established regime operated effective state institutions that could reassert territorial control after the chaos of ground fighting ended. The chances of continued warfare remain very high in Yemen, but there is ultimately no military solution to the country's divisions because of shifting alliances on rugged mountain terrain. For all of these reasons, it is necessary to reopen discussions about the future structure of the Yemeni state.

For decades, Yemenis debated federalism as a solution to problems of national unity. Thus, the idea did not appear from nowhere at the NDC in 2013. At the heart of the six-region federal plan and draft constitution, there was an inherent problem due to public perceptions of outside interference. This included the role of G-10 ambassadors, primarily representing GCC and NATO member states, as well as the UN Security Council and the UN secretary-general's special envoy to Yemen. Despite the fact that hundreds of Yemeni delegates who attended the all-Yemeni NDC desired a federal devolution of power, many citizens perceived any change in state structure as something forced upon the country by foreign interests. A big part of the problem was poor public relations and domestic media coverage of the NDC outcomes. By agreement of the G-10, the task of supervising public relations and media was given to the Russian ambassador who was not inclined to prepare the ground for success. As a result, Yemenis did not receive good information.

The draft constitution of January 2015 might conceivably help restart talks about future state structure. It contained good ideas that appeal to all antagonists of the war, including Huthi leaders who so adamantly opposed the federal plan. Contrary to common mistaken perceptions, especially among Huthi leaders and their supporters, the NDC-derived constitution envisioned a federal state with a relatively strong central government in Sana´a balanced against six institutionally weak regional governments. While Huthi leaders denounced the plan as a scheme to destroy Yemeni unity, their own actions did far more harm. Through a multi-tier financing scheme, the draft constitution would have allowed the central government to retain control of revenues collected from valuable resources like oil and gas at sub-regions, called *wilayat* (*Draft Yemeni Constitution,* 2015, Article 391, p. 74). In other words, the government in Sana´a could have bypassed the authority of new regional parliaments, which merely served as symbolic representatives of people living in different regions.

Today, implementation of the NDC-derived constitution is a lost option. But it is not necessary to revive the document word for word. It is only necessary to restart political discussions concerning the future structure of the state. Amendment of the draft constitution is required due to dramatic changes on the ground which leave Yemen more fragmented than any time in the past half century, since the 1960s when foreign military intervention aggravated an earlier civil war. A summer 2020 report by the International Crisis Group suggested that one way to arrange a lasting cease-fire, and perhaps end the war, is to empower existing elected bodies in more than twenty provinces, allowing them to administer the country over the short term, while postponing negotiations on a long-term state structure (International Crisis Group, 2020). This option would make a federal outcome with a strong central government more likely because over time it would become easier to revive the capacity of national institutions to regulate small provincial authorities.

Given the current fractured conditions with a minimum of five separate authorities on the ground, it may be necessary to grant greater power at a regional level encompassing three or more provinces. This option would be more likely to lead to a future confederation of states, if not multiple states with full independence. Some might propose four or five regional capitals at Sana´a, Marib, Ta´izz, Aden, and possibly al-Mukalla, while allowing varying degrees of executive authority over territory in neighboring provinces. Elected assemblies in these four or five capitals need greater autonomy than capital cities of provinces like Hajjah, Ibb, Al-Jawf, Al-Bayda, Shabwah, and Al-Mahrah. The key is to devise a plan capable of stimulating economic growth and social development, while maintaining security. Technocrats in Yemen worked on such a plan during the post-2011 transition, and results of their work should be consulted (Taleb, Personal interview, 2019).

References

Bin Mubarak, Ahmed, Yemeni Ambassador to Washington, DC (2019, March 11), Interview by author [In person].

Day, S. (2012), *Regionalism and Rebellion in Yemen: A Troubled National Union*, New York: Cambridge University Press.

Day, S. (2014, January 27), "The 'Non-Conclusion' of Yemen's National Dialogue," *Foreign Policy*.

Day, S. (2015, February 23), "What's Behind Yemen's Recent Political Turmoil," *The Washington Post*.

Day, S. and N. Brehony (2020), *Global, Regional, and Local Dynamics in the Yemen Crisis*, New York: Palgrave-Macmillan.

Draft Yemeni Constitution (2015), translated by the United Nations.

International Crisis Group (2020, July 2), Rethinking Peace in Yemen, Middle East Report 216, Brussels.

Lackner, H. (2014), *Why Yemen Matters: A Society in Transition*, London: Saqi Books.

Office of the Special Envoy of the Secretary-General for Yemen (2018, December), *Full Text of the Stockholm Agreement*.

Rasmussen, S. E. and S. al-Batati (2019, August 11), "Fragile Truce in Yemen after Separatist Soldiers Capture Presidential Palace," *The Wall Street Journal*.

Salisbury, P. (2017), *Yemen: National Chaos, Local Order*, London: Chatham House.

Taleb, Saadeddine, Former Yemeni Minister of Industry and Trade (2019, January 15), Interview by author [By telephone].

Chapter 3

SECTARIANISM, TRIBALISM AND THE RISE OF THE HUTHIS

Hussein Alwaday and Maysaa Shujaa Al-Deen

Introduction

The current Yemeni conflict is often defined as a sectarian and regional proxy war between Saudi Arabia and Iran. Such a depiction is misleading and disregards the real motivations and the local roots of this devastating war. The sectarian factor in Yemen was always associated with external regional influences: the spread of Salafism from Saudi Arabia to all parts of Yemen, including the Zaydi areas, and the impact of the Iranian revolution on a certain group of the Zaydis. The September 26, 1962, revolution put an end to the Zaydi imamate that had ruled north Yemen for almost three centuries and had briefly controlled the whole of Yemen in the seventeenth century. It was a radical transformation that led to massive social and cultural change, weakening the predominant social hierarchy and the position of the *sada* (or Hashemites) that the Huthis have been seeking to revive. Revolution and its aftermath together with wider social influences affected the tribal system so that tribes are now less organized, much weaker, and more exposed to influence by religious groups. It is mistaken to assume that Huthis represent the Zaydi population or that they are in close alliance with all the Zaydi tribes. Opponents of Huthis come from different backgrounds and are motivated by different causes.

Hence, in this chapter we examine how the growth of sectarianism in the period since 1962, and particularly after the Youth revolution in 2011, has affected political developments, with a special focus on Yemen's tribes. We analyze the features that are most likely to be relevant in post-conflict Yemen, focusing on how sectarianism has affected the position of the Zaydi Shi´a in northern Yemen and led to the rise to power of the Huthi movement.

The Tribal and Sectarian Background

Tribes are best described as a people anchored in a certain geographical area (cf. Varisco 2017: 231) and organized on kinship ties and a shared system of customs and values, the *qabyalah* (Adra 1985). There is much academic literature on tribal ideology (Adra 1985), the tribes' social structure, and their relationships with each other and the state (Dresch 1989; Weir 1997; Brandt 2017); and the status of "protected" non-tribal individuals living in tribal areas (Bédoucha and Albergoni, 1991). In particular, the role of the *sada*, descendants of the Prophet Muhammad, is extremely relevant when examining the emergence and strength of the Huthi movement. From the end of the ninth century to 1962, Zaydi imams were selected from among the Hashemites.

Upper Yemen is home to the two largest tribal confederations: Hashid and Bakil (once known as the "two wings" of the Zaydi imamate).[1] Not all northern tribes belong to these confederations—for instance, the Khawlan bin Amir in the northwest—and individual tribes have strong identities that transcend the confederations to which they belong, such as the Khawlan Al Tayyal of the Bakil and the Usaimat of the Hashid. Tribal structures are not limited to Upper Yemen: of particular significance are the Abida and Bani Murad tribes to the east; the Aulaqi in Shabwah and the Yafa'i in Lahij/Abyan. Tribal influence is important in Al-Bayda and Marib, as well as in the interior regions of Hadhramaut, Al-Mahrah, and Al-Jawf. However, millions of Yemenis do not claim tribal affiliation. Densely populated urban areas of Lower Yemen lack significant tribal social structures: the inland cities of Ibb and Ta'izz, the western region of Tihama, and the cities of Aden, Sana'a, Mukalla, and Saiyun.

From the seventeenth century onward, following the first Ottoman occupation, the imams relied to a large extent on the power of the Hashid and Bakil to carry out their armed expansion into Lower Yemen and the Tihama. Yemen's history is often recounted as a struggle between the resource-scarce mountainous north and the fertile, resource-rich west and interior (cf. Numan 1965: 25–6 quoted in Dresch 1989: 12); the region around Ta'izz, Ibb, and Jibla is Yemen's "bread basket" (Dresch 2000: 12). The Zaydi imams would mobilize tribes to plunder and seize agricultural land (Dresch 1989: 22–29) on which northerners might then settle (Dresch 2000: 14). Even though Imam Yahya (d. 1948) claimed the right to rule all Yemen (ibid.: 11), eastern areas, particularly Marib, were largely left alone because of the nature of their tribal arrangements, sectarian makeup—powerful tribes were Sunni—and limited resources. With the exception of what is now the governorate of Dhala, larger and stronger tribes of southern Yemen, such as the Yafa'i and Aulaqi, often rejected rule by the imam. They were independent in 1839 when the British took over Aden and later "protected" these tribes (Dresch 2000: 10), a step toward creating a distinct south Yemeni identity.

While the majority of tribespeople in Upper Yemen are Zaydi, those of Lower Yemen, the Tihama, and the eastern territories (Al-Jawf, Marib, and Shabwah) are largely Sunni Shafi'is. However, tribal relationships are based more on shared interests and pragmatism than sectarian considerations. For instance, some Shafi'i tribes converted to Zaydism in the seventeenth century (Dresch 1989: 14). In recent decades, the paramount sheikh of the Hashid, Abdullah al-Ahmar, and many sheikhs in the Arhab area have joined the Muslim Brotherhood-affiliated Islah Party, even though their tribes are located in the Zaydi heartland (Dresch and Haykel 1995). Consequently, to use the terms Zaydi and Shafi'i can be misleading when applied to tribes.

The September 26, 1962, Revolution and even more unification in 1990 accelerated a longer-term process of the intermixing of sects and population groups, making it particularly difficult to categorize cities such as Sana'a, Ta'iz or Hodeida and even smaller settlements and rural areas as predominantly Zaydi or Shafi'i. People assimilated to the point that mosques were no longer designated as Sunni or Shi'a.

According to al-Qasir (2006), two main approaches have been adopted for understanding Yemen's political and social conflicts. One is typically "orientalist," as it views pre-national state structures such as tribe, family, or sect, as the main drivers of the conflict. The second is more "functionalist" and focuses on contemporary configurations such as parties, military organizations, merchants, and middle-class intellectuals (ibid.: 17). The reality, however, is that neither of these two approaches provides an adequate understanding of the roots of Yemen's drawn-out conflict.

Historically, relations between Zaydis and Shafi'is have largely been peaceful, with a few exceptions. One was Imam al-Mutawakkil's well-known *fatwa* declaring the Shafi'is "exegetical infidels" and making it permissible to take their money (al-Masudi 2006: 113–15). Another was Imam Yahya's subjugation of Shafi'i territories after the Turks withdrew from Yemen at the end of the First World War although that can be interpreted as a part of state expansion and a reversion to the pattern of Upper Yemen seeking to control Lower Yemen. "Classic" sectarian identities were rarely a driver of conflict. Even today, the Huthis combine a new version of political Islam grounded in "modern" sectarian narratives but use multiple other strategies to gain influence and power.

Tribes Under the Imams and Saleh

Imams and, then, presidents have at times sought to co-opt tribes and at others to try to sow division among them, notably between the Hashid and Bakil. Following the overthrow of Imam Ahmad, five republican presidents were appointed between 1962 and 1978. Three of them were from the Hashid confederation: Abdullah al-Sallal (1962–67) and Ali Abdullah Saleh (1978–2011) from the Sanhan tribe, and Ahmad al-Ghashmi (1977) from Hamdan. Abdulrahman al-Eryani (1967–74) and Ibrahim al-Hamdi (1974–77) were non-tribal *qadis*,[2] who appointed notables and elders from the Bakil to strike a balance with the Hashid. For example, the Abu Luhum, a prominent Bakil family, had significant influence during the al-Eryani era and the beginning of the al-Hamdi era. On the other hand, Saleh drew on his family and the Sanhan to create an "inner circle" of military and security commanders (Phillips 2011: 24) and used his patronage networks and divide-and-rule tactics to stir up Hashid-Bakil rivalry.[3]

An instrumental relationship with the tribes was a characteristic of the imamate and it was reinforced by distinctions grounded in descent and lineage, rather than in sectarian considerations. The imams—all of them descendants of the Prophet Muhammad's daughter Fatima as demanded by the Zaydi school—often condemned tribal customs and common law (*urf*) because these did not derive legitimacy from religion. However, the logic behind their rhetoric was contradictory: when the tribes rebelled against the religious leadership, they were considered infidels; but when they fought alongside them, they were praised as God's soldiers. Similarly, the tribes were very pragmatic. At times they fought for spoils, as during the famous 1948 siege of Sana´a (Wenner 1967: 105). At other times they accused the imams of being unjust, overtly challenging their authority—as provided for by the Zaydi principle of *khuruj* (Brandt 2017: 42). To guard against this, each imam would take the sons of prominent tribal sheikhs and their relatives as "hostages of obedience" to ensure their tribes' loyalty (ibid.: 41). This was one of the main reasons for tribal discontent toward the imamate system.

To be sure, during the 1980s, Saleh placed a great emphasis on tribal belonging and even affirmed that "The state is part of the tribes, and our Yemeni people is a collection of tribes" (Dresch 1989: 7). He expanded the structure and budget of the Tribal Affairs Agency and added a larger number of sheikhs to the state's payroll (Alaug 2014: 16). Using patronage in the form of money, services, jobs and favors he harnessed the influence of tribal sheikhs to his own advantage. They gradually became "palace sheikhs" residing for much of their time in luxury in Sana´a and became detached from ordinary tribesmen living in areas lacking even the most basic of services. As a result, many sheikhs came to be seen as representing the interests of the government and not of the tribe.

Despite this trend, former president Saleh continued consolidating traditional community forces at the expense of the state and its institutions, privileging tribal custom over the rule of law even in major cities and the capital. This added to the post-1962 atmosphere of tribal turmoil that made the imamate era appear as more orderly, devout, and law-abiding, giving a strong impetus to the Zaydi revival movement that emerged at the beginning of the 1980s.

Sectarianism in Yemen Today

Today, Shafi´ism and Zaydism differ remarkably from their "classic" manifestations during the *ancien régime* (897–1962), and post-conflict Yemen will be deeply influenced by these transformations. Though it can be argued that the roots of sectarianism were planted at the moment that Imam al-Hadi—the founder of the Zaydi school in Yemen—entered Sa´ada at the end of the ninth century, the momentous events of 1979 played a major role in shaping its modern form and will remain influential in the new Yemen. In 1979, Ayatollah Khomeini returned to Tehran to establish the first theocratic state of the twentieth century; Juhayman al-Otaybi and his followers seized the Grand Mosque in Mecca, demanding the downfall of the ruling Al Saud; and Soviet forces had recently invaded Afghanistan.

The seminal events of 1979 transformed the politics of the Arab and Islamic world over the next forty years and gave rise to an "Islamic ideology" based on three pillars: the religious rule of the caliphate or imam in place of democracy or nationalism; the application of *Shari´a* law instead of modernization; and the

Islamization of culture and society or, more accurately, the reintegration of Muslims into Islam. Yemen's traditional Zaydi and Shafi'i sects were deeply affected.

In Yemen, 1979 saw the creation of the Islamic Front made up from tribal militias that were established to confront the Marxist National Democratic Front (NDF), which was supported and directed by the People's Democratic Republic of Yemen (PDRY). It was successful in helping the Saleh regime to eliminate the NDF threat by 1983. As a reward, the Saleh regime allowed Islamists to play an influential role in the Ministries of Education and Religious Endowments (Dresch 2010: 173), giving them the freedom to spread their Islamic ideas in the society and thus to transform political discourse from a nationalist to an Islamist ideology. Consequently, the 1980s witnessed a process of Islamization in the fields of law, education, and even dress.[4]

In early 1979, Sheikh Muqbil al-Wadi'i was expelled from Saudi Arabia. He was close to Juhayman and there was conflicting information about his participation in the seizure of the Grand Mosque. On his return to his hometown in the Dammaj district of Sa'ada governorate, in 1980, he established the country's first Salafi institute, Dar al-Hadith—a kind of "Trojan horse" of Saudi interests (Bonnefoy 2009: 322). The installation of what was seen as a Salafi proselytization center in the Zaydi heartland sparked sectarian strife.

Zaydi religious authorities mobilized to defend their sect. In 1982, a Zaydi scholar from Sa'ada created a study group on the Iranian revolution—what was to become the first nucleus of the Huthi movement (Lux 2009: 376). Following the establishment of Yemen's multi-party system in 1990, two Zaydi parties were also formed: Hizb Al-Haqq (the Party of Truth) and the Union of Popular Forces (UPF). In 1993, Zaydi summer camps were arranged and became known as the Believing Youth Forums, which led to a process of Zaydi revival and favored the spread of Hussein al-Huthi's anti-imperialist message (Nevola and Shiban 2020). The subsequent events are well known and led to the six Sa'ada wars (2004–10) and to the Huthis taking over Sana'a in September 2014.

"Classic" and "modern" sectarian affiliation—or political Islam—are often played off against each other. Some prominent leaders within the Muslim Brotherhood and the Salafi movement in Yemen hailed either from traditional Zaydi families or from Shafi'i families. Both abandoned their sect's traditional frameworks and adopted new sectarian identities. Abd al-Majid al-Zindani is a clear example of this trajectory: though hailing from a Zaydi town and family, he became a leading figure in the Muslim Brotherhood and of the Islah's Shura council, conducting a vicious campaign against Zaydism. There were similar attacks on Zaydism by Muqbil al-Wadi'i and Yahya al-Hajouri (al-Wadi'i's successor as head of the Dar al-Hadith). The situation was mirrored within the Shafi'i leadership. Yasin al-Qubbati (a leader of the Muslim Brotherhood from Ta'izz), Abdullah al-Udayni (a religious sheikh and Islah MP), and Hani bin Bureik (a former Dammaj student and deputy head of the Southern Transitional Council (STC)) have all attacked expressions of traditional Shafi'i religiosity, such as Sufism, saint blessing, and folk practices (referred to derogatorily as "old time religion"). With regard to Zaydism, the traditional clergy has lost its power to the Huthi movement's leader, Abd al-Malik al-Huthi, who maintains authority over many well-known traditional Zaydi religious leaders; very few have openly resisted the Huthis.

The interplay of "classic" and "modern" sectarianism also framed the Huthi advance in Sunni-majority areas in Lower Yemen and in the Tihama (Al-Bayda, Ta´izz, Ibb, and Hodeida). On the one hand, the Huthis evoked memories of the conflict between the imamate and peoples from those same territories prior to the 1962 revolution. On the other hand, they attempted to justify their advance as an operation to counter the Muslim Brotherhood and al-Qaeda. Eventually, al-Qaeda and, to a lesser degree, the Islamic State of Yemen (ISY) saw this as an ideal opportunity to position themselves as the bulwark for Sunnis against the invasion of the "Shi´a heresy" (Kendall 2018).

Sunni Islamic Political Movements in Yemen Today and in the Future

The main Sunni Islamic political movements present in Yemen are the Muslim Brotherhood through its role within the Islah Party and Salafism, which is less organized than the Muslim Brotherhood and takes multiple forms. Islah is a paramount example of how tribalism, politics, and sectarianism pragmatically overlap in the Yemeni context. The party was formed in 1990 and structured around three "wings": the tribalists, like the party's first president Abdullah Hussein al-Ahmar; traditional Muslim Brothers, like Yasin al-Qubati; and more radical figures, like al-Zindani. Islah garnered influence in the north through al-Ahmar's tribal networks and in the south by speaking for the dispossessed (Dresch 2010: 187). Al-Ahmar was joined by other Zaydi sheikhs from both the Hashid and Bakil, indicating that membership was not based on the party's religious doctrine but, rather, on the sheikhs' highly pragmatic political positioning.

Salafism, on the other hand, took several forms. Salafist movements can adopt two main approaches to politics and violence (Meijer 2009). The first and most radical strand, Salafi jihadism, has given rise to al-Qaeda in the Arabian Peninsula (AQAP) and ISY. Al-Qaeda assigns more significance to the distant enemy, especially the United States and its Western allies, whereas ISY prioritizes the sectarian war against Shi´a and other sects. Furthermore, ISY views empowerment and force as necessary ingredients for the establishment of an Islamic State, while al-Qaeda takes a more pragmatic and nuanced approach. AQAP is far more active than ISY (Kendall 2018: 9-10).

The second strand—scriptural Salafism—limits itself to religious learning and stringent orthodox practice based on full obedience to rulers. One part of this strand rejects all political participation, whether in elections or party politics, while another is politically engaged, but does not participate in combat without permission from the ruler.

Initially, most Yemeni Salafis, such as those associated with the Dar al Hadith Institute in Dammaj, rejected any kind of political participation. However, in 2011, the Salafi movement underwent several important changes against the backdrop of the Arab Spring. Some Salafis chose to continue along the path of political nonparticipation, while others decided to engage in politics and form political parties, such as the Al-Rashad Union and the Peace and Development Party.[5] The Salafi movement also went on to incorporate members of many well-known Zaydi tribes, like Yahya al-Hajouri from Hajjah (Muqbil al-Wadi'i was from a Zaydi family from Sa'ada), as well as Shafi'i tribal members, most notably Abd al-Wahhab al-Humayqani, one of the founders of the Al-Rashad Union. al-Humayqani, a tribal sheikh from Al-Bayda, was highly influential in his tribe and persuaded many of its members to join the Salafi movement.

Following the Huthi advance, the Salafis split. Some represented by Mohammed al-Imam in Ma'bar (Dhamar) and Mohammed al-Mahdi in Ibb continued to withhold from engaging in the conflict and to focus on teaching and education. Others took up arms against the Huthis as a form of jihad. It was the expulsion of Salafis from Dammaj in January 2013 that marked the transition of many scriptural Salafis into combat leaders on battlefronts in central and southern regions of the country. Today, there are concentrations of Salafis on most fronts of the war: the Tihama, Dhala, Ta'izz, Al-Jawf, Hajjah, and Sa'ada. Notable Salafis who made this transition include Adil Fara Abu al-Abbas, the famous leader of the eastern front in Ta'izz; Sadiq Mahyub, or Abu al-Saduq, who is also active in Ta'izz; and Hani bin Bureik in Aden. When suspected links later began to emerge between Abu al-Abbas and al-Qaeda, he was added to the US sanctions list (al-Daghashi 2020). Al-Humayqani, also on the US list, is another member of the Salafi leadership who has fought the Huthis and represents more of an activist Salafi. He is associated with the Muslim Brotherhood via the Al-Rashad Union and leads the resistance movement against Huthis in Al-Bayda alongside powerful local tribes from the area.

Divisions within Salafi ranks have at times dissolved and at other times deepened based on political developments. For instance, southern Salafis have fought on most of the northern fronts, such as Ta'izz, the west coast, and Sa'ada, though they have since withdrawn to join the battle in the south. The Salafi Giants Brigades, led by Abu Zara'ah al-Mahrami on the west coast, handed over their positions to the forces of Tariq Saleh and returned to the south. Likewise, the Salafi commanders Mahran al-Qabati and Bassam al-Mahadhar withdrew from the Buqaa frontline in Sa'ada governorate, enabling a northern Salafi commander to take over. It might seem that Salafi leaders, like Hesham al-Sayyed, al-Qabati, al-Mahrami, and al-Mahadhar, who made their reputations after the launch of Operation Decisive Storm, are the primary military power in the south. However, the situation is much more complicated because of the presence of other military forces such as those associated with Aidarus al-Zubaidi, the leader of the STC (see Chapter 2).

Just as the Salafi movement has evolved over the years, so too has the relationship between Salafis and the Muslim Brotherhood. The ongoing struggle between the Muslim Brotherhood and the Salafi militia led by Abu al-Abbas in Ta'izz is a good example of how their relationship has occasionally shifted from cooperation and support to feuding and betrayal. This has undermined the anti-Huthi forces fighting in the city. It has also led to conflict in the south, exacerbated by the UAE's antipathy to Islah and Islah's support for the IRG, and the influence of Salafism within the Security Belt forces of the STC, which regards Islah as an enemy.

Tribes and Al-Qaeda

There are two main features of the relationship between tribes and al-Qaeda (and ISY). The first involves the permission given by tribes to these groups to operate within their territories. Tribes normally do not allow this kind of arrangement out of fear of getting thrust into the conflict (Kendall 2018: 12),[6] but, in some instances, they permit it to help protect the tribe. The second derives from the recruitment of tribal members by jihadist groups, sometimes for religious reasons and at others for worldly considerations.

Osama bin Laden viewed the social structures of Yemeni tribal areas as the ideal social model for Afghanistan. The mountainous terrain made it difficult for governments to exercise control and tribes were disenchanted over marginalization by governments and thus ripe for recruitment when revenues from oil and gas production had not led to a better life for them. Even when would-be recruits were not particularly devout, they could be motivated to join the fight. Like the Huthis, al-Qaeda recruited members by stoking anger over political and social marginalization and by exploiting the weakening relations between sheikhs and tribespeople.

These factors help explain the growth of al-Qaeda and AQAP in the eastern regions of Marib, Al-Bayda, and Shabwah. Although tribes generally seek reconciliation before conflict, their readiness to fight makes them well suited for recruitment within jihadist organizations. As discussed in Chapter 4, al-Qaeda was able for a time to gain control in regions with weak tribal structures such as Zinjibar in Abyan (2011), Al-Odayn in Ibb (2014), and Mukalla in Hadhramaut (2015) (Dawsari 2020). AQAP has also successfully inserted itself into inter-tribal discord as it did within the Al-Dhahab tribe in Al-Bayda (Al Salih 2017).

It was once thought that a so-called "black line" prevented political organizations from penetrating tribal structures, thus preventing them from undermining the authority of the sheikhs. This is clearly no longer the case. The current conflict has disrupted the long-standing balance of power within the majority of the tribes in areas like Arhab and Al-Humayqan as well as weaker tribes like those in the outskirts of Ta'izz. Tribes are still the biggest reservoir for new recruits for Salafis. The Huthi presence has further helped al-Qaeda and other Salafi jihadist groups with this process and given them increased popularity in certain areas.[7] Though AQAP and ISY have been weakened since 2016 (Chapter 4) they are far from finished and could again emerge as serious threats after the end of the war.

The Huthis

Badr al-Din al-Huthi was a *sayyid*, a renowned Zaydi scholar and an important tribal mediator, widely respected among the Sa'ada tribes. He married twice from tribal families of the Khawlan bin Amir and twice from families of *sayyid* origin. His first wife, from Bani Bahr, gave birth to Hussein, the founder of the Huthi movement, who died during the first rounds of fighting in the Sa´ada war in 2004; his fourth wife, from the Hashemite al-Ijri family, gave birth to Abd al-Malik, the current leader of the movement (Brandt 2017: 139–144).

Members of the Huthi family succeeded in taking up the role that *sada* played in tribal areas: their non-tribal backgrounds and revered religious status made them natural mediators among the tribes (Brandt 2017: 121). This was reminiscent of the role played by Imam al-Hadi, the original founder of the Zaydi state in Yemen in 897 CE, who was asked by the tribes at the time to mediate between them to resolve their differences (Zayd 1981: 59).

Some of the *sada* received protection from the tribes in exchange for the vital religious and political role they played after Zaydism began to expand throughout the northern tribal region of Yemen. These *sada* resided in protected enclaves within tribal territory known as *hijrah* (Bédoucha and Albergoni, 1991).[8] The *Sada* retained a prominent role in the Zaydi school for another reason. Imams had to fulfill several requirements in order to assume political leadership in the Zaydi imamate: they had to be members of the Prophet's lineage and have a legislative reference in matters of Zaydi jurisprudence. In genealogical terms, the *sada* are considered "northern Arabs"—thus outsiders in Yemen—and named after their eponymous ancestor, Adnan. Southern Arabs, who consider themselves the autochthonous inhabitants of Yemen, are named, instead, after their ancestor Qahtan. During the 1940s, the mythical opposition between Adnan and Qahtan was revived by the political opponents of the imamate and gained new strength (Serjeant 1979: 94–9). As a result, after the 1962 revolution, republican rhetoric drew on this distinction to redefine the people of Yemen as the "Sons of Qahtan" (Orkaby 2015), depicting the "sons of Adnan"—the *sada*—as outsiders and oppressors. The Zaydi revival in the 1990s helped bring the conflict out in the open by framing it as a Zaydi defense against the persecution of the *sada* and their perceived exclusion from state decision-making by the Saleh regime.

In truth, it was initially difficult to differentiate between the objectives of Zaydi revivalism and the aim of restoring *sada* families to political power and wealth. To sort out this ambiguity, in 1990, some prominent Zaydi scholars, and among them Majduddin al- Mu´ayyadi,[9] signed a manifesto dismissing the core condition for access to the Zaydi imamate: being a learned descendant of the Prophet (Dorlian 2013: 30; Brandt 2017: 114).[10] However, with the rapid developments that accompanied the Huthi movement, the role of lineage in the conflict became increasingly clear, particularly after the group released its ideological and cultural charter in 2012, which was signed by its leader, Abd al-Malik al-Huthi, and several other Zaydi scholars, and affirmed that those from the Prophet's lineage were the chosen and rightful rulers (Nashwan 2020).

Ideological differences between the Huthi movement and the traditional Zaydi leadership represented by Majduddin al-Mu´ayyadi began to emerge as even "Qahtani" Huthi leaders—including Mohammed Azzan, Abdulkarim Jadban, and Ali Ahmed al-Razihi—complained about being marginalized by the Hashemite leaders

(Ayesh 2007). Perhaps this explains the marginalization of some founding members of the leadership. The most prominent was Abdullah Aidha al-Razami, a former MP for Hizb Al-Haqq and a tribesman, who was nominated to succeed Hussein al-Huthi after his death. While al-Razami was considered second in command of the movement after Hussein, in 2005 he was ultimately ruled out in favor of the former leader's younger brother, Abd al-Malik (Brandt 2017: 125). Later, he lost his position as a military leader and disappeared under mysterious circumstances in 2016.

Overt control over the Huthi movement by a few Hashemite families led some of its members to view it as a movement based on *sayyid* lineage, rather than a Zaydi group. It is telling that the most prominent defectors from the movement have been non-*sayyid*: such as Mohammed Azzan, Mohammed Ayesh, and Ali al-Bukhayti, all of whom had important media roles during the movement's rapid expansion from Sa´ada to Sana´a.

It can be argued that the Huthis comprise a broad political Islamic movement rather than one specific to Zaydism—in the same way that the Muslim Brotherhood presents itself as a cross-sectarian organization. It should not be forgotten that the Huthis established three "Islamic councils" after they took power, representing the two main sects in Yemen: Zaydism in the north, Shafi´ism in the south and interior with a separate council for Sufism in Hadhramaut, Ta´izz, and Tihama (Ayesh 2010). These councils maintain strong loyalty to the Huthi movement and support all of its goals and operations (Zaydiah 2020). They also do not adhere to any national framework but, instead profess support for a transnational Shi´a solidarity. This was captured in their announcements criticizing the execution of the Saudi Shi´a Sheikh Nimr al-Nimr and condemning the repression of the Bahrain uprising (Al Thawra 2016). Scholars heading the three councils all belong to *sayyid* families: Sheikh Ahmed Saleh al-Nahari is the head of the Shafi´i Islamic Council; Mohammed Yahya al-Juneid and Sahel Ibrahim Aqil, who was appointed as a Shafi´i Mufti in Yemen, lead the Sufi Islamic Council; and Shams al-Deen Sharaf al-Deen presides over the Zaydi Islamic Council.

The Huthi movement is thus distinct from the pre-1962 imamate rule in Yemen in that it does not seek to rule only in the name of Zaydism. Rather, it endeavors to incorporate all sects into its rule and reorganize them based on its own governance ideology. On the other hand, the Huthis are trying to revive the concept of the superiority of the Prophet's family and rely on irregular security and military forces recruited from Zaydis.[11]

It is important to distinguish between Islamic ideology (Islamism) and traditional Islamic sects. Islamic ideology is a kind of political activism by groups who believe that personal, public, and political life should be guided by Islam's instructions. Given that, Islamist movements do not position themselves as part of this or that traditional sect. Instead, they present themselves as the representatives of the "true" and only Islam, and claim that this holistic representation of Islam gives them the power to reformulate Islam even outside their traditional sect. This is one of the reasons why the Huthi movement is crossing the red sectarian lines between Zaydis and Shafi´is and, therefore, working to impose its ideology even in the traditional Shafi´i areas. The Huthis—like the Muslim Brotherhood—are not sects or traditional Islamic schools: they are modern political movements with totalitarian ideologies that claim the right to control all aspects of life based on their interpretation of Islam.

Given that the Huthi philosophy of rule pivots on the exclusive right of the Hashemites to hold power, solidarity across the major *sayyid* families is used to influence the other religious sects in Yemen and adapt them to the Huthi concept of authority (cf. al-Alam 2018). Huthis not only spearhead change within Zaydism by reshaping the sect in accordance with their interests, but also attempt to reformulate the other sects within their jurisdiction. This is achieved by empowering *sayyid* religious figures who subscribe to the concept of Hashemite political domination and are endowed with the authority to issue *fatwas* and Quranic interpretations. This includes the reinterpretation of Sufism and Shafiʿism as political sects that center on the concepts of loyalty, learning, and closeness to the descendants of the Prophet.

We are not arguing that Yemen is sectarian, but, rather, that sectarian identities have been weaponized as the conflict's primary rallying cry. The war could still descend into a sectarian imbroglio as there are concentrations of Islamists on the front lines. Whether these fighters belong to the Muslim Brotherhood, the Salafi movements or groups like al-Qaeda and ISY, they all view the fight against the Huthis as a battle against Shiʿa Islam as a whole (Abi-Habib 2015). The Huthis' attempt to eradicate their ideological "other" (Salafism) has generated support for the latter who position themselves as *mujahideen* fighting on behalf of Sunni Islam (Ghalib 2015). Even international actors involved in Yemen have started subscribing to this sectarian logic and have made calls for the implementation of a sectarian political order along the lines of the "Lebanese model" to resolve the conflict (Khoury 2015).

While at the start of the war the international community tended to play down Iran's role in the Huthi movement (cf. Terrill 2014), there is now a growing recognition of Iran's ideological, political, and military influence over the Huthis. Undoubtedly, Iran's relationship with the Huthis is relatively different from its relationship with Hezbollah. While Hezbollah openly pledges loyalty to the Iranian politico-religious doctrine of *Wilayat Al Faqih* and receives most of its funding and weaponry from Tehran, the Huthis pledge no such allegiance and have secured independent sources of revenue through their control of state taxation and exports (Hiltermann and Alley 2017). These differences, however, do not negate the fact that Iran has tried to exert influence on the Huthis and support them politically and militarily—and will attempt to do so in a new Yemen. UN Experts have pointed to evidence of the smuggling of weapons, and there have been interceptions of shipments of Iranian arms and missile parts (UNPoE 2018).

The Significance of the Huthi-Saleh Alliance and Zaydi Solidarity

At the start of the Zaydi revival in the 1990s, discussions took place about ruptures in Zaydi areas between the religious authority and *sada*, on the one hand, and the tribal confederations on the other. Some tribes had become deeply concerned by the spread of Salafi and Wahhabi learning in Yemen. This stemmed from the fact that government leaders in Sana'a, most of whom were from Zaydi areas, were allied with Sunni Islamic political groups,[12] indicating that belonging to Zaydism was often more regionally motivated than it was doctrinally.

When the Huthis allied with former president Saleh in 2014, it was effectively a union between a sectarian-dynastic coalition represented by the Huthis and a tribal-regional bloc represented by Saleh. Politically, the Huthis and Saleh allied because of their shared enemy: the Islah Party. Saleh viewed the Islah as the main catalyst for the 2011 protests, while the Huthis considered it their most significant political and sectarian rival. Saleh allied with the Huthis in an attempt to undermine the GCC political transition process by creating chaos that would help catapult him back into power to end the turmoil of the post-2011 period. The Huthis recognized that they were militarily strong but politically weak, and by joining Saleh they became positioned to seize power rather than settle for the more limited gains they could expect from participating in electoral politics. The proposal to divide Yemen into six federal regions was also important for understanding this unfolding dynamic (Baron 2019 and Chapter 2). The plan left the Azal region,[13] which is largely Zaydi, isolated from the coastline and lacking the petroleum reserves of neighboring Al-Jawf. The population of Azal felt they would be isolated and marginalized if this federal concept were imposed and gave rise to a regional solidarity among those in the Sana'a region and its northern hinterlands which was further consolidated by UN sanctions on the Huthis and Saleh in the leadup to the intervention of the Saudi-led coalition on March 26, 2015.

Saleh and his supporters were well represented within state institutions. Later, Saleh and Huthis formed the Supreme Political Council to structure their authority. When the National Salvation government was set up in July 2016 (while peace negotiations were taking place in Kuwait), it reflected the heavy representation of Saleh supporters within state institutions. The Huthis possessed the ability to mobilize troops for the front lines and gained legitimacy and a strong local and regional presence. Saleh's influence began to wane as the Huthis amassed more power, enlisted more fighters, and increased their sources of funding. On December 2, 2017, Saleh announced his intention to "turn the page" and break the alliance with the Huthis. Just two days later the Huthis killed him (Nevola and Shiban 2020: 244).

The Huthis benefited in the short term in that it gave them sole control over most of Upper Yemen. However, in the long run, it generated enmity and weakened their relations with tribal confederations. Their pact with Saleh had given them a strong network of tribal alliances that they had exploited for their own purposes. With Saleh's death, the sectarian policies of the Huthis began to undermine the regional solidarity that had been created by their pact with Saleh.

Implications of the Struggle Over Hajour for Fragmentation of Zaydism

The non-sectarian and ideological nature of President Saleh with the nostalgia for the perceived relative stability of his regime had made him more popular than the Huthis by the time of his death. Therefore, his killing caused many challenges to the Huthis: demonstrations in Sana´a, social unrest in Ibb, and the Hajour tribe's rebellion in the Huthis' northern heartland, which we now examine.

Yemeni tribes always defend the independence and integrity of their respective territories and rarely fight outside of them. The Hajour regions of Hajjah, which make up approximately 200 square kilometers southwest of Sa´ada, are of particular strategic importance to the Huthis in that they tie Sa´ada to the nearest coastline on the Red Sea and to Harad on the Saudi-Yemeni border, as well as to the Amran governorate, a key route to Sana´a.(Shujaa al-Deen 2020)

During the 2011 popular uprising, the Huthis first took control of Sa´ada and replaced the state-appointed governor with one of their choice, Faris Mana (Brandt 2017: 333) and then sought to take over other key areas, the most prominent of which was the Salafi Dar al-Hadith Institute at Dammaj. At the end of 2011, they moved into Hajjah where they attacked the Hajour tribes. The assault was ended in January 2012 by tribal mediation in a cease-fire and an agreement that each side would adhere to its own territory; Huthi men and weapons were banned from passing through Hajour tribal areas. However, fighting restarted in January 2019 and ended on March 8 when the Huthis announced that they had taken control of the territory. At this point, the Huthis started summarily executing their rivals and blowing up their houses.[14] Each side claimed that the other had broken the 2012 agreement. The Huthis accused the Hajour sheikhs, singling out a former Saleh ally (Sheikh Fahad al-Dahshoush), of receiving money from Saudi Arabia in exchange for setting up security checkpoints. In turn, the Hajour accused the Huthis of sneaking into their territory and claimed that some of their non-tribal supporters from a *sayyid* family were stockpiling weapons in one of their villages.

Whatever the direct cause, the conflict was probably inevitable. Relations had deteriorated significantly between the tribes and Huthis in the area after Saleh's death. In addition, Saudi Arabia had begun expanding its control in the Harad region in an effort to establish a buffer zone between the border and Sa´ada and potentially enable coalition forces to cut the route between Sa´ada and Amran City. The Hajour tribes had gone to great lengths to protect the independence of their land. While this imperative is shared by all tribes, it had become interwoven with sectarian and political interests. For instance, one of the Huthis' most prominent opponents was Abu Muslim al-Zakari. He belonged to a Zaydi tribe in Hajour but had embraced Salafism after studying at the Dar al-Hadith Institute—an interesting example of the extent of Salafi influence in a Zaydi region. In a further twist illustrating the overlapping political, tribal and sectarian interests, al-Zakari had a strong rapport with the Huthis before the death of Saleh and was also close to Saleh's nephew, Tariq Saleh, and had fought in his National Resistance Forces. The Hajour incident shows how the Huthis' enemies multiplied in the north after Saleh's death and the extent to which regional and political considerations often trumped sectarian ones.

The fact that the battle of Hajour lasted two months despite the Huthis' far greater military strength is a testament to the tribes' perseverance and the increasing opposition to the Huthis in these areas. It also was indicative that Saudi intervention was starting to affect the situation: one month after the eruption of the battle, the coalition began providing the tribes with munitions and equipment—which helps explain why the fighting lasted so long. It is also likely that Saudi intervention may have hindered tribal mediation from being successful.

In yet another twist illustrating the complexities of the situation in the north, Salafis and former Saleh supporters were backed by the UAE while the internationally recognized government and Islah Party were supported by Saudi Arabia. After the battle, the pro-Hadi minister of electricity, Saleh Samea, appeared on Al-Jazeera and requested the government to bring an end to the UAE's involvement in the coalition, as it was no longer committed to restoring the government (Shujaa al-Deen 2019). One explanation for this tension with the UAE is that Hajour territories fell within the sphere of influence of Vice President Ali Mohsen, who is seen as representing the main military arm of the Islah Party, with which the UAE refuses to cooperate.[15] The Huthi success in Hajour could thus be portrayed by UAE-backed groups as a failure by Islah and Mohsen to protect potential allies even though they had troops close to the areas. This inaction may have been caused by Islah's fear that if they had deployed Salafi groups to aid the Hajour tribes, the Salafis might have taken over the territory afterward (ibid.). Whether that is true or not is uncertain, but it illustrates the degree of distrust within the anti-Huthi forces and the sectarian issues that are likely to affect the post-conflict situation.

The Huthi State Model

The Huthis exercise control over state institutions and local government through a system of supervisors who are chosen for their loyalty to the Huthi cause—many were Huthi fighters in the Sa´ada wars (2004–10). Supervisors were first appointed when the Huthis took over Sana´a in 2014, and many more after Saleh's death in December 2017 using both ideologically committed Huthis and those members of the General People's Congress who allied with the Huthis (Nevola 2020). The main mission of the supervisor system is to connect the Huthi inner circle and the local governance system. It has a structure and hierarchy of leadership who are appointed by the Supreme Revolutionary Committee headed by Abd al-Malik al-Huthi. A general supervisor is on the top of his district's supervisors' network and is responsible for forming the popular and revolutionary committees and lower level supervisors in his district. There are also supervisors for educational social affairs and security.

The system of supervisors was inspired by Hezbollah's policy of creating parallel structures to the Lebanese state institutions. It has evolved into a sophisticated system of control. Initially, the supervisors ensured that the administrations taken over functioned in ways that met Huthi aims. As it has evolved, Huthi loyalists have replaced previous government officials and taken more direct charge. Since the death of Saleh, they have taken full control of the military, and security and intelligence services.

More than half the supervisors are *sada* and most of the rest are drawn from tribesmen. Nearly all are from Zaydi-dominated governorates—50 percent from Sa´ada (Nevola 2020). There are important kinship and marriage connections between the supervisors and main Huthi leaders. For example, the current president of the Huthi-run Supreme Political Council, Mehdi al-Mashat, is from the Khawlan bin Amir tribes which have numerous marital links with the Huthi family. Other significant *sayyid* families—again with connections through marriage to the Huthis—are well represented among the supervisors: for example, al-Mutawakkil, al-Ajri, and al-Tawwus (Nevola 2020).

What Next?

The Huthis have been strengthening their control of the north since the death of Saleh and are using that control to bring about changes in society that could be long-lasting. Several changes have been made to the education curriculum and school textbooks such as adding new chapters about "Imam al-Hadi," the founding father of the Zaydi imamate in Yemen. National events and celebrations are centering around the *sada* with moves to privilege the Hashemite families, which make up fewer than 10 percent of the population under Huthi control. One example is the new law on *zakat* of April 2020 which imposes an *Al-khums* tax ("one-fifth," or 20 percent) on revenues from minerals, gas, oil, water, and fishing to be used predominantly for the benefit of the Hashemites. *Zakat* is one of the five pillars of Islam and obliges every individual to donate a portion of his wealth annually (Sanaa Center Economic Unit). The new law is an unusual and controversial interpretation of *Al-khums* under Zaydi doctrine, but the political effect is that the tax will increase the burden on some economic sectors for the benefit of the Hashemite minority. This new law is seen by many as one step in a complex and organized process to impose doctrines imported from Iran. If the Huthis continue in this direction, they will inflame sectarianism and greatly complicate any political deal over the future governing of Yemen.

At the same time in the region under the control of IRG, Islah, with its links to the Muslim Brotherhood, is becoming increasingly influential in Marib, Ta´izz, and parts of Shabwah, Hadhramaut, and Al-Mahra. Salafism in various guises continues to spread, especially in the south and among those fighting for the STC. In central Yemen, the conflict is directly between the Huthis and Sunni-dominated militias.

Conclusion

The current conflict in Yemen is as complex as the country's own social, tribal, and sectarian structures. Political calculations intertwine with sectarian motivations against the backdrop of increasingly intricate domestic and international developments. The assumption that the Huthi movement is synonymous with

Zaydism and northern tribes is distorted and overlooks the diversity of the tribes and groups involved. It is essential that this is recognized when considering the post-conflict situation.

The Huthi takeover can be understood, in part, as a reaction to the state's support for Sunni Islamic groups and the growth of Salafism and Wahhabism within Yemen, particularly in its traditionally Zaydi areas. The legacy of the imamate, to which many Huthis believe they are the heirs, also factors heavily into the equation. In addition, there are important developmental and political aspects that helped give rise to extremist groups that, in turn, have exploited people's frustrations and feelings of injustice to gain power and influence.

Although the Huthi movement presents itself as representing the repressed Zaydi population, it seems more concerned with restoring *sayyid* social and political dominance and dividing society along sectarian and regional lines. The Huthis were remarkably successful in rallying tribes to support their march to power by making use of an ideological and nationalistic vocabulary of fighting corruption and taking on foreign intervention. However, by representing a limited cadre of *sada* and a small number of allied tribes, the Huthis have demonstrated that their mission amounts to little more than a regional-sectarian struggle against Sunni Islam, which is not only at odds with traditional Zaydi doctrine but has also sown violent discord from Sa´ada to Dhamar to Sana´a. Undeniably, the gap between Huthi interests and those of destitute tribes has grown wider through the former's implementation of mandatory *zakat* tax, levies on agricultural products and land, and the growing demand for "blood tax," which refers to the practice of recruiting tribal members to join the front lines. The Huthis ultimately do not represent the interests of these tribes and can come to blows with them, as happened in Hajour. There are other examples from Arhab and Amran and more seem likely in the future.

All sides in the conflict seem to be using sectarian affiliations to legitimize their rule. The tribal nature of society has helped them to perpetuate such practice. The deterioration of democratic experience in Yemen after 1994 war caused people to revert to sectarian and tribal affiliation to fill the gaps created by the weak state and a weakened culture of citizenship. Tribal and sectarian roots as sources of their identities had lost ground as national identity was promoted and education spread—but had not disappeared. The failure of governments to secularize the political sphere will continue to draw Yemenis toward their own religious and sectarian roots. With the continuing decline of the state, traditional/premodern affiliations have reemerged. There is even speculation that Yemen could emerge from the conflict with three states or federal regions: one in the Zaydi-dominated Upper Yemen; a Sunni entity in Lower Yemen; and another in the south, replicating the fluid divisions of Yemen before the modern era.

The situation has been further exacerbated by the intervention of regional powers. To Saudi Arabia, the growing influence of the Huthis in 2014 and 2015 was alarming and ultimately led it to launch a war. It is difficult to compare Iran and Saudi Arabia's respective interventions and justify one or the other's involvement given that they have different histories in Yemen. Saudi Arabia developed its influence over time both as the large and wealthy country along the northern border and through an investment of political, financial, and religious resources into Yemen and its tribal and Islamic groups. Iran, on the other hand, has had a more recent sectarian-regional involvement that has taken the form of funding and support for armed sectarian groups in their revolt against the government. As support for these rebel groups increased, so did Iran's power and influence. Iranian support for the Huthis is increasingly visible, not least in the appointments of ambassadors in Tehran and Sana'a. There are even reports of renewed Turkish and Qatari interest: there is an active branch of Islah associated with the Muslim Brotherhood in Turkey, which has been showing new interest in territories that were once part of the Ottoman Empire. Qatar is sympathetic to the Muslim Brotherhood but was also active in mediating a solution to the Sa'ada wars in the late 2000s. The current Yemeni prime minister has accused Doha of supporting the Huthis and of trying to sow chaos in the country.

It is unlikely that the Yemen conflict will be resolved through negotiations between the major stakeholders within the country (IRG, Huthis, and the STC). For this reason, Yemeni talks must include regional powers, such as Saudi Arabia and Iran, to have any real impact. Relying on regional powers to hold talks is particularly important in light of the United Nations' failure and inability to apply real meaningful pressure on parties to the conflict. Saudi Arabia and Iran have the ability to quickly reach mutual agreements that may not satisfy all sides but can achieve meaningful progress. In the event that an agreement is made, however, Yemen will remain in a fragile state of peace due to the spread of heavy weapons in the country as well as the number of political groups based on identity and religion rather than political plans and initiatives. A change is needed from Western countries as well. The way the West treats the Huthis and southern separatists as the two main forces in the country because of their "minority" or "persecuted" status ignores fundamental complexities of the war, assumes that the STC represents the whole south, and mistakes the Huthis as being representative of the north, its tribes, and Zaydism writ large. That has to change.

Notes

1   In genealogical terms, Hashid and Bakil were brothers and descendants of Hamdan; the north-eastern region of Yemen was thus described as the land of Hamdan (Dresch 1989: 5, 24). A third confederation, the Madhhij, which is dispersed between the country's east, west, south, and interior (Al Iryani 2003: 2589) has now greatly weakened, as has the Kindah of Hadhramaut (Abdullah 2003: 2459-2461).

2   The so-called *qadis* share with the tribesmen a common descent from Qahtan, but during the imamate they were ranked above because of their learning and role in the state (Weir 1997: 52).

3   This tension between the Bakil and Hashid was stoked by the enlisting of the Bakil tribes and opponents of the Hashid in the Sa'ada wars of 2002–10 to oppose an assembly of fighters known as the Popular Army and led by Hussein bin Abdullah bin Hussein al-Ahmar, which fought alongside the army.

4   The *niqab* was made compulsory and Western dress banned, particularly among women.
5   For a detailed analysis of developments to Salafism after the Arab Spring, see Abu Rahman (2013: 22–28) and Bonnefoy (2011).
6   According to a survey of the Yemeni Polling Center, Yemenis are more afraid of airstrikes and drones than of terrorism (Heinze and Albukari 2018, quoted in Kendall 2018: 7).
7   Qayfa district, in Al-Bayda, is a paramount example of how anti-Huthi rhetoric favored the acceptance of al-Qaeda and ISIS by local tribes (Kendall 2018: 20).
8   The Huthi family was a family of *muhajjar sada*, placed under the protection of certain Sa'ada tribes during the 1990s (Brandt 2017: 142). In the ancient Yemeni language, *hijrah* means "protected areas" (Zayd 1981).
9   Al-Mu'ayyadi (1913–2007) was a prominent Zaydi religious scholar. Though hailing from Al-Jawf, he spent most of his life teaching in Dahyan in Sa'ada (Brandt 2017: 113).
10 Significantly, Badr al-Din al-Huthi did not sign the document (Dorlian 2013: 36).
11 Naji, Sultan (2004). Al Tareekh Al Asskari li Al Yemen. P. 45–49. Sanaa. Da'irat Al Tawjeeh al Ma'nowi.
12 The alliance between a Zaydi-majority government and Sunni Islamic groups can be explained by two factors. First, the central government is tied to the support and funding from Saudi Arabia. Second, Zaydi doctrine is still strongly associated with the imamate and with the power of the Hashemites, and thus it decreases the legitimacy of the republican government.
13 The Azal region would comprise of Dhamar, Sana'a, Amran, and Sa'ada governorates.
14 The destruction of opponents' houses had long been a practice since the time of Imam al-Hadi and had been used by tribes as a form of punishment for people outside who violated its customs or committed a disgraceful act (Zayd 1981: 79). The goal of the demolitions was to drive the offender out of the host tribe's territory. Another significant example of the demolition of houses was that of the house of Sheikh Abdullah bin Hussein al-Ahmar by the Huthis in February 2014.
15 Mohsen is a member of the GPC but is strongly associated with Islah.

References

Abdullah, Y. M. (2003), "Kindah," in H. A. Al Wadi'i et al. (eds), *al-Mawsu'a al-Yemeniyya, 2459–2461*, Sana'a: Alafif Cultural Foundation.

Abi-Habib, M. (2015), "Al Qaeda Fights on the Same Side as Saudi-Backed Militias in Yemen," *Wallstreet Journal*, July 16. Available online: https://www.wsj.com/articles/al-qaeda-fights-on-same-side-as-saudi-backed-militias-in-yemen-1437087067 (accessed February 25, 2020).

Abu Rahman, M. (2013), *Salafis and the Arab Spring: The Question of Religion and Democracy in Arab Politics*, Beirut: Center for Arab Unity Studies.

Nevola, L. (2020), "The Houthi Supervisory System: The Interplay of Formal State Institutions and Informal Political Structures Thematic Report," June 17. Assessment Capability Projects. Available online: https://www.acaps.org/sites/acaps/files/products/files/20200617_acaps_yemen_analysis_hub_the_houthi_supervisory_system.pdf

Adra, N. (1985), "The Concept of Tribe in Rural Yemen," in N. S. Hopkins and S. E. Ibrahim (eds.), *Arab Society: Social Science Perspectives*, 275–85, Cairo: The American University in Cairo Press.

Al-Alam (2018), "Al-Majalis al-Islamiyya al-Yemeniyya Tubarik Injazat al-Jaysh al-Yemeni," July 27. Available online: https://www.alalamtv.net/news/3691601/%D8 %A7%D9%84%D9%85%D8%AC%D8%A7%D9%84%D8%B3-%D8%A7%D9%84%D8 %A5%D8%B3%D9%84%D8%A7%D9%85%D9%8A%D8%A9-%D8%A7%D9%84%D9 %8A%D9%85%D9%86%D9%8A%D8%A9-%D8%AA%D8%A8%D8%A7%D8%B1 %D9%83-%D8%A5%D9%86%D8%AC%D8%A7%D8%B2%D8%A7%D8%AA-%D8 %A7%D9%84%D8%AC%D9%8A%D8%B4-% (accessed January 16, 2020).

Alaug, A. S. (2014), "The Tribal Engagement in the Yemen National Dialogue Conference," Draft paper for the MESA conference. Available on line: https://www.academia .edu/12716741/Tribal_Engagement_in_the_Yemen_Politics_National_Dialogue _Conference (accessed March, 2021).

Ayesh, M. (2007), "Majd al-Din al-Muʿayyadi: Nuṣf Qarn min Ṣiyaghat al-Hawaya al-Muʿaṣira li-l-Zaydiyya," *Mohammed Ayesh Blog*, November 1. Available online: http://ayeshpress.blogspot.com/2010/11/blog-post_01.html (accessed February 25, 2020).

Ayesh, M. (2010), "Laḥẓat al-Taṭawwur al-Faṣila min ʿal-Hadawiyya' ila ʿal-Ḥuthiyya': Ḥarb Ṣaʿda wa Ithraha fi Taḥwilat al-Zaydiyya al-Diniyya," *Mohammed Ayesh Blog*, February 25. Available online: http://ayeshpress.blogspot.com/2010/11/blog-post.html (accessed February 25, 2020).

Baron, A. (2019), "Mapping the Yemen Conflict," *European Council on Foreign Relations*, July. Available online: https://www.ecfr.eu/mena/yemen (accessed February 25, 2020).

Bédoucha, G. and G. Albergoni (1991), "Hiérarchie, médiation et tribalisme en Arabie du Sud: la hijra yéménite," *L'homme*, 31 (118): 7–36.

Bonnefoy, L. (2011), *Salafism in Yemen*, London: Hurst & Company.

Bonnefoy, L. (2009), "How Transnational is Salafism in Yemen?" in R. Meijer (ed.), *Global Salafism: Islam's New Religious Movement*, 321–41, London: Hurst & Company.

Brandt, M. (2017), *Tribes and Politics in Yemen: A History of the Huthi Conflict*, London: Hurst & Company.

Al Daghashi, A. M. (2020), "Al-Tiyar al-Madkhali al-Musallah," *Ruya for Research & Studies*, January 16. Available online: https://ruyaa.cc/Page/4814/ (accessed February 25, 2020).

Dawsari, N. (2020), "Foe Not Friend: Yemeni Tribes and Al-Qaeda in the Arabian Peninsula," January 10. Available online: https://pomed.org/pomed-report-foe-not -friend-yemens-tribes-and-al-qaeda-in-the-arabian-peninsula.

Dorlian, S. (2013), *La mouvance zaydite dans le Yémen contemporain: Une modernisation avortée*, Paris: L'Harmattan.

Dresch, P. (1989), *Tribes, Government, and History in Yemen*, Oxford: Oxford University Press.

Dresch, P. (2000), *A History of Modern Yemen*, Cambridge: Cambridge University Press.

Dresch, P. and B. Haykel (1995), "Stereotypes and Political Styles: Islamists and Tribesfolk in Yemen," *International Journal of Middle East Studies*, 27 (4): 405–31.

Ghalib, S. (2015), "Wajhat al-Naẓr: Mashruʿ al-Harb fi Zaman Iḥtikar al-Tamthil fi al-Yemen," *BBC*, March 10. Available online: http://www.bbc.com/arabic/middleeast /2015/03/150310_yemen_politics (accessed January 16, 2020).

Heinze M. and H. Albukari (2018), "Yemen's War as Seen from the Local Level: Politics, Governance, and Reconstruction in Yemen," *POMEPS*, January 29. Available online:

https://pomeps.org/wp-content/uploads/2018/02/POMEPS_Studies_29_Yemen_Web
-REV.pdf (accessed March 5, 2020).

Hiltermann, J. and A. L. Alley (2017), "The Huthis Are Not Hezbollah," *Foreign Policy*,
February 12. Available online: https://foreignpolicy.com/2017/02/27/the-Huthis-are
-not-hezbollah (accessed January 16, 2020).

Al Iryani, M. A. (2003), "Madhḥij," in H. A. Al Wadiʿi et al. (eds.), *al-Mawsuʿa
al-Yemeniyya, 2588–2589*, Sanaʿa: Alafif Cultural Foundation.

Kendall, E. (2018), *Contemporary Jihadi Militancy in Yemen: How Is the Threat Evolving?*
Washington: Middle East Institute.

Khoury, N. (2015), "Lebanonizing Yemen May Save It," *Atlantic Council*, May 28. Available
online: http://www.atlanticcouncil.org/blogs/menasource/lebanonizing-yemen-may
-save-it (accessed January 16, 2020).

Lux, A. (2009), "Yemen's last Zaydi Imam: The shabab al-muʾmin, the Malazim, and ʿhizb
allah' in the thought of Ḥusayn Badr al-Din al-Ḥuthi," *Contemporary Arab Affairs*,
2 (3): 369–434.

Al Masudi, A. Q. (2006), *Al-Shawkaniyya al-Wahabiyya: Tiyar Mustajidd fi al-Fikr
al-ʿArabi al-Hadith*, Cairo: Maktabat Madbula.

Meijer, R. (2009), "Introduction," in R. Meijer (ed.), *Global Salafism: Islam's New Religious
Movement*, 1–32, London: Hurst & Company.

Nashwan News (2020), "Nuṣṣ al-Wathiqa al-Fikriyya li-l-Ḥuthiyyin: al-Iṣṭifaʾ ʿala
al-ʿAlamayn," January 15. Available online: https://nashwannews.com/newsold
/138874/ (accessed February 25, 2020).

Nevola, L. (2019), *From Periphery to the Core: A Social Network Analysis of the Houthi
Local Governance*. A working paper, VERSUS .

Nevola, L. and B. Shiban (2020), "The Perspective of 'Coup Forces,' Saleh and Houthi
Elements," in S. Day and N. Brehony (eds.), *Global, Regional and Local Perspectives of
the Yemen Crisis*, London: Palgrave Macmillan.

Numan, M. A. (1965), *Al-Aṭraf al-Maʿniyya fi al-Yemen*, Beirut: Muʾassasat al-Ḍabban.

Orkaby, A. (2015), "A Passing Generation of Yemeni Politics," *Middle East Brief*, 90.

Phillips, S. (2011), *Yemen and the Politics of Permanent Crisis*, New York: Routledge.

Al Qasir, A. (2006), "Al-Qabila fi al-Yemen laysat al-Mushkila: Al-Muʿaḍila al-Niẓam
al-Siyasi alladhi Yastakhdimha li-ʿArqalat Taṭawwur al-Mujtamaʿ al-Madani," *CIA*,
August 24. Available online: https://www.cia.gov/library/abbottabad-compound/55
/55EA8EE670A074B3EB5DA8498DE18493_qds17.pdf (accessed January 16, 2020).

Al Salih, H. (2017), "Man Hiya Usrat al-Dhahab allati Istahdafha al-Jaysh al-Amriki fi
al-Yemen?" *Al Arabiya*, January 31. Available online: https://www.alarabiya.net/ar/
arab-and-world/yemen/2017/01/31/%D9%85%D9%86-%D9%87%D9%8A-%D8%A3
%D8%B3%D8%B1%D8%A9-%D8%A7%D9%84%D8%B0%D9%87%D8%A8-%D8
%A7%D9%84%D8%AA%D9%8A-%D8%A7%D8%B3%D8%AA%D9%87%D8%AF
%D9%81%D9%87%D8%A7-%D8%A7%D9%84%D8%AC%D9%8A%D8%B4-%D8
%A7%D9%84%D8%A3%D9%85%D9%8A%D8%B1%D9%83%D9%8A-%D9%81%D9
%8A-%D8%A7%D9%84%D9%8A%D9%85%D9%86%D8%9F.html (accessed March
5, 2020).

Sanaa Center Economic Unit (2020), "Yemen Economic Bulletin: Tax and Rule – Houthis
Move to Institutionalize Hashemite Elite With "One-fifth" Levy." Sanaa Center for
Strategic Studies.

Serjeant, R. B. (1979), "The Yemen poet Al-Zubayri and his polemic against Zaydi imams,"
Arabian Studies, 5: 87–130.

Shuja Al Deen, M. (2020), "Tasaʿud al-Maʿarik al-Huthiyya al-Qabaliyya fi al-Yemen," *Carnegie Endowment for International Peace*, April 23. Available online: https://carnegieendowment.org/sada/78970 (accessed January 20, 2020).

Terrill, A. W. (2014), "Iranian Involvement in Yemen," *Orbis*, 58(3): 429–40.

Al Thawra (2016), "Al-Majalis al-Islamiyya fi al-Yemen Tudayyin Iʿdam al-Sulṭat al-Saʿudiyya al-Allama Nimr al-Nimr," January 2. Available online: http://althawrah.ye/archives/369740 (accessed March 5, 2020).

UNPoE (2018), *Final Report of the Panel of Experts on Yemen* (S/2018/68). Available online: https://www.securitycouncilreport.org/atf/cf/%7B65BFCF9B-6D27-4E9C-8CD3-CF6E4FF96FF9%7D/s_2018_68.pdf (accessed June 1, 2019).

Varisco, D. M. (2017) "Yemen's Tribal Idiom: An Ethno-Historical Survey of Genealogical Models," *Journal of Semitic Studies*, LXII (1): 217–41.

Weir, S. (1997), *A Tribal Order: Politics and Law in the Mountains of Yemen*, Austin, TX: University of Texas Press.

Wenner, M. W. (1967), *Modern Yemen, 1918–1966*, Baltimore: Johns Hopkins Press.

Zayd, M. A. (1981), *Muʿtazila al-Yemen: Dawlat al-Hadi wa Fikruhu*, Beirut: Dar Al ʿOuda.

Zaydiah (2020), "Bayan Idana al-Majalis al-Islamiyya al-Yemeniyya Ightiyal al-Qaʾidin Sulaymani wa-l-Muhandis." Available online: http://www.Zaidiah.com/news/7671 (accessed January 16, 2020).

Chapter 4

AQAP AND GOVERNANCE IN YEMEN

POST-CONFLICT CONSIDERATIONS

Dr. Joana Cook

Introduction[1]

Terrorist governance has gained worldwide attention due to Islamic State (ISIS) seizing, holding, and governing territory in Syria and Iraq for nearly five years between 2014 and early 2019. Yet, while to date it is the most successful case of terrorist governance, it was certainly not the first. Yemen is one of the earliest, most important, and often overlooked case of such jihadist governance. In addition, from al-Shabaab to al-Qaeda, jihadist groups and their offshoots around the world have increasingly attempted to create proto-states and engage in differing levels of governance, melding their ideology with practical services and public works. While a specifically jihadist ideology may be strongly rejected by the populations these groups are attempting to co-opt, such efforts may nonetheless fill gaps in local governance or human and physical security in areas riven by conflict and power vacuums and demand particular considerations for addressing such groups.

In Yemen, to different extents and for differing lengths of time, al-Qaeda in the Arabian Peninsula (AQAP) has implemented governance in some parts of the country and it is the development of this, and considerations for countering AQAP going forward, that is the focus of this chapter.[2] AQAP has also notably adapted its actions and approach over the years. This was seen, for example, when it attempted to minimize the enforcement of Islamic punishment (which had brought much criticism), instead working to "correct" what it viewed as un-Islamic behaviour through more structured judicial means. It also began to provide public services ranging from the judicial to security in areas facing gaps in these public goods. As AQAP leader Nasser al-Wuhaishi noted, "providing these necessities will have a great effect on people and will make them sympathize with us and feel that their fate is tied to ours" (Associated Press 2012).

AQAP remains a viable (though currently diminished) presence in Yemen due, in part, to its evolution in governance. Since its first significant governance attempt in 2011 during the Arab Spring, AQAP has controlled diverse territory on multiple occasions, implementing various aspects of governance—some much more expansive than others. Its most successful effort to date has been holding the provincial capital of Mukalla for a year, from 2015 to 2016, following the onset of the conflict in Yemen that has been officially ongoing since March 2015.

Following a brief discussion of jihadist proto-states and rebel governance, this chapter draws from publicly available reports and current academic literature to outline AQAP's jihadist approach to governance and its evolution. It will specifically analyze the most significant case studies including Jaar, Zinjibar, and Mukalla, and consider how the ongoing conflict has impacted AQAP's approach in the country. Finally, it will discuss the responses that must be considered in Yemen going forward, including post-conflict stabilization, governance, and counterterrorism.

Terrorist Proto-states and Rebel Governance

It is worth briefly reviewing terrorist (specifically jihadist) proto-states and broader rebel governance.[3] Lia notes that these often share several characteristics. First, they are deeply ideological projects that publicize the ways they implement Sharia law and destroy un-Islamic icons (tombs, statues, etc.). Second, they are internationalist projects and may seek foreign fighters, cooperate or compete with other jihadist proto-states, or commit to internationalist causes.[4] Third, such states are often a significant security concern for neighboring states and the international community. Finally, jihadist proto-states commit to effective governance consisting of civilian services, justice systems, administrative and military roles, tribal mediation, and so forth. These "states" help them attain influence and power over rivals, including in terms of material resources (money and equipment) and supporters (foreign fighters or members) (Lia, 35–6.). Karmon (2015) has referred to this as "competing for hearts and minds," comparable to insurgencies to some extent. These groups may use "charitable service provisions as a tool to shift the position of local populations along a 'continuum of community acceptance,'" gaining support for other elements of their wider agenda through the physical and material support of the population (Flanigan 2006). The provision of such services also directly impacts the social contract between a population and its government and undermines "a key source of state legitimacy" (Grynkewich 2008).

Groups derive three main benefits from the provision of social services: they highlight the failure of the state to provide these; they increase legitimacy among their target population; and they can "trade needed social services for recruits, support, and sympathy from the population" (ibid., 353–5). To manage this, states must eradicate these social services by non-state actors, Grynkewich argues, while increasingly replacing these with their own (ibid., 351). Mampilly (2012) also discusses three essential "goods" required as part of "effective governance": some force able to provide security and stability to the population; a dispute resolution mechanism; and public goods that extend beyond security. All three of these essential goods have been provided by AQAP, and remain relevant areas of concern, particularly in the south where such state-provided goods have been particularly lacking.

A significant number of Islamist militant organizations have engaged in this type of governance. ISIS has thus far proved to be the most successful in both scope and longevity (Caris and Reynolds 2014). The Taliban (Johnson 2013) and Hamas (Berti 2015), Hezbollah (Wiegand, 2016), Al-Shabaab (Hansen, 2013), and Boko Haram (Ladbury et al. 2016) have also governed to varying extents (also see Cook and Maher 2021). In short, there is nothing new or novel about terrorist governance. It is often functional, and aims to challenge the legitimacy and support for local authorities through the provision of services usually provided by legitimate government actors. This governance varies in scope, duration, actors, and implementation. Such governance is often attempted and implemented in areas that are experiencing human security and governance shortfalls, often during conflict, and can interact with other local actors such as tribes. The extent of this governance may also have clear implications for post-conflict actors. The next section looks at how this has unfolded in Yemen via AQAP.

Al-Qaeda's Long Shadow in Yemen

Al-Qaeda's presence in Yemen long preceded 9/11, emphasizing the longevity and evolution of the organization, and its domestic and international streams of focus. A dual attack in 1992 on the Gold Mohur and Aden Movenpick hotels is considered to be the first al-Qaeda-linked attack against the United States (Clark 2010, 163). A Yemeni member of al-Qaeda was implicated in the 1998 US embassy bombings, and a subsequent attack by al-Qaeda on the USS *Cole* in the Port of Aden in October 2000 remains the deadliest attack against US personnel in the country. Following 9/11, numerous al-Qaeda links to the country were exposed. In 2006, twenty-three key al-Qaeda figures escaped from a Sana´a prison, and in 2009, Saudi and Yemeni al-Qaeda elements established AQAP.[5] Al-Qaeda has frequently targeted internationals in the country, including a 2007 attack on Spanish tourists that killed ten, a 2008 attack on the US embassy, and a 2009 attack on South Korean tourists that killed five. AQAP has since been viewed as an international threat and at times the most dangerous branch of al-Qaeda globally, specifically due to the abilities of its key bomb maker, Ibrahim al-Asiri (d. 2017), who threatened international aviation and concealed bombs in packages sent to the United States. Samir Khan and American-Yemeni preacher Anwar al-Awlaki, and English-language online magazine *Inspire*, were also widely acknowledged to open AQAP recruitment to an English-speaking audience and were connected to numerous plots, including the 2009 shooting at Fort Hood by Nidal Hassan and other lone actor attacks. Links to the *Charlie Hebdo* attack in Paris in 2015, and a December 2019 attack in Pensacola Naval Air Station by a lieutenant from the Royal Saudi Air Defense Forces, are recent examples of the international reach of AQAP.

However, the most significant threat from AQAP remains within Yemen, where it has attacked police, military, and government targets and operated in a manner more akin to an insurgency.[6] A May 2012 attack on a military parade rehearsal saw 120 killed and 200 injured, and the brutal 2013 attack on a ministry of defense hospital, which killed fifty-six, show just how deadly AQAP can be. The group has also continued to increase its membership over the years, from only 300 members in 2009 (Johnsen 2013) to around 7,000 members by 2020 (Analytical Support and Sanctions Monitoring Team, 2020), demonstrating its continued and growing attraction.

AQAP has demonstrable global and local ambitions, and effective counterterrorism will have to deal with this threat through distinct streams of effort. We now focus on AQAP's internal dynamic within Yemen whilst keeping in mind the interconnectedness of local dynamics with AQAP's ability to project itself abroad.

Appealing to Local Hearts and Minds

From as early as 2006, AQAP's predecessors have exploited popular grievances and emphasized jihad as a solution (Koehler-Derrick 2011, 41). As al-Dawsari notes, central state security structures in the country have historically been minimal, if not fully absent in many tribal areas, and this security gap was often filled by tribes who have a much stronger presence in rural areas.[7] Many of these tribes, she notes, had sought increased government security and service delivery (Dawsari 2018). AQAP, in particular, has been able to exploit weak or absent government presence to build support in local communities.

There has been a perception that some tribes have partnered with AQAP to achieve various ends. These have included for near-term interests, where from a tribe's perspective, "a working relationship with AQAP can mean an ally against any government, warlords, or other tribes, and does not necessarily mean they agree with AQAP's principles and objectives" (Cigar, 2018, 11). Kendall has discussed this in terms of an "understanding" with local tribes, nurturing this through marriage and kinship ties. Where tribesmen have accidentally been killed in operations, AQAP has in some cases provided the payment of blood money and issued formal apologies (Kendall 2018, 6–7). While al-Dawsari pushes back on the idea that tribes have been key to AQAP's success thus far in Yemen, she does note that among foreigners and urban Yemenis, AQAP has been able to recruit individual tribesmen to the group by tapping into local discontent. In addition, she highlights how AQAP has offered even the relatively unobservant religious an outlet for grievances related to poor economic prospects; lack of development; feelings of isolation or injustice in society; and deaths of family members or friends via counterterrorism efforts or Huthi attacks. Joining AQAP's calls for action allows such people to reclaim their dignity and seek justice (al-Dawsari 2018). Unless thematic issues—including those related to human security, governance, dignity and justice—are adequately addressed, the risk for non-state actors to exploit these remains.

AQAP has provided practical assistance and responses to "the economic, social, and emotional needs of frustrated tribal youth." These have included helping "tribal youth who join [AQAP] build their own homes, get married, and receive decent stipends, sometimes reaching thousands of dollars." Perhaps most importantly, however, AQAP has offered them a "sense of purpose and a way to become influential in their communities" (ibid.). AQAP communicated this in locally resonant ways, such as through the use of poetry, which can further connect with local communities, and solidify jihadist identities (Kendall & Stein, 2015), or draw on their personal tribal identity to align themselves with local communities.

AQAP attempts to portray itself as a governing alternative to redress and correct local grievances. Such governance can help secure commitment and dedication to the group, exploiting the ills of the Gulf region's poorest state. Some authors suggest that the lack of governance by Islamic State in Yemen (ISY) contributed to its failure to gain support from local populations (Kendall 2019, 79), and may impact ISY to gain influence in Yemen.

AQAP has two primary strategic tracks: global and local. The first is directed internationally at the "far enemy," whether trying to blow up planes en route to the United States, kidnapping foreign tourists, or targeting foreign embassies or citizens. The local track was initially focused on terrorism, but as its membership grew it adopted a populist approach through its governance and increasingly resembled an insurgency within the country that utilizes terrorism as a key tactic. AQAP demonstrates a flexibility of approach in its efforts to retain local support, while pursuing al-Qaeda's wider global ambitions. Such evolutions have clear implications for response to the group today and in the future. However, it is first prudent to better understand the scale and contours of this governance historically as was seen in its first large-scale effort in 2011 in the cities of Jaar and Zinjibar.

Jaar and Zinjibar 2011 and 2015

The withdrawal of military and security units from Abyan as Ali Abdullah Saleh and General Ali Mohsen al-Ahmar maneuvered against each other in mid-2011 provided AQAP with an ideal opportunity.

AQAP had long been seeking to establish an Islamic State in southern Yemen: in 2009 it worked to mediate tribal disputes. In 2010, it had offered to help bring teachers to Rafadh (in Shabwah province), where even basic education was unavailable (Worth 2010). AQAP had been dissuaded from going further by Osama bin Laden, who believed the group did not have enough public support.

The situation in Yemen after January 2011 changed that equation. In March 2011 Ansar al-Shariah announced over the radio its establishment of an "Islamic Emirate" in Abyan and renamed the city of Jaar to "Islamic Emirate of Waqar." Trying to distinguish itself from past errors, AQAP had rebranded itself (a common practice for the group), as Ansar al-Shariah ("The Supporters of Islamic Law"). Abu Zubayr Adel, Sharia official for AQAP, had stated, "The name Ansar al-Shariah is what we use to introduce ourselves in areas where we work to tell people about our work and goals." State security forces put up little resistance when the group moved in and they quickly seized the city. Khalid Abd-al-Nabi (aka Abu-Basir al-Yazidi), who was described as "the field commander of the mujahidin in Jaar District," stated in an April 2011 interview, "The state has fallen here. If we didn't take over, others will take over. We have tried secular rule and we have tried Socialist rule. Now we need to try Islamic rule because we have no hope but through the Koran and the Prophet's teachings" (BBC Monitoring Research 2011). Abyan had been a victim of years of state neglect, particularly post-1986.

Abu al-Zabir, AQAP's then religious leader, noted that this governance was established to "attract people to Sharia rule" in areas they controlled, and had been influenced by the Afghan Taliban and al-Qaeda in Iraq (AQI). Many of those involved in Ansar al-Shariah at this time had themselves reportedly lived under Sharia law in Afghanistan or Iraq (al-Shishani 2012). This suggests they were able to learn from past errors and now understood the benefits of engaging in governance, even when unsuccessful (as it had been in Afghanistan and Iraq). Major General Muhammad al-Sawmali, commander of the 25th Mechanical Division, noted that AQAP's cadres included foreigners, including Saudis, Pakistanis, Egyptians, and Somalis.

Alongside this statement by al-Zabir was an advisory to women to stay at home and to be accompanied by a male relative when in public. Public gender segregation became a consistent theme in AQAP governance in its various locations (BBC Monitoring Research 2011). AQAP implemented Sharia law, including *hudud* punishments, but did so gradually, after first educating the populace (al-Abab 2011). For those caught stealing, this could mean a public lashing or the amputation of a hand, even though funds were given to one such victim to "start a new life" subsequently (ibid.; Johnsen 2013: 279).

In April, Adil al-Abab, AQAP's chief cleric, announced that the group had seized power in Jaar and stated, "The largest problem that we face here is the lack of public services such as sewage and water, and we are trying to find solutions." Al-Abab noted that they had "full plans for projects we want to achieve for the people. We want to make contracts with investors so as to arrange these affairs" (al-Abab, 2011). Adel noted that in places such as Abyan, AQAP had "moved our work from the elitist work to the populist" (ibid.) He admitted that AQAP may not be "open or fully visible because we lack the administrative staff and financial resources that would make us able to provide services to the people" (ibid.). AQAP's presence could be worthwhile only when it could show that it had the capacity to provide security and governance.

AQAP also took over a local radio station in Abyan in April 2011, calling for media experts and professionals to help run it (Al-Abab, 5, 2011). Finally, according to one "judge," the group also focused extensively on providing justice mechanisms, reporting that it resolved forty-two cases in two weeks. Providing a formal justice mechanism also appeared to deter a spiral of revenge killings, according to al-Dawsari (Simcox 2012, 62). Yet, AQAP also conducted particularly brutal acts. It was *hudud* punishments, such as amputations and crucifixions (including of those accused of being spies), that eventually turned local populations against AQAP.[8]

Alongside violence normally associated with jihadist groups in Jaar and Zinjibar, Ansar al-Shariah began publicizing public works and services it stated it was carrying out.[9] These included distributing water and resolving complaints about stolen property, in some cases trying to recover the property for the aggrieved party. It also focused on more substantial infrastructure projects, such as digging water courses and establishing electrical lines for residences that had previously been denied such services by the central government (Johnsen 2013, 279). The group also reportedly installed sewage pipes, ensured there were teachers for local schools, ran the local police force, connected telephone lines, and even collected garbage (Simcox, 2012: 62). It delivered pamphlets warning against "usury in trade and money exchange" and the sale of "lewd" magazines and newspapers, and warned against collecting taxes where only the distribution of "zakat" to the poor was allowable (Makram, 2011).

This was the first time al-Qaeda as an organization had been able to govern to a notable extent. Preceding efforts had been undertaken by al-Qaeda in Iraq (AQI). Renamed Islamic State of Iraq (ISI) from 2006, ISI had explicit aims: to gain and hold territory, establish a caliphate, and provide governance following the departure of US forces. The framework it established included small public works projects; resources and care for families of deceased martyrs;[10] calls for foreign fighters around the world to join the cause; and the recruitment of persons with administrative and scientific backgrounds (an approach later promoted by ISIS) (Fishman 2016, 90). However, this Iraqi project was exceptionally limited in its scope and implementation, and local communities rose up against ISI. Instead, Yemen proved to be the first notable success of governance by al-Qaeda and its diverse branches and affiliates.

Local Yemeni forces, besieged in their bases around Jaar and Zinjibar in this period, continued to fight Ansar al-Shariah forces, which had severely damaged infrastructure in the area, including hospitals, schools, and mosques. Popular Committees (groups of local residents from multiple tribal backgrounds who come together to implement local security) played an important role in preventing Ansar al-Shariah's further expansion to other regions and ultimately expelled the group from Abyan (al-Dawsari 2014). In September 2011, General Ali Mohsen and his forces pushed into the city to little resistance as Ansar al-Shariah cadres melted away into the mountainous countryside (Johnsen 2013, 282). They were still able to hold pockets of territory and conduct diverse (though smaller scale) aspects of governance. The death toll of civilians, military personnel, and fighters was in the hundreds in this period (Roggio 2012). AQAP also took to destroying local religious symbols. In 2012 several Sufi shrines and tombs in Jaar were destroyed, which was publicized by the group (ibid.). Different religious sites in Mukalla were also destroyed by AQAP in 2015 and 2016. Extremists outside of AQAP mirrored these actions and wrecked the mosque of Sheikh Abdulhadi al-Sudi in Ta'izz in 2016.

The takeover of Jaar and Zinjibar was repeated in December 2015, while the group simultaneously held Mukalla. By this time Yemen was in the throes of the civil war enabling Ansar al-Shariah to capitalize on the ensuing chaos. The initial entry into Jaar was reportedly due to AQAP's search for leaders belonging to Popular Committees, which had previously pushed back against AQAP onslaughts into the city and provided local security (Almosawa & Fahim, 2015). AQAP held Jaar for only a few days before it withdrew, but was able to retain its presence in Zinjibar until August 2016. In this city it allowed local government officials to operate as they had done previously. Drawing from lessons learned earlier in Jaar and Zinjibar, AQAP renamed itself the "Sons of Abyan" (Al-Batati 2015b) (a similar exercise took place in Mukalla). Local journalist Anwar al-Hadhrami noted the group's more progressive approach in 2015: "In 2011 al-Qaeda stormed military camps, stopped teachers from teaching some subjects, imposed a curfew during prayer times and strictly enforced Sharia law including amputating thieves' hands, executing murderers, and whipping those who commit minor crimes," he said (ibid.). Now, it was being acknowledged for its attempts to build water infrastructure, dig wells, and provide residents with water (Fergusson 2015). In Zinjibar, AQAP increasingly tried to implement governance and infrastructure works for the local community—a progressive approach that could be replicated in the future if such opportunities were to arise again.

Rada 2011–13

AQAP was involved in the city of Rada, Al-Bayda (population 60,000), sporadically but did not seek to hold and administer it. Between 2011 and 2012 AQAP conducted local conflict resolution, led largely by Tariq al-Dhahab (d. 2012), brother-in-law of Anwar al-Awlaki.[11] It mediated between tribes and provided blood money to facilitate the ending of feuds.[12]

In January 2012, AQAP took over the al-Amiriyah castle in downtown Rada for one week, an occupation that ended following tribal mediation and the release of fifteen AQAP prisoners in Sana'a (Xinhua 2012). Local tribes mobilized their members to guard public facilities, including military camps, to prevent AQAP from taking over the whole city, demonstrating that such incursions by AQAP did in fact meet with continued local resistance, even as some residents may have welcomed limited aspects of their presence.

AQAP reappeared in Rada sporadically in 2013 and 2014. In 2013, there were reports of local residents, frustrated with local justice mechanisms, seeking out AQAP mediation to settle local disputes. One resident who had a land dispute resolved noted, "I went to Al-Qaeda and they were able to resolve the dispute. Since then, I have gone to them as an alternative to court" (al-Sakkaf, 2013).[13] Support for AQAP may not have been widespread, but it must be acknowledged that an absence of public works, services, and justice mechanisms is likely to increase some level of support for non-state actors who are able to implement such efforts.[14]

It withdrew from the town after a prisoner release was negotiated via tribal mediation (Yemen Post 2013)—showing how AQAP could use the holding of territory as a bargaining tool. However, in September 2014, AQAP still had a presence in Rada: on September 26 after Friday prayers the group led anti-Huthi protests in the streets with its supporters (al-Mushki 2014).

Rada is an example of how AQAP uses small-scale governance to achieve its aims. Individual examples are often overlooked, yet when taken as a whole (see

Cook 2019b, appendix), there were numerous cases of small-scale governance. When conducted effectively AQAP can gain some support and a positive reputation.

Mukalla 2015

Mukalla proves to be the most successful case of AQAP governance to date and marked an evolution in the way it implemented governance. In August 2014, AQAP militants looted the international bank in Mukalla, the capital of Hadhramaut (Yemen Post 2014). Then, in April 2015, AQAP moved into the port city, population 300,000, relatively unopposed by local security forces and the Hadhrami Tribal Alliance.[15] It released 300 prisoners, including leading AQAP figures Khalid Batarfi and Ibrahim al-Abyan, and raided the central bank of Mukalla from which it stole a total of approximately $100 million. It then overran the local radio station and six army and security barracks and seized weapons (Amr 2015). Over the next month it took over a number of public buildings, the airport, and seaport.

Initially, AQAP took a "softer" approach in the city—black flags were not raised, music was allowed, and women were able to walk on the streets (Al-Batati 2015b). Its governance became more sophisticated over the course of the following year as it engaged local partners to help implement governance in ways it had not done previously. By early May 2015, AQAP had rebranded itself as the "Sons of Hadhramaut" (Al-Batati, 2015a), thus assuming a local identity. The Sons of Hadhramaut themselves did not govern; instead (and uniquely), they agreed to a political transition and left governance largely to a locally established group named the Hadhramaut National Council (Middle East Eye 2015). This Council otherwise claimed to have no link to AQAP, and had received a guarantee from AQAP that they would depart from Mukalla in one year's time.[16] This Council ran Mukalla with a civilian body that included sixty unelected local members, and a power-sharing scheme that saw a more hands-off approach in the day-to-day governance of the city by AQAP (Amr 2015). The Hadhramaut National Council also reportedly had branches in Shihr, Ghayl Ba Wazir, Shohair, Raida, and Qusair also held by AQAP (Al-Batati, 2015a), of which Shihr, with its oil export facilities, was the second most significant. All these branches were comprised of local residents unaffiliated with AQAP.[17]

The Hadhramaut National Council acted as a separate governing intermediary—conducting day-to-day governance for AQAP, while still able to engage outside political actors, including President Hadi's office. While it was viewed by some as being another front organization for AQAP, others saw it as a locally established council comprised of unelected local Sunni Salafi scholars, tribal leaders, and other dignitaries. The International Crisis Group (ICG) reported that the Council included local dignitaries and prominent non-AQAP Hadhramis; and local members were appointed as religious police. In fact, most citizens viewed the Hadhramaut National Council as an AQAP front but concluded that it was an "acceptable way to deal with the outside world" (ICG 2017, footnotes 42 and 46).

When the Sons of Hadhramaut took over the city, the Hadhramaut National Council secretary-general, Abd al-Hakeem bin Mahfood, stated that a delegation of local citizens (who eventually formed the Hadhramaut National Council) approached AQAP to express concern that AQAP's presence would lead to military intervention, which would cause considerable damage to the city and its residents. They did not want Mukalla to face a fate similar to Jaar and Zinjibar.[18] It was subsequently agreed that the Hadhramaut National Council would manage the administration and security of the city, while AQAP would focus on fighting the shared Huthi threat. This increased the appeal and acceptance of AQAP's presence.

The Council also claimed that President Hadi "praised the Council for its efforts in restoring peace and security in the city," (Al-Batati, 2015a) and that Council members had met in Riyadh with both Saudi and Yemeni authorities to discuss their role in local governance. These interactions were led by Omar bin Shakal al-Jaidi, head of the Council, and were not widely publicized. Instead, these were described more in terms of the Council "passing a message" from the Sons of Hadhramaut to the Hadi government, rather than direct discussions or negotiations.[19] Yet, they are a clear example of government engagement and dialogue via a third party who had a widely known relationship with al-Qaeda.

This interaction raises important questions about legitimacy and pragmatism in official engagements with non-state actors that enable groups like AQAP to feel that they gain some legitimacy. Yet, if such interactions also reduce civilian harm and suffering by allowing the continuation of public services, they need to be assessed in terms of the potential local benefits of some unique and limited dialogue with AQAP. In short, how, when, under what circumstances, and to what ends non-state actors could be engaged with is not clear-cut. There is a need to balance the consequences of legitimizing or raising the profile of non-state actors and the immediate security and needs of local populations.

AQAP's governance of Mukalla was the most extensive to date, and created a more sophisticated financial model than seen previously. It extorted money from the national oil company—$1.4 million according to one estimate (Bayoumy, Browning & Ghobari 2016). Its management of the Port of Mukalla and the corresponding coastline proved to be its most profitable source of income. While the port was initially managed by the Council for several months (including the import of oil), the Sons of Hadhramaut eventually took direct control. The taxation of goods and oil coming into the port earned the group up to $2 million per day, according to some reports (ibid.), though others have placed this more modestly at $700,000 (Trew 2018b). The Sons of Hadhramaut also, from the onset, took control of all military and security facilities in the areas.

The Sons of Hadhramaut returned the airport and Central Bank to Hadhramaut National Council control and then even arranged for some of the money stolen from the bank to be reinstated to pay striking cleaners and civil servants (Middle East Eye 2016). The Council also received money from fuel imported into the city and $3.7 million directly from AQAP (Al-Batati 2015a). In May 2015, it was claimed that control of the port had been returned to the Hadhramaut National Council (BBC Monitoring 2015).

In an interview with ICG, one local resident spoke positively of the work of the Council during the ongoing war:

> We view the [Hadhramaut National] Council positively, because it has managed to continue to pay government salaries. . . . It has kept public services at a much better level than what is available in the rest of the country. . . . The AQAP judicial system is fair and swift and therefore preferred over the government's corrupt system. Many prominent cases that had lingered for years were resolved in a single day. (International Crisis Group, 2017)

On the other hand, many people continued to struggle financially. A local journalist observed, "Many suffered to feed their families and so even joined AQAP due to a lack of jobs just to get the paycheck" (Trew 2018b).

During AQAP control of Mukalla, harsh *hudud* punishments were not as publicized as those doled out by ISIS, who recorded and disseminated punishments widely and theatrically. However, local residents did state that journalists, radio presenters, opposition figures, and religious figures, among others, were threatened, detained, or killed by the group. One doctor reported seeing a woman accused of adultery stoned to death, and noted that women had been heavily restricted in their movements (ibid.). There was greater emphasis on the segregation of women, and unrelated males and females could not be seen together in public (Amr 2015). Religious policing was carried out by an organization called the Committee for the Promotion of Virtue and Prevention of Vice (ibid.). The Sons of Hadhramaut imposed a ban on *qat* and seized quantities of it from the local populace.

In total, AQAP ended up "conquering" an area of 700 kilometers, stretching from the Oman border to Aden, including multiple town centers, particularly in the southern coastal region (Trew 2018c). AQAP also launched a social media campaign promoting its public works in Mukalla. AQAP's Twitter account reportedly featured their governance works in 56 percent of their 2016 Tweets, emphasizing the community development carried out by the group (Kendall 2018, 7). Through the al-Ather "news" agency Twitter feed, the group showcased handing out food to the needy and showed itself improving local electrical access, street work, and management of public waste in garbage trucks (Joscelyn 2016). Local citizens were featured praising the quality of public works, the speed with which they were implemented, and the lack of corruption among local contractors (who could face severe punishment for corruption or poorly conducted work).[20]

Yet, disillusionment gradually set in and accelerated when AQAP became more visible and sidelined the Council. While the populace praised the services carried out in the city, it was *hudud* punishments and corruption that generated resistance to the Sons of Hadhramaut. On October 12, 2016, local residents protested against AQAP's corruption in public marches, which included chanting and carrying anti-AQAP banners.[21] Mukalla represents another important learning opportunity for AQAP, regarding a strategic and adaptive approach to governance. While up to 2016 AQAP's governance projects had ended in failure, these also proved informative for how they could adapt their governance attempts in the future if governance continued to feature in their local strategy, and if such opportunities arose again.

The manner of AQAP's departure from Mukalla raises further important considerations for future interactions with the group. The Associated Press found that the group's withdrawal from Mukalla and subsequently from six other towns was actually negotiated. AQAP agreed to pull out of the city (taking guns and other seized loot), if the United States did not conduct strikes on those leaving. Under the arrangements, 10,000 local tribesmen, including 250 AQAP militants who had "repented," would be integrated into UAE-backed Security Belt Forces (Michael, Wilson & Keath 2018).

By 2018 the UAE admitted that it had, after what it stated was extensive vetting, allowed some low-ranking AQAP youth into its ranks for pragmatic reasons, including winning over the population and reducing the number of AQAP members.[22] Brigadier Ali, a UAE commander in the counterterrorism operation, noted, "When we cleared al-Qaeda out of urban areas, they left behind many of these men and it made sense to recruit them, because it sent a powerful message about the Yemeni commitment to liberation" (Trew 2018b). AQAP's governance in Mukalla thus ended in 2016. It was AQAP's last major and most prolonged effort at governance at the time of writing.

Implications for Security in Yemen

The earlier literature on terrorist and rebel governance emphasizes the importance of wartime activities of non-state actors for determining post-war outcomes. In the case of Yemen, wartime activities by the Huthis and other state-oriented actors will have the greatest impact on long-term stability. Here, I examine the potential impact of AQAP's experience of governing in terms of post-war Yemen, considering AQAP's own ambitions and the implications for how counterterrorism is conceived and conducted on a broader scale.

Future Governance Ambitions

AQAP governance appears to have been influenced by several factors. One is the experience of some of its more senior members of living under Sharia law as enforced by the Taliban in Afghanistan and AQI in Iraq, and the perceived appeal of this intergenerationally. Subsequently in Yemen it can draw lessons from its own successful aspects of governance discussed earlier. It may further be informed by external case studies—drawing on what it may have observed from how other jihadist groups, including ISIS, practiced and implemented governance. AQAP has noted the potential appeal and benefits of governance. This would fall in line with its country-focused ambitions and could be utilized to regain support and membership, even if AQAP also maintains some focus on international targets. They have learned to be long-term, and pragmatic in their approach, aiming at winning hearts and minds of the population rather than co-opting people through fear and force. As highlighted by the UN's Analytical Support and Sanctions Monitoring Team in 2018, "Against the backdrop of a security vacuum and a lack of public services in many areas, AQAP sponsors and participates in public activities, seeking to build a reputation for humanitarianism and governance" (Fitton-Brown, 2018). In 2020, AQAP was focusing on recruitment (in competition with ISY) via "youth outreach and the provision of public services in areas under its control" (Analytical Support and Sanctions Monitoring Team, 2020). This appeal to local populations through its projected humanitarian and governance activities will likely remain an active focus for the group for both public relations/support and recruitment purposes.

Simultaneously, AQAP is now the weakest it has been for many years, and has the lowest recorded rates of activity since 2015.[23] It has lost high-profile leaders to targeting by UAE, Yemeni military, and US forces—believed to be due (in part) to spies that had infiltrated AQAP's ranks, lending to a crisis of trust within the group. The death of AQAP leader Qasim al-Raymi in January 2020 saw Khalid Batarfi—an individual believed to have much less support within the group—take up leadership of the Yemeni branch (Analytical Support and Sanctions Monitoring Team, 2020). In 2020, they continue to have difficulty maintaining control over even small areas. Clashes have also continued with ISY (which, in the case of Al-Bayda, have actually contributed to diminishing ISY's influence),[24] and as Kendall (2020) notes, July 2018 to early 2020 saw what she describes as an "all-out war" between the groups which focused their attacks almost exclusively on each other. This rivalry has also included AQAP defense of key strategic logistic lines in Al-Bayda, which ISY attempted to seize in early 2020 (Analytical Support and Sanctions Monitoring Team, 2020). By mid-2020 some analysts believed that AQAP and ISY were potentially even being "weaponized by regional powers" (Kendall 2020), suggesting a significant change in the level of independence of the group seen previously. In central Yemen, AQAP has been degraded and dispersed but is still able to attract new members by positioning itself as a defender of Sunnis against Huthi incursion.[25]

AQAP will need to regroup and rebuild its resources and support in one of its most challenging periods, and its continued interaction with ISY will further impact its resources, focus, and activities in the country. AQAP may, further, see advantages in continuing to exploit current and future gaps in governance to offer itself as a viable option in seeking new members and support, which in the past has also included the recruitment of child soldiers (General Assembly 2016). Counterterrorist strategies will need to prevent that happening, even as all signs are currently pointing toward continued governance failings in the country, and an unstable post-conflict situation—if or when the conflict subsides.

Full-spectrum Counterterrorism

AQAP's shift toward governance has implications for future full-spectrum approaches to counterterrorism, which includes both "hard" or "direct," and "soft" or "indirect" lines of effort that must work together cohesively. Direct efforts include military, defense, law enforcement, and criminal justice approaches, dealing with the more immediate threats through appropriate means and neutralizing security concerns. Indirect approaches involve more preventative efforts to deter the recruitment of persons, and steps to reduce the appeal that terrorist groups may offer to potential supporters or members. Indirect approaches often fall under the scope of preventing/countering violent extremism (P/CVE) policies, and can include a broad array of initiatives, such as education, development, and good governance, to name but a few. The undertaking of governance by groups such as AQAP has significant implications for how an overarching counterterrorism strategy in the country should develop. As I highlighted elsewhere (Cook, 2019a), this means that those involved in balancing, coordinating, and implementing diverse streams of effort must be constantly aware of the impact and implications of one stream on the others.

Good governance, economic development, and effective state justice mechanisms (among other indirect approaches) will still be required in Yemen to ensure long-term stability and must be owned and led by the Yemeni government with the support of international partners. In 2020 COVID-19 slammed Yemen, creating yet another humanitarian crisis, and the government's limited response to the virus has only opened another avenue for local grievance to be potentially exploited. Basic good governance for the whole population will require capacity-building, leadership, job skills, and empowerment for often marginalized groups such as women and the youth. Such policies will dry up the pool from which AQAP may recruit. However, while such work may in the long term reduce concerns related to terrorism, these should not be presented and driven as aspects of counterterrorism but, instead, as normal, sensible, and essential means of contributing to societal stability more broadly. Local partners implementing these reforms may face threats if they are seen to be associated with counterterrorism. Long-term security and stability should thus ensure long-term, consistent funding and support for enabling and maintaining good governance and economic development, while avoiding the controversial, even problematic, labelling of programs as "counterterrorism" where possible.[26]

Rights-based, Accountable Counterterrorism

Human rights-based and legally compliant approaches to counterterrorism become increasingly important for the perception, legitimacy, and efficacy of state actors and their work. These relate to the perceived legitimacy of the Yemeni government and other foreign actors conducting counterterrorism operations in the country, both of which can contribute either to intensify or to lessen grievances against the state (and its partners). Defense-related efforts tend to dominate the overall perception of programming in a country, even if development, humanitarian assistance, and other forms of support are also present. As such, when defense efforts are correlated with injustices in the minds of local populations, this may generate sympathies for groups like AQAP and continue to feed into future recruitment, while also tainting indirect efforts.

In Yemen, there have been many instances of problematic or highly contested counterterrorism practices related to the state and its partners. This could be seen, for example, with US drone strikes in the country, which have killed upward of 1,389 persons (including up to 225 civilians and fifty children), persons who have not faced trial (The Bureau for Investigative Journalism, 2021).[27] As highlighted in Cook (2017), the gendered, secondary, and tertiary impacts of such policies are not generally acknowledged. Where primary male breadwinners are killed and large families are left behind, AQAP has aimed to provide succour, trying to earn local support in addressing grievances generated by US actions. The intergenerational grievances caused by such actions must also be acknowledged. It is also notable that the high rate of US air strikes in the country in 2017 deeply affected local perceptions of the United States. More recent reports from 2018 have highlighted the presence of US mercenaries in an "assassination program" run by the UAE in Yemen that targeted a number of al-Islah members, clerics, and terrorists (Roston, 2018).

Reports from Mukalla in 2017 also highlighted significant concerns of human rights violations by UAE troops in secret prisons around the country. Here, up to 2,000 men were reportedly swept up and detained in the search for AQAP militants. Information about these individuals was not made accessible to their families. Former inmates also described unsanitary conditions, abuse, and even sexual assault at the hands of UAE or UAE-backed forces (Michael 2017). Human Rights Watch further documented at least four children who were detained or who forcibly disappeared (Human Rights Watch 2017). Such transgressions should be fully investigated, and any wrongdoing held to account in order to ensure that local populations can maintain trust in Yemeni authorities.

These concerns echo many of the negative legacies of US counterterrorism in the early years of the global War on Terror, ones that still cast a long shadow on US efforts today.[28] Such actions by these international partners reduce local support for the Yemeni government and drive grievances that some may seek to reconcile through membership or support of such groups as AQAP, which may be regarded as defending them. Compounded by a "hearts and minds" approach from AQAP, it is likely that support for AQAP will increase if the Yemeni government and its partners do not uphold human rights in their security operations. Furthermore, in the past, counterterrorism operations have been instrumentalized by the Saleh government for their own political aims. Such cases include the 2010 killing of Jabir al-Shabwani, a prominent tribal sheikh and deputy governor of Marib province, after Saleh fed misleading intelligence to US forces (Entous, Barnes & Coker, 2011).

A Nuanced Approach to AQAP

People join AQAP for a variety of reasons and counterterrorist policy needs to take this diversity into account. Some join for pragmatic reasons, such as to earn a wage to feed their families while some are ideologically motivated. A few may think that AQAP governance has righted wrongs or injustices caused by the government, and others join AQAP to defend Sunni Islam against the Huthis.

Viewing AQAP in all its complexity can help us better understand the group and its members and distinguish between what may be the hard-core, ideologically motivated, and dangerous supporters and those who may be weaned away the group. Counter terrorism may thus include deradicalization and reintegration for low-level members who have not been implicated in serious, violent, criminal activities; kinetic and criminal justice options for immediate and serious threats; and an overall emphasis on meaningfully responding to local grievances. A kinetic-dominated approach will likely be ineffective and even counterproductive and risks targeting an ever-widening pool of varied supporters.

The inclusion of previously neglected local and tribal figures can prove to be particularly beneficial. The increased engagement of and consultation with relatively neglected actors such as women, the youth, and members of civil society through formal government channels when developing or implementing full-spectrum counterterrorism activities may help create new nodes of trust between governments and communities. It can also ensure that the needs and concerns of all aspects of society are considered and accounted for in these practices, and thereby bolster long-term peace.

Women and the youth are key demographics that have historically been neglected in this space, even though youth are most at risk from AQAP recruiters. Women also suffer disproportionately from the instability that high levels of terrorism bring and can play influential roles in the family and in the community, including mediation, which can help prevent local conflicts from escalating (Cook 2016). Youth and women should be actively engaged and consulted in all full-spectrum approaches to counterterrorism as part of a broad attempt to ensure that society at large is engaged and has a stake in countering this concern and improving public safety and security (Cook, 2019a. See also Huckerby & Fakih, 2011).

Both the United States and the United Arab Emirates have also made extensive efforts over the years to train Yemeni security forces—a key component of good governance. While the United States has historically emphasized training and equipping counterterrorism-specific forces, the United Arab Emirates has more recently been training security forces (the Security Belt forces in and around Aden and the Elite forces in Hadhramaut and Shabwah, which were 90,000 strong in mid-2019) (France 24, 2019). In Mukalla, local police have been recruited and trained—some enlisting in response to the activities of AQAP in the city, including the murder of local security forces (Trew 2018b).

Lessons can be gleaned from this in terms of best practice and accountability to local communities, including new actors who may not have historical or damaged relationships to the previous Saleh government. However, caution should also be exercised with regard to how these new forces are managed and supported going forward. For those who previously had close ties to AQAP in Yemen, and were integrated into the UAE's Security Belt Forces, their perception and satisfaction with the post-conflict outcomes could impact their willingness to remain with these forces, or return to AQAP—now with additional military training and experience.[29] Unpaid salaries in the Security Belt Forces have already been cited as one reason the Southern Transition Council announced its self-administration in the south of the country, and could continue to generate grievances in the country.

State security forces were largely perceived to abandon towns like Zinjibar and Mukalla when AQAP entered these cities; rebuilding local trust will take time. Furthermore, new security forces remain relatively young, inexperienced, and were dependent on UAE support until September 2019,[30] but the UAE withdrawal from the country leaves the future status and funding of these forces less secure. Two additional initiatives would prove beneficial going forward. First, bringing new faces into security forces, such as women, will also provide an important outlet for all members of society to feel like they have access to these security forces. Second, forces that have participated in controversial practices or abuses and violations of human rights must also be held accountable in order to rebuild trust with local communities. The UN documented extensive violations of international human rights law by all parties in Yemen between 2014 and 2020, including some committed by Security Belt Forces, which highlights the extent and gravity of this ongoing concern, the implications for long-term reconciliation, and the perception of justice and trust in the country for government actors (Human Rights Council 2020).

Conclusion

For Yemen, the most important step toward reducing present and future threats from AQAP is to end the current war. Until that happens there will continue to be opportunities for AQAP and ISY to seek power, influence, and a safe space from which to regroup and grow. Such opportunities for influence and activity may also be exploited by a growing number of Salafist militant groups that have emerged in the country since the onset of the current conflict. These have been particularly visible in Ta'izz where numerous groups have members with suspected ties to al-Qaeda (al-Maqtari 2017).

While military and police-dominated efforts will likely be required to address immediate threats, they should be part of a thoughtful, long-term, and balanced full-spectrum approach to security that will emphasize the importance and value of multiple streams of effort. Such an approach will recognize that diverse actors have a stake in a unified approach to security. Ensuring that these diverse streams of effort, including defense, diplomacy, governance, the economy, and development elements, work cohesively together toward similar ends and meaningfully engage a broad array of stakeholders—including local tribes, civil society, women, and the youth, among others—will be crucial to the full-spectrum approach's success. Such a strategy should ensure that these streams of effort are prioritized and receive sustained funding and resources. This report can help inform and shape long-term efforts to prevent and respond to terrorism specifically, and security and stability more broadly, in the country.

Notes

1 This chapter expands from Cook 2019b. As such, the author would like to thank Nadwa al-Dawsari, Adam Baron, Saeed al-Batati, and Elisabeth Kendall for their initial valuable comments and feedback.

2 This was largely concentrated in Abyan, Azan in Shabwah, and Mukalla, and to a much lesser extent in Qaifah in Baydha. A more comprehensive list of cases is featured at the end of Cook 2019b.

3 For a more expansive literature review, particularly discussing rebel governance, see Cook, Haid, and Trauthig 2020; Cook and Maher 2022 (forthcoming).

4 Yemen is a particularly noteworthy example from this perspective, as will be demonstrated below; AQAP have tended to be more locally focused in their governance attempts.

5 For a more detailed history of al-Qaeda in Yemen, see Johnsen, 2013; Koehler-Derrick, 2011; and Murphy, 2010.

6 See START, 2019, at the University of Maryland for greater detail on attack frequency and targeting.

7 In some cases, tribal figures were also members of the state's security apparatus.

8 This local rejection of barbaric violence is one of the reasons why ISY has been unable to gain much support in the country.

9 There should always be a degree of skepticism when analyzing the positive works and services being carried out that are promoted by such groups. Even as these are being conducted by groups like AQAP they may be limited, small-scale, or, in fact, driving greater insecurity.

10 This practice of paying for the care and support of "martyred" members, particularly those killed in US raids and drone strikes, is one which also featured in Yemen and continues to this day.

11 In this case, Tariq al-Dahab had been embroiled in a family feud and had partnered with AQAP to gain leverage over his opponents—a clear case of tactical and political expediency. Al-Muslimi & Baron: 2017.

12 Thanks to Nadwa al-Dawsari for highlighting this point.

13 This issue of jihadist courts is discussed at length in Cook et al. 2020.

14 Tribal justice mechanisms have a long history in Yemen and have often filled this role. However, tribal justice mechanisms too may face some resistance from local residents if seen as ineffective or unfair.

15 While local armed tribesmen had entered Mukalla forty-eight hours later in response to AQAP's invasion, their presence was short-lived. Ghobari and Mokhashaf 2015.

16 Thank you al-Batati for highlighting this point.

17 Thank you al-Batati for highlighting this point.

18 Thank you al-Batati for highlighting this point.

19 Thank you Al-Batati for highlighting this point.

20 Thank you al-Batati for highlighting this point.

21 Thank you Al-Batati for highlighting this point.

22 Kendall highlights how AQAP tried in multiple statements in 2017 to dissuade tribes in Hadhramaut from joining UAE forces. Kendall, 2018: 11.

23 At its peak in 2015, AQAP was active in eighty-two of Yemen's 333 districts. In November 2020, this was forty, according to figures from Carboni and Sulz 2020, p. 5.

24 Kendall 2019 further elaborates on a discussion of this rivalry between AQAP and ISY.

25 AQAP activity against the Huthis was particularly overt in locations such as Ta´izz and Aden.
26 For further discussion, see Cook, 2019a.
27 For further discussion of the gendered implications of counterterrorism in the country, see Cook 2017.
28 This sentiment is also echoed by Hartig, 2018.
29 For more on persons with ties to al-Qaeda in the Yemeni forces see Trew 2018a.
30 The payment of Security Belt and related forces has now been taken over by Saudi Arabia, with the UAE continuing to pay the STC salaries.

References

al-Abab, A. Z. (2011), "Online question and answer session with Abu Zubayr Adel al-Abab, Shariah Official for Member of al-Qaeda in the Arabian Peninsula (AQAP)." *Jihadology*. Available online: https://jihadology.net/wp-content/uploads/_pda/2011/04 /ghorfah-minbar-al-ane1b9a3c481r-presents-a-new-audio-message-from-al-qc481 _idah-in-the-arabian-peninsulas-shaykh-abc5ab-zc5abbayr-adc4abl-bc4abn-abdullah -al-abc481b-en.pdf (accessed January 18, 2021).

Al-Batati, S. (2015a), "Al-Qaeda in Yemen launches a 'hearts and minds' campaign." *Middle East Eye*, December 27. Available online: https://www.middleeasteye.net/news/ al-qaeda-yemen-launches-hearts-and-minds-campaign (accessed January 18, 2021).

Al-Batati, S. (2015b), "When Al Qaeda Stormed My City: Reporter's Notebook." *New York Times*, April 10. Available online: https://www.nytimes.com/times-insider/2015/04/10/ when-al-qaeda-stormed-my-city-reporters-notebook/ (accessed January 18, 2021).

al-Dawsari, N. (2018), "Foe Not Friend: Yemeni Tribes and Al-Qaeda in the Arabian Peninsula, POMED: Project on Middle East Democracy." Available online: http:// pomed.org/wp-content/uploads/2018/02/Dawsari_FINAL_180201.pdf (accessed June 28, 2018).

Almosawa, S. and K. Fahim (2015), "Militants From Qaeda Affiliate Seize 2 Yemeni Towns." *The New York Times*, December 2. Available online: https://www.nytimes.com /2015/12/03/world/middleeast/militants-from-qaeda-affiliate-seize-2-yemeni-towns .html (accessed January 18, 2021).

al-Maqtari, Bushra (2017), "The Evolution of Militant Salafism in Ta´izz." *Sana´a Centre for Strategic Studies*, September 29. Available online: https://sanaacenter.org/ publications/analysis/4843 (accessed January 18, 2021).

al-Mushki, A. (2014), "Reactions to Al-Qa'ida-Huthist clashes in Yemen's Al-Bayda." *Yemen Times*, September 30. Available online: https://monitoring.bbc.co.uk/product /80282776 (accessed January 18, 2021).

al-Muslimi, F. and Baron, A. (2017), "The Limits of US Military Power in Yemen: Why Al Qaeda in the Arabian Peninsula Continues to Thrive." *Sanaa Center for Strategic Studies*. Available online: https://sanaacenter.org/publications/analysis/86 (accessed January 18, 2021).

al-Sadmi, Y. (2011), "Yemen Army Commander Says Al-Qa´idah in Zinjibar Region Will Soon Be Defeated." *Al-Siyasah*, October 4. Available online: https://monitoring.bbc.co .uk/product/80109548 (accessed January 18, 2021).

al-Sakkaf, N. (2013), "Yemen's Rada District Locals Turn to Al-Qa'idah to Settle Disputes." *Yemen Times*, October 10. Available online: https://monitoring.bbc.co.uk/product /80235580 (accessed January 18, 2021).

al-Shishani, M. (2012), "Profile: Ansar al-Sharia." *BBC Arabic*, March 18. Available online :
   https://www.bbc.co.uk/news/world-middle-east-17402856 (accessed January 18, 2021).

Amr, A. (2015), "How al Qaeda Rules in Yemen: Letter from Mukalla." *Foreign Affairs*,
   October 28. Available online: https://www.foreignaffairs.com/articles/yemen/2015-10
   -28/how-al-qaeda-rules-yemen (accessed January 18, 2021).

Analytical Support and Sanctions Monitoring Team (2020), *26nd comprehensive report*,
   UN, New York: New York. Available online e: https://undocs.org/S/2020/717 (accessed
   January 18, 2021).

Associated Press (2012), "Al-Qaida Papers." *Associated Press*, August 6. Available online:
   https://www.longwarjournal.org/images/al-qaida-papers-how-to-run-a-state.pdf
   (accessed January 18, 2021).

Bayoumy, Y., N. Browning and M. Ghobari (2016), "How Saudi Arabia's War in Yemen Has
   Made al Qaeda Stronger – and Richer." *Reuters*, April 8. Available online: https://www
   .reuters.com/investigates/special-report/yemen-aqap/ (accessed January 18, 2021).

BBC Monitoring (2011), "Yemeni Militants, Rebels Take Control of Two Local Radios."
   Media Feature, BBC Monitoring, April 14. Available online: https://monitoring.bbc.co
   .uk/product/m19ldltg (accessed January 18, 2021).

BBC Monitoring (2015), "The Extent of Al-Qa'idah Control of Yemeni City of
   Al-Mukalla." *BBC Monitoring Insight*, May 15. Available: online https://monitoring.bbc
   .co.uk/product/m1cg42tc (accessed January 18, 2021).

Berti, B. (2015), "Non-state Actors as Providers of Governance: The Hamas Government
   in Gaza between Effective Sovereignty, Centralized Authority, and Resistance." *The
   Middle East Journal*, 69 (1): pp. 9–31.

The Bureau for Investigative Journalism (2021), "Drone Strikes in Yemen," January 18.
   Available online: https://www.thebureauinvestigates.com/projects/drone-war/yemen
   (accessed January 18, 2021).

Caris, C. and S. Reynolds (2014), "ISIS Governance in Syria." *Middle East Security Report*
   22: pp. 4–41.

Carboni, Andrea and Matthias Sulz (2020), "The Wartime Transformation of AQAP in
   Yemen." ACLED, December. Available online: https://acleddata.com/2020/12/14/the
   -wartime-transformation-of-aqap-in-yemen/ (accessed January 18, 2021).

Cigar, N. (2018), *The Enemy Is Us: How Allied and U.S. Strategy in Yemen Contributes to
   AQAP's Survival*, Florida: JSOU Press 18 (4).

Clark, V. (2010), *Yemen: Dancing on the Heads of Snakes*. Great Britain: Yale University
   Press.

Cook, J. (2017), "Shifting Priorities: Reconstituting Security Agendas and Security Sector
   Reforms in Yemen," in S. N. Romaniuk et al. (eds.), *The Palgrave Handbook of Global
   Counterterrorism Policy*. London: Palgrave Macmillan.

Cook, J. (2016), "Analyzing the Formal and Informal Roles of Women in Security and
   Justice in Yemen: Reflections for Future Considerations," *The Canadian Network for the
   Study of Terrorism, Security and Society* 16: 8. Available online: http://tsas5.wpengine
   .com/working-papers/analyzing-the-formal-and-informal-roles-of-women-in-security
   -and-justice-in-yemen/ (accessed January 18, 2021).

Cook, J. (2019a), *A Woman's Place: US Counterterrorism since 9/11*. London: Hurst.

Cook, J. (2019b), "Their Fate Is Tied to Ours': Assessing AQAP Governance and
   Implications for Security in Yemen." The International Centre for the Study of
   Radicalisation, King's College London. October 2019. Available online: https://icsr.info
   /2019/10/28/their-fate-is-tied-to-ours-assessing-aqap-governance-and-implications
   -for-security-in-yemen/ (accessed January 18, 2021).

Cook, J., Haid, H. and Trauthig, I. (2020), "Jurisprudence Beyond the State: An Analysis of Jihadist 'Justice' in Yemen, Syria and Libya." *Studies in Conflict & Terrorism*. Available online: https://www.tandfonline.com/doi/abs/10.1080/1057610X.2020.1776958.

Cook, Joana and Shiraz Maher (forthcoming 2022), *Islamist Approaches to Governance*. London: Hurst.

Dawsari, N. (2014), "The Popular Committees of Abyan, Yemen: A Necessary Evil or an Opportunity for Security Reform?" Middle East Institute. Available online: https://www.mei.edu/publications/popular-committees-abyan-yemen-necessary-evil-or-opportunity-security-reform (accessed January 18, 2021).

Entous, A., Barnes, J. E. and Coker, M. (2011), "U.S. Doubts Intelligence That Led to Yemen Strike," *The Wall Street Journal*. Available online: https://www.wsj.com/articles/SB10001424052970203899504577126883574284126 (accessed January 18, 2021).

Fergusson, J. (2015), "Yemen Is Tearing Itself Apart over Water." *Newsweek*, January 20. Available online: https://www.newsweek.com/2015/01/30/al-qaida-plans-its-next-move-yemen-300782.html (accessed January 18, 2021).

Fishman, Brian H. (2016), "The Master Plan: ISIS, Al-Qaeda, and the Jihadi Strategy for Final Victory." Yale University Press, USA.

Fitton-Brown, E. (2018), "Analytical Support and Sanctions Monitoring Team, 22nd Report." UN Security Council, July 27. Available online: https://undocs.org/pdf?symbol=en/s/2018/705 (accessed January 18, 2021).

Flanigan, S. (2006), "Charity as Resistance: Connections between Charity, Contentious Politics, and Terror," *Studies in Conflict and Terrorism* 29 (7) (October–November 2006): 642.

France 24 (2019), "Dozens Killed in Attacks on Security Forces in Yemen's Aden." *France 24*, January 8. Available online: https://www.france24.com/en/20190801-yemen-aden-two-deadly-attacks-police-jihadists-shiite (accessed January 18, 2021).

General Assembly (2016), "Children and Armed Conflict," Report of the Secretary General, April 20. Available online:: https://www.un.org/ga/search/view:doc.asp?symbol=s/2016/360&referer=/english/&Lang=E (accessed January 18, 2021).

Ghobari, Mohammed and Mohammad Mukhashaf (2015), "Yemeni Tribes Enter Coastal Town to Drive Out al Qaeda." *Reuters*, April 4. Available online: https://www.reuters.com/article/uk-yemen-security-mukalla/yemeni-tribes-enter-coastal-town-to-drive-out-al-qaeda-idUKKBN0MV08O20150404 (accessed January 18, 2021).

Grynkewich, A. (2008), "Welfare as Warfare: How Violent Non-state Groups Use Social Services to Attack the State," *Studies in Conflict & Terrorism* 31(4): 350–70.

Hansen, S. (2013), *Al-Shabaab in Somalia: The History and Ideology of a Militant Islamist Group*. Oxford: Oxford University Press.

Hartig, L. (2018), "Justice Dept Must Open Criminal Investigation Into Potential War Crimes by U.S. Mercenaries in Yemen," October 16. Available online: https://www.justsecurity.org/61761/full-accounting-needed-us-uae-counterterrorism-partnership-yemen/ (accessed January 18, 2021).

Huckerby, J. and L. Fakih (2011), *A Decade Lost: Locating Gender in US Counter-Terrorism*. New York: NYU Center for Human Rights and Global Justice. Available online: https://chrgj.org/wp-content/uploads/2016/09/locatinggender.pdf (accessed January 18, 2021).

Human Rights Council (2020), "Situation of Human Rights in Yemen, Including Violations and Abuses since September 2014," Report of the Group of Eminent International and Regional Experts on Yemen, September 28. Available online: https://www.ohchr.org/Documents/HRBodies/HRCouncil/GEE-Yemen/2020-09-09-report.pdf (accessed January 18, 2021).

Human Rights Watch (2017), "Yemen: UAE Backs Abusive Local Forces. Resolve 'Disappearances', Grant Access to Detention Sites." *Human Rights Watch*, June 22. Available online: https://www.hrw.org/news/2017/06/22/yemen-uae-backs-abusive -local-forces (accessed January 18, 2021).

International Crisis Group (2017), "Yemen's al-Qaeda: Expanding the Base," International Crisis Group (174), February 2. Available online: https://www.crisisgroup.org/ middle-east-north-africa/gulf-and-arabian-peninsula/yemen/174-yemen-s-al-qaeda -expanding-base (accessed January 18, 2021).

Johnsen, G. (2013), *The Last Refuge: Yemen, Al Qaeda and America's War in Arabia*. New York: W Norton.

Johnson, T. (2013), "Taliban Adaptations and Innovations," *Small Wars & Insurgencies* 24 (1): 3–27.

Joscelyn, T. (2016), "AQAP Provides Social Services, Implements Sharia While Advancing in Southern Yemen," FDD's Long War Journal, February 3. Available online: https:// www.longwarjournal.org/archives/2016/02/aqap-provides-social-services-implements -sharia-while-advancing-in-southern-yemen.php (accessed January 18, 2021).

Karmon, E. (2015), "Islamic State and al-Qaeda Competing for Hearts & Minds," *Perspectives on Terrorism* 9(2): 71–9.

Kendall, E. and E. Stein (2015), "Yemen's al-Qa'ida and Poetry as a Weapon of Jihad." *Twenty-First Century Jihad: Law, Society and Military Action*, 247–69. I B. Tauris.

Kendall, E. (2018), "Contemporary Jihadi Militancy in Yemen: How Is the Threat Evolving?" Policy Paper 2018–7, Middle East Institute.

Kendall, E. (2019), "The Failing Islamic State Within the Failed State of Yemen," *Perspectives on Terrorism* 13(1): 78–84.

Kendall, E. (2020), "ISIS in Yemen: Caught in a Regional Power Game," Center for Global Policy, July 21. Available online: https://cgpolicy.org/articles/isis-in-yemen-caught-in-a -regional-power-game/ (accessed January 18, 2021).

Koehler-Derrick, G. (2011), *A False Foundation? AQAP, Tribes and Ungoverned Spaces in Yemen*. Military Academy, West Point, NY Combating Terrorism Center.

Ladbury, S. et al. (2016), "Jihadi Groups and State-building: The Case of Boko Haram in Nigeria," *Stability: International Journal of Security and Development* 5(1): 1–19.

Makram, F. (2011), "The Yemeni Army Faces Hard War with Al-Qa'idah In Abyan," *al-Hayat*, June 30. Available online: https://monitoring.bbc.co.uk/product/80090641 (accessed January 18, 2021).

Makram, Faysal (2011), "Yemeni Army Reportedly Fights Difficult War with Al-Qa'idah in Abyan," Al-Hayat London (Arabic). Available online: https://monitoring.bbc.co.uk/ product/80090641

Mampilly, Z. (2012), *Rebel Rulers: Insurgent Governance and Civilian Life during War*. Ithaca: Cornell University Press.

Michael, M. (2017), "In Yemen's Secret Prisons, UAE Tortures and US Interrogates," Associated Press, June 22. Available online: https://www.apnews.com/4925f7f0fa65485 3bd6f2f57174179fe (accessed January 18, 2021).

Michael, M., Wilson, T. and Keath, L. (2018), "Yemen: U.S. Allies Spin Deals with al-Qaida in War on Rebels." *Associated Press*, August 6. Available online: https://pulitzercenter .org/reporting/yemen-us-allies-spin-deals-al-qaida-war-rebels (accessed January 18, 2021).

Middle East Eye (2015), "MEE EXCLUSIVE: Al-Qaeda pulls out of key government buildings in south-eastern Yemen." *Middle East Eye*, May 12. Available online: https://

www.middleeasteye.net/news/mee-exclusive-al-qaeda-pulls-out-key-government
-buildings-southeastern-yemen (accessed January 18, 2021).
Murphy, C. (2010), "AQAP's Growing Security Threat to Saudi Arabia," *CTC Sentinel* 3(6):
1–4.
Roggio, B. (2012), "AQAP Destroys Tombs in southern Yemen." *FDD'S Long War Journal*,
June 15. Available online: https://www.longwarjournal.org/archives/2012/06/aqap
_destroys_shrine.php (accessed January 18, 2021).
Roston, A. (2018), "A Middle East Monarchy Hired American Ex-Soldiers to Kill Its
Political Enemies. This Could Be the Future of War." *Buzzfeed News*, October 16.
Available online: https://www.buzzfeednews.com/article/aramroston/mercenaries
-assassination-us-yemen-uae-spear-golan-dahlan (accessed January 18, 2021).
Simcox, R. (2012), "Ansar al-Sharia and Governance in Southern Yemen," Hudson
Institute. Available online: https://www.hudson.org/research/9779-ansar-al-sharia-and
-governance-in-southern-yemen (accessed January 18, 2021).
START (2019), "Global Terrorism Database." University of Maryland. Last accessed
September 3, 2019. Available online: https://www.start.umd.edu/gtd/search/Results
.aspx?page=1&casualties_type=b&casualties_max=&dtp2=all&country=228
&perpetrator=20032&count=100&expanded=no&charttype=line&chart=overtime
&ob=GTDID&od=desc#results-table (accessed January 18, 2021).
Trew, B. (2018a), "Former al-Qaeda Foot Soldiers Have Been Allowed into Yemen Forces,
Admits UAE Military." *The Independent*, August 16. Available online: https://www
.independent.co.uk/news/world/middle-east/yemen-civil-war-al-qaeda-soldiers-uae
-military-emirati-a8494481.html (accessed January 18, 2021).
Trew, B. (2018b), "Mukalla: Life after al-Qaeda in Yemen." *The Independent*, August 17.
Available online: https://www.independent.co.uk/news/world/middle-east/mukalla
-yemen-al-qaeda-civil-war-before-after-jihadi-terror-group-a8495636.html (accessed
January 18, 2021).
Trew, B. (2018c), "How the Conflict in Yemen Could Lead to the Return of al-Qaeda."
The Independent, August 17. Available online: https://www.independent.co.uk/
voices/yemen-conflict-al-qaeda-saudi-arabia-uae-southern-separatists-war-violence
-a8496476.html (accessed January 18, 2021).
Wiegand, K. (2016), *Bombs and Ballots: Governance By Islamist Terrorist and Guerrilla
Groups*. Routledge: London.
Worth, Robert F. (2010), "Is Yemen the next Afghanistan?" *New York Times Magazine*.
Available online: https://www.nytimes.com/2010/07/11/magazine/11Yemen-t.html
(accessed January 18, 2021).
XINHUA (2012), "Official Says Al-Qaidah Agrees to Withdraw from Yemeni Town."
BBC Monitoring, January 24. Available online: https://monitoring.bbc.co.uk/product/
f1a7gmfw (accessed January 18, 2021).
Yemen Post (2013), "Tribal Mediation Reportedly Ends Yemeni Forces' clashes with
Qa'idah in Al-Bayda." *Yemen Times*, January 30. Available online: https://monitoring
.bbc.co.uk/product/80192532 (accessed January 18, 2021).
Yemen Post (2014), "Al-Qa'idah Militants Attack, Loot Bank in Yemen's Al-Mukalla."
Yemen Post, August 14. Available: https://monitoring.bbc.co.uk/product/80276606
(accessed January 18, 2021).

Chapter 5

THE ROLE OF WOMEN IN POST-CONFLICT YEMEN

Bilkis Zabara and Sabria Al-Thawr

Introduction

Yemen ranked 179 (out of 189) in the Human Development Index in 2020, and it has been ranked last in the World Economic Forum's Global Gender Gap index for thirteen successive years. The Gender Inequality Index (GII) value for Yemen is 0.834, ranking the country 162 out of 162 countries in the 2019 index (UNDP, 2020). Once the war is over, there will be many challenges that could hinder the full participation of women in rebuilding the country and will add to the multidimensional insecurities women have long had to endure. Changes in social norms caused by the war have been positive in allowing women to assume new roles but also negative in giving rise to new threats. Yemeni women have demonstrated levels of resilience during the current war, as they have across history, that could provide for a more active inclusion process in peace building and reconstruction. Yemeni women are not a homogenous group as they reflect the geopolitical and cultural diversity in Yemen. Just as their circumstances were different before the conflict, they have experienced the war differently (al-Gawfi, Zabara, & Yadav, 2020).

In this chapter, we examine the preexisting norms, laws, and issues of accountable justice toward women and girls and the positive and negative implications of war on women, and suggest how women can play an active role in the peace process and in then building a new Yemen.

Yemeni Women: A Tireless Struggle

Yemen had made some significant progress in closing gender gaps such as female literacy rates and life expectancy. However, there were challenges in remedying the substantial differences between boys and girls in school enrollment and educational attainment, responding to unmet reproductive and child health needs, reforming discriminatory laws, and eliminating legal restrictions on women's participation in the labor force and in political life (World Bank, 2014). Successive governments failed to ensure provision of quality services to people as a result of political and economic instability since unification in 1990, the misuse of resources, and rampant corruption. Such failures were exacerbated in rural areas, where the majority of people live, although the impact could vary greatly from region to region.

Gender inequality in any society keeps women and girls in poverty, deprives them of their rights, and weakens their capacity for change (OXFAM, 2019). In Yemen, only 19.9 percent of adult women have reached at least a secondary level of education compared to 35.5 percent of their male counterparts (UNDP, 2019). The only female member of Parliament passed away in 2015. Persistent drought and poverty in rural areas contributed to men's internal and external migration to look for work leaving responsibilities of family care, land cultivation, and other productive roles to women. Less than 1 percent of agricultural landholders in Yemen are women despite the fact that women undertake 60 percent of labor in crop farming and 90 percent in livestock rearing. They form only 10 percent of waged labor (FAO, 2019): their contribution is perceived as being part of women's unpaid domestic duties. Women in rural areas need to travel to access quality health services that exist only in main cities, but depend on the approval and ability of male relatives to escort them—for protection—due to the unavailability of safe public transportation (Aulaqi, 2014).

Women are described in the Yemeni constitution as "sisters of men" and more commonly as "half of the society." At first glance, these phrases affirm the equality of men's and women's rights, but legal texts and cultural practices tell a different story. Restrictions and controls forced on women are often justified by reference to the need for conformity with Islamic requirements (Freedom House, 2005; World Bank, 2009; Dahlgren, 2013). Conservative interpretations of Islam prevailing in Yemen (as elsewhere in the region) are not necessarily women-friendly (Strzelecka 2013); rather, they encourage patriarchal control over women and limit women's mobility and public participation.

Yemen has been perceived by scholars as one of the most patriarchal societies in the Arab region (Dresch and Haykal 1995; Carapico, 2003, Würth 2003; Longley 2007; Gressmann, 2016), where the controlling tribal ideology and leadership are male-dominated, and grant women limited power. Contrary to this Western perspective, some other anthropologists view rural women from a local angle: "rural women in Yemen do not behave as victims. They are unusually assertive, stand tall, walk with long strides and express themselves loudly and with confidence" (Adra 2016, p. 318).

Men's control over women increased from the 1970s onward, when Yemen started to open up to the west. Yet in the 1990s Yemen was seen as a democratic model in the Arabian Peninsula and Yemeni women were the first in the region to obtain the active and passive right to vote.

Discrimination and gender-based violence were prevalent before the war both in law and in practice. Yemen has no law designed specifically to protect women from gender-based or domestic violence. Early marriage has been the norm and 52 percent of Yemeni girls marry before they are 18, and 14 percent before they are 15 (Ministry of Public Health and Population, 2013; CARE, 2015). The texts of the

Penal Code provide general protection for men and women that criminalizes the infliction of physical harm. Likewise, provisions in the Penal Code can increase the vulnerability of women to violence: article 232, for example, allows for reduced and lenient sentences for men convicted of so-called "honor killing." It provides that a man who murders or injures his wife, mother, daughter, or sister, or her partner after finding them in the act of committing adultery should receive a maximum prison sentence of one year or a fine.

Despite previous efforts to enhance women's rights such as the establishment of the National Women's Committee in 1996 and the Supreme Council for Women in 2003 and the development of various national strategies, poor enforcement of legislations and the entrenched cultural and religious norms failed to provide women with equal rights to men (Gressmann, 2016). Women need the authorization of their male guardian (usually their husband or father) in order to obtain an identity card or passport (Human Rights Watch, 2015). Women cannot marry without permission from their male guardian who also controls women's rights to divorce, inheritance, and child custody. The lack of enforced legal protection mechanisms leaves women and girls at risk of domestic and sexual violence (Gressmann, 2016). Tribal law is predominantly concerned "with the maintenance of honour, the sanctity of the given word, and protection of the 'weak'" (al-Zwaini, 2006:3). "Weak" includes women, children, and people who provide manual services to the tribe, which is bound to protect them. Harming "weak" persons is a violation or *ayb* (shame, dishonor), that is usually classified as mounting degrees of gravity (al-Zwaini, 2006). Such norms categorize women as weak and can deprive them from receiving their inheritance among other rights in the tribal system. On the other hand, women in tribal areas can instigate conflict (encouraging relatives to seek revenge) or act as peacemakers within their families and communities; and older women may intervene in solving violent disputes (Al-Dawsari et al, 2011). However, women's access to tribal justice usually requires the support of male members of their family.

One example of the limiting effects of social norms is the gender segregation in public life including schools and social and religious gatherings. Women's representation in the state institutions is limited with no influence on policies and decisions made by legislative institutions such as the Parliament and the judiciary (Freedom House, 2005). Efforts to engage women have been led by the international community: for example (see later), it was the UN that imposed the thirty percent quota for participation of women in the National Dialogue Conference (NDC) (Kangas & Stevens, 2018). Women's participation in political and civic life is limited and consequently has weakened their influence on policy decision-making. In Yemen, meetings of members of official institutions and civil society organizations are often held in men-only afternoon *qat* sessions, where women's access is not allowed by social custom (Freedom House, 2005). Women's exclusion from these sessions inhibits their capacity to participate and influence decisions made in these forums. There are no alternative similar spaces available for women to practice politics and to engage in public activities. In many areas of Yemen, women are not perceived as being intellectually able compared to men—a consequence of conservative and strict gender norms that limit women's role to the domestic sphere (World Bank, 2014).

The Women's Movement in Yemen has been shaped by the fluctuating political and economic history of the country and characterized by its fragmentation (al-Ashtal, 2012) so that it can be best described as activism often through extensive women's networks rather than a movement. Women remained resilient and adopted the tactic of a patient and quiet struggle, instead of direct confrontation with the state and society (al-Ashtal, 2012). Women were more active in civil society because of the unwillingness of political parties to create space for female political participation (Yadav, 2010; Heinze, 2016).

Small gains have been won by Yemeni women since the revolutions of the two parts of Yemen in 1962 and 1967. Unfortunately, the achievements gained by women in the People's Democratic Republic of Yemen (PDRY) were blown away with the adoption of more conservative laws after unification in 1990. The PDRY constitution called upon women to build society alongside men and issued the most progressive "Family Code" among the Arab countries in 1974. This gave women greater rights and better control over issues of marriage, custody of children, and divorce. The family code in the Yemen Arab Republic (YAR) was enacted in 1978: it was a mixture of Islamic law and customary conventions regulating family life compared with the code in the south (Dahlgren, 2013). However, after unification in 1990, women's advancement was marginalized (Lackner, 1995) and only women with ties to power structures were permitted to take up state positions (Dahlgren, 2018). Women's political participation before 2011 had been limited to select members of the elite (Yadav and Clark, 2010; Awadh and Shujaadeen, 2019) and political debate was confined to male-dominated gatherings and TV programs or newspapers articles. Other factors that contributed to the increased exclusion of women after unification were conservative attitudes among some members of Parliament and influenced by the popularity of political Islam as noted (see Chapter 3 in this volume) that called for restricting women's mobility and expression (Adra, 2006; Panday, 2009).

The Uprising and Transitional Period

The 2011 uprising and the transition period that followed were instrumental in giving a new voice to women that it was thought might endure. Women were among the first to take to the streets in the uprising in a wholly unprecedented pattern that paved the way for an active participation. This enabled them to "challenge the system that initially excluded them," to achieve representation in the NDC (al-Naami and Moodley, 2017: 2) and to articulate their demands in the outcomes of the NDC and the new draft constitution. For some, women's active participation in the 2011 uprising brought "a new dimension to the average Yemeni woman's life" (al-Sakkaf, 2012), but the average Yemeni woman saw little real change.

Women's participation in the NDC was impressive as demonstrated by the high level of women's representation, including chairing three out of the nine working groups of the conference as well as membership in the supervisory team chaired by President Hadi. At the end of the NDC in 2014, Yemeni women celebrated the achievements of ten months of hard work and advocacy, particularly in modifying discriminatory laws and opening up more space for women's inclusion by approving a 30 percent quota for women at all levels of government. Four of the seventeen members of the constitution drafting committee were female activists and legal experts who did their utmost to translate the NDC outcomes into the articles and texts of the draft constitution—including the 30 percent quota for all decision-making and elected positions.

Unfortunately, two years later, with the outbreak of the war in Yemen, women's hopes were shattered, and many women activists feared that the gains made during the transitional phase would be the first to go in political compromises among the warring parties (Rohwerder, 2017; Heinze, 2016; Alwazir et al, 2016). Deteriorating security and economic conditions have significantly inhibited women's activism. No political faction, regardless of ideology or capacity, has worked to uphold the NDC's promises of women's economic, social, or political equality (Ghanem, 2019).

Impact of the War on Women

Yemeni women bear the heaviest burden of war and suffer disproportionately from its impact. UNHCR reported in April 2018 that "over one-third of displaced Yemenis live in female-headed households including many headed by female children below the age of eighteen."[1] (UNHCR 2018) The suspension of the payment of salaries for the government employees in 2016, the dramatic decline in the currency value, and rampant inflation have further exacerbated the plight of Yemenis (UNOCHA, 2018). The war has significantly and disproportionately reshaped the lives of women across different geographical regions and social groups (al-Ammar, Patchett & Shamsan, 2019). While their suffering is discussed in the international community extensively, their social and economic support to individuals and society, however, is often overlooked and weakly documented. In the sections that follow, we describe some areas where women have overcome challenges and developed coping strategies amid the deteriorating living conditions during six years of a devastating war.

In addition to the impact of casualties—military and civilian—caused by the conflict, women experienced enormous physical and psychological stress. Following the first airstrikes on major cities of Sana'a, Aden, Sa'ada, and Ta'izz, women, children, and the elderly fled to more secure rural areas (often their place of origin) or cities that were not then directly affected by the conflict such as Hodeida, Ibb, and Hadhramaut. Some families were displaced more than once as the conflict widened. The men who stayed behind kept an eye on the family property to prevent looting. The huge number of IDPs added to the burden as rural women often provided immediate food aid and housing to them. This kind of volunteering enhanced social cohesion and increased women's self-esteem (al-Gawfi, Zabara, & Yadav, 2020). Wealthier women who could afford to flee Yemen along with their families, or even alone, settled mostly in one of the few countries accessible to Yemenis such as Egypt, Jordan, Saudi Arabia, Turkey, and Malaysia. After one year of the war, many families returned to Yemen because they had run out of savings or had not been able to adapt to the new foreign culture. Cases of women seeking asylum are also known, particularly in Europe. Further, the relative stability in major cities such as Sana´a and Ibb encouraged IDPs to return. This added an increased pressure on resources such as water and fuel.

On the other hand, middle-class urban women suddenly have had to perform domestic tasks in primitive ways. Some found that they were forced to collect firewood and fetch water, exposing them to the risk of gender-based violence (GBV) (Gressman 2016: 43 in Rohwerder 2017).

Access to Basic Services

The destruction of public infrastructure and war-related economic hardships have adversely affected women's lives in cities. Using the excuse of insecurity, women were among the first employees in both the public and private sectors to lose their jobs or to take compulsory leave. With the collapse of the electricity supply, health and water and sanitation services reduced and malnutrition increased, obliging women to assume new roles to support their families. In northern cities women went to collect water from free-of-cost distribution points (Zabara 2018).[2] Women queued up for several hours to buy cooking gas bottles or fuel for their own or their husbands' cars or for domestic electric generators. In Sana´a, since the beginning of the fuel crisis, only one petrol station has been allocated to serve women, while men have access to several stations, a questionable procedure that could indicate attempts to normalize the sidelining of women's visibility.

During the war, women's ability to access health services have become extremely limited (al-Naami and Moodley, 2017: 6 in Rohwerder 2017, p.10), especially with the looting of public hospitals in Aden and with airstrikes on hospitals including those targeting military areas close to al-Sabeen Hospital for Maternity and Childhood in Sana´a—forcing the immediate evacuation of patients and exposing them to a high risk of unsafe delivery at their homes. Pregnant women died during surgery as a consequence of sudden fuel shortage. The total loss of public power supply disproportionately affected the poorest women as the wealthier women could afford better-equipped private facilities. In 2017, the UNFPA recorded 1.1 million severely malnourished pregnant women and 52,800 cases of high-risk pregnancy (UNFPA, 2017). Many women have become more reluctant to seek necessary medical interventions unless it is a matter of life and death.

In 2020, the global pandemic COVID-19 hit Yemen's population hard adding to the economic, health, and social burdens of women and men. IOM reported 2030 cases and 587 deaths as of September 19, 2020 (IOM, 2020), but reliable statistical data for the number of cases is not available. UN Women, UNICEF, UNFPA, UNDP, and other international and local organizations as well as both governments in the north and the south of Yemen, and individual initiatives stepped in with relief programs and actions to protect the population from the pandemic. Women took over the production of personal protective equipment for medical staff (UNDP, 2020) across the country, filling the market gap for these emergency items. Women have taken the lead—as always during the war in Yemen—in providing care mostly to infected people at home due to shortage of hospital care and medicines, whether in the cholera outbreak in 2017–2019 or in dealing with COVID-19 during the peak period in April–June 2020. Meanwhile, women in rural areas often suffered especially badly. War damage blocked roads making it difficult to get access to cities to buy cooking gas and supplies or to access health facilities. In the period from March 2015 to August 2016 airstrikes on agricultural land (Mundy, 2017) hit food production (where as noted earlier, women provide the bulk of the labor) and threatened to push part of Yemen into famine.

Women's access to education has always been restricted by social norms and with the poor capacity of the state to ensure equal opportunities for all, their situation worsened during the war. Women's literacy rate was less than 30 percent across Yemen before the war, and it fell again as conflict disrupted education: schools were among the targets hit and teachers went unpaid; undamaged schools in both urban and rural regions were used as shelters for IDPs. More recently, as the education system started to function again, boys were the first to be sent back to schools to secure education as they were perceived as future breadwinners by their families. Many parents are firmly convinced that their daughters cannot protect themselves and should stay at home, thus adding to the number of illiterate female adults who will have to struggle even harder to access services (Rohwerder 2017). On an individual level, female teachers and secondary school graduates volunteered to teach children at schools after the government stopped paying salaries. In later stages of the war, parents have had to contribute money to keep the education system running. Mothers were foremost in ensuring the education of their daughters. Female teachers and mothers took the initiative of collecting old schoolbooks to support the continuation of education and providing countless numbers of breakfasts for poor students.

New Roles: New Threat of GBV

The collapse of the economy by nearly 50 percent, as a result on the ongoing war (World Bank Group, 2019), has forced thousands of women to take over the role of breadwinners (Rohwerder, 2017); (al-Gawfi, Zabara, & Yadav, 2020) whilst coping with the lack of food, insecurity, and the fear of being caught in the military conflicts that can suddenly break out. From 2016, the non-payment of civil servants' salaries has had severe consequences for those directly and indirectly affected (Rageh, Nasser and al-Muslimi 2016). Most civil servants were men, who felt helpless with no income to support their families, leaving them with the option of joining the army or militias or relying on humanitarian organizations to provide a food basket or a small amount of money to buy food. The "manhood" image was distorted in a society in which it is a matter of sociocultural honor that boys are raised to protect their mothers, sisters, and daughters (Adra 2016: 316). One effect was an increase in domestic violence, as frustrated men sought to reassert their masculinity (Al-Ammar, Patchett and Shamsan 2019).

Women have had to take on new roles outside the house that have added to their normal domestic duties. In most families, women have to get up several hours earlier to do these household tasks before leaving for work—and they continue to do them when they return home. Failure to do so exposes women to domestic violence or even divorce—some even fear for their lives. Though women have long faced such problems the war has exacerbated them.

The conflict has narrowed the presence of women in local government authorities as these are now entirely dominated by men (Gressmann, 2016). As a consequence, women have been pushed into playing a major role in the informal sector such as subsistence farming and caring for close vulnerable, brittle, and fragile relatives, both old and young, and now COVID-19 patients. However, the harsh living conditions during the conflict have forced women to break with social norms: "leaving their private home sphere" exposing themselves to new threats of harassment and uncertain outcomes hoping for the survival of their family (Heinze & Stevens, 2018). Only those who are strong and determined can escape subordination to men—and the opposition of some female relatives. Not all community members (men and women) oppose women working outside the house; some men are supportive, particularly if it results in a good income and no loss of prestige. Women have had to change the way they travel to work. Some have sold their dowry jewelry or used their private savings to buy a small car for themselves or for their male relatives who in their turn drive female relatives to work. The less fortunate have to walk, ride behind their husbands or brothers on a motorbike, or take several shared minibuses, which can be expensive and time-consuming as well as involving a struggle for seats between males and females. Such coping mechanisms are not entirely without risk of harassment, both inside automobiles and at bus stops. Unfortunately, no significant action has been taken so far to protect female victims. On the contrary, this has given rise to more subordination and oppression by men and occasionally even by women.

Mobility between governorates if not escorted by a male relative or *mahram* is barely acceptable socially. The lack of security combined with weak or, rather, nonexistent state control in many parts of the country has exacerbated women's struggle to travel without fear, particularly in northern regions. They face harassment, arbitrary detention, and torture by various security forces (Harb, 2019) as well as at the countless armed checkpoints all over the country (Gressmann, 2016; al-Naami and Moodley, 2017; Nasser, 2019).

During the conflict, more cases of the violation of women's rights and gender-based violence were reported (OHCHR report of Eminent Group, 2018), despite informal customary or tribal norms that have often been protective of women: for example, putting women and children at risk during conflict is considered a "Black Shame" (ADRA 2006; Lackner 1995; Al-Dawsari, 2012). However, many of the armed groups, whether Shi´a or Salafi, associated with legitimate authorities or affiliated to non-state actors have violated tribal and social norms that protect women. These groups regularly shame women who do not conform to their ideology in order to render them voiceless. Ansar Allah, for example, to avoid being stigmatized as committing a "black shame,"[3] has utilized armed female units to attack women who raise their voice against them. (The New Arab, 2015)

Violence is also exerted against women in the Yemeni media by smear campaigns and hostile attacks against female activists and activism (al-Gawfi, Zabara & Yadav, 2020). To protect their lives, many female journalists and activists have fled to more secure regions in the south or even outside the country. Some have managed to continue working in their profession but others have given up or shifted to social media, where they have more space to express themselves freely (Farhan, 2017). Women working in radio broadcasting and online media in Sana´a, Ibb, and Hajjah claim that males monopolize leadership positions. In other words, they are not part of shaping the policies and programs of Yemeni media. To respond to such structural violence, the Gender Development Research and Studies Center at Sana´a University (GDRSC) has attempted to consolidate gender concepts among male and female media workers in these cities in a number of training workshops. The Hadhramaut Establishment for Human Development (HEHD), a local non-profit organization, succeeded in empowering female journalists in Mukalla to express themselves freely. Trainees felt they could contribute more professionally and "highlight women's stories" (UNESCO, 2017). The war has thus destroyed the limited gains that women had struggled to achieve during the transitional phase. It has prevented them from using the small steps gained to work toward wider and more effective participation of women. Norms have been breached in order for women to survive but also in order to instrumentalize women for political purposes or to discredit opposition. The war has undermined the social fabric that helped protect women and made them more vulnerable. However, a glimpse of hope has kept women fighting and challenging this backlash. Many young women have become strong human rights activists and social helpers (Pandya 2018).

Women in the Post-Conflict Yemen

In this section, we examine the implications of the gains and losses made by women during the war on the post-conflict situation. Will the situation return to the prewar situation? What cannot remain and what will change? How will women be able to play a role in peace building and then in building a new Yemen? What are women's priorities in the design of the future state and its different sectors?

Despite the economic insecurity during the war, women have managed to open new windows (al-Jawfi, Zabara & Yadav, 2020). For example, young women have shown that they can compete very well with their male counterparts in entrepreneurship. This was obvious in the way young women presented how they have started their own small companies in the field of IT, interior and fashion design, and online trade in the "Rowad Aamal Show-2019" organized by a Yemeni firm for the Global Entrepreneurship Week held in Sana´a. Many urban women have started home-based businesses (sewing, incense making, baking, jewelry designing, etc.), making products which they sell primarily to female customers in the neighborhood or through social media. Women of the lower social classes sell their products directly on the local market alongside men while others delegate the selling to their male relatives. A few women have entered new fields of work such as mobile phone and automobile repairs, construction (Al-Gawfi, Zabara, & Yadav, 2020), hotel and café services, and catering. They imitate the work of men or join capacity-building workshops (paid or unpaid) to learn how to perform better. Their success often gives them self-esteem and confidence—which they fear they could lose after the war stops. They share most of their income with their families while keeping some for their personal use. On the other hand, for those women who have been forced to generate an income to feed their families, work can become an extra and exhausting burden. They often have no money left for their own needs. Some of those who have taken refuge abroad have managed to find work as teachers or physicians and others have started postdoctoral research or continued their master's degree. Whether women will be able to continue and develop this into sustainable change depends on the willingness of the ruling power to support a more active future role for women. A conservative government may push women back to their reproductive roles. A more open and liberal government would eventually support women's rights and boost a gender-inclusive, sensitive, and responsive policy approach. Unexpectedly, the new IRG cabinet assigned in December 2020 excluded women for the first time in the past twenty years. Female activists across Yemen strongly denounced this move. Therefore, women should be more proactive in defining their priorities and demands, and in combining their efforts to strengthen their advocacy and lobbying skills.

Despite the immensely increased involvement of women in the informal sector in times of war, they are unlikely to receive a pension when they retire or fall ill. There is a need for the development of an appropriate and applicable social security system as women, like most of the population, were denied any kind of insurance even before the war.

As the war escalated, women were in the forefront of responding to the humanitarian crisis (Heinze, 2016). Driven by the helplessness of injured and hungry victims, women mobilized a network of volunteers to provide food, first aid, accommodation, and access to other basic necessities (Pandya, 2015:1-2). They work in collectives of women or family members but also individually to support their extended families and the neediest poor. This was first enabled by the charitable support of individual men and women and has since then been sustained by the support of local and international organizations.

Many humanitarian aid initiatives were established by women at the neighborhood level; parents' and teachers' groups have helped people affected by the war. Local people have come together to build the potential to support the helpless, whilst building new friendships. A younger generation of female students and employees started new initiatives within their own social networks and neighborhoods to collect and distribute clothing and blankets during the winter in mountainous regions. They opened WhatsApp and Facebook groups to call for urgent medical assistance and to attract donations from inside and outside the country. This has been quite helpful in collecting cash for some urgent medical procedures. The majority of those who need to travel abroad for medical treatment cannot afford it or face the hazards of inland journeys to Aden and Sayoun airports, given the ongoing siege on Sana´a international airport. Female medical and health care students joined forces with each other or their male colleagues and volunteered to treat the sick and collected medication and distributed it for free. Volunteering in itself is a dedication to help others and promote social and economic cohesion. Voluntary work will eventually decline as a consequence of improving services in post-war Yemen. However, volunteering could be adopted as a system by the state to encourage people, including women of all ages, to make a difference to society. This should be recognized and in return be awarded, ultimately by providing scholarships or financial incentives or discounts in some services.

Despite the hardships faced, some women have managed to get recognition for their contribution to strengthening social cohesion and paving the way for peace through conflict and dispute resolution (al-Jawfi, Zabara & Yadav, 2020). While women are always portrayed as victims of the war and in need of assistance and protection, they have acquired some unconventional roles in the current war which has been little researched. Pictures of women wearing military uniforms and carrying weapons appear in the media and social media channels of different political factions, suggesting the utilization of women in different armed groups such as Elite Female Unit of the Security Belt and Aden Security (The New Arab, 2015), *Zainabyatt* in Ansar Allah, and as part of the popular resistance groups in Ta´izz (The Conversation, 2018). More recently, some women have been involved in private security companies: one is reported to be led by a woman who was supported to open her own company/small project (UNFPA, 2019).Women used to be part of the Special Forces or female security groups prior to the conflict, but now they are more invisible, and they may not be functioning as they used to be. We assume that women will be part of a broader security reform and play a greater role in security in the future in all cases though this might be limited to certain functions or tasks such as supporting the inspection of women at check points, airports, sensitive state buildings, or events, etc. Meanwhile, some studies indicate the importance of depoliticizing women's role in security provisions to enable sustainable peace building (Cook 2014 in al-Gawfi, Zabara, & Yadav, 2020).

Regardless of such radical gender roles that are somehow encouraged by different armed groups, women are still not permitted to engage in peace building; they are not allocated seats at the negotiation table regardless of the pressure[4] from the international community. There have been mixed fortunes for women in local mediation. Although there are examples of female mediators resolving crimes of honor and SGBV, and disputes between students and families in Shabwah and Marib, these appear to be exceptions. Even in Shabwah, where women have traditionally played such roles, they act more as social activists than mediators. Female mediation in Al-Jawf has become less common than in the past. However, in Sana´a and Hajjah, women have participated in negotiating prisoner exchange and resolving tribal conflicts (Awadh, Shujaadeen and al-Refaei, 2019, p. 33, 34). In other areas controlled by Ansar Allah, conducting some forms of peace activities such as studies, training, and awareness are not accepted as they are perceived as being part of the agenda of hostile outside states. Informal peace building initiated by women will most likely continue after the war ends. However, it does not seem that women will have a strong voice in formal peace negotiations in the short or medium run.

There are also implications for how international agencies approach the post-conflict situation. Observations suggest that during the conflict, development and humanitarian interventions addressed women's needs from a reductionist perspective. For example, restricting humanitarian aid to women in reproductive age groups, while clearly necessary, tends to strengthen the idea that women are recognized only as mothers. This accords with social norms in Yemen that do not recognize women as capable individuals who can manage their lives, make decisions and choices that matter for them, and be independently accountable for such choices. On the other hand, gender is commonly used in the aid context as a buzzword (Cornwall, 2007; Abi Rafeh, 2009) to make project proposals and planned interventions more appealing and increase the likelihood of it being funded—without seriously considering the actual needs and impact on women's and men's lives. International agencies need to adopt a more critical approach toward monitoring project outcomes from a gender perspective.

Building a New Yemen

Women will need and want to take their share of responsibility in building a new Yemen after the war. But they are aware of the uncertainties over how the war will end, how peace will be stabilized, and how governing structures may be organized and the economy rebuilt. Women will want to see suitable frameworks that respond to women's priorities and develop the mechanisms to ensure the full and inclusive participation of women. The following actions address these requirements taking into account the prewar situation and the changes wrought by the war.

Securing Peace: Peace Building and Diplomacy

The new Yemen will start with the peace building process, which must begin as soon as possible and not wait until there is an overall peace deal. The inclusion of women as active participants increases the sustainability of peace agreements (Krause and Bränfors, 2018). Therefore, women need to be proactive to start developing a common and inclusive peace agenda for all Yemenis. Not only the urban educated but also the rural illiterate women and those representing different socioeconomic diversities must be involved (Aboueldahab, 2019). This strategic priority should focus on serious efforts to develop consensus mechanisms for the inclusion of women as formal and informal independent participants in peace processes and mediation at various levels (Alwazir, A., et al., 2016). Further to that, post-war reconstruction planning should be gender-mainstreamed across the various sectors for immediate implementation after the peace agreement.

Women can cross the divides in Yemen, as they are perceived to be less active politically in the conflict compared with men, but women have excellent access to local communities. Their engagement should be enhanced in local peace building initiatives, particularly where women work as mediators such as in tribal areas of Al-Jawf and Marib, or in strengthening the social fabric through activism in humanitarian intervention (such as collectively distributing food baskets), or in prisoner exchange and resolving community conflicts (Awadh, Shujaadeen and al-Refaei, 2019).

It is thus essential that the culture of recognizing women's work in peace building is disseminated. Investments should be made available to equip women with peace education while enhancing women's negotiation skills and opening channels of respectful communication between fighting parties and women.

Constitutional, Legal and Security Reform

Building a new Yemen will require a critical gender review of all discriminatory constitutional texts and laws. It should start by revising the relevant outcomes of the NDC and the draft constitution of 2014 (Alwazir, et al., 2016). To achieve this goal and ensure that their needs are taken into account, women should be included in the reviewing of existing laws and the drafting of new laws and should take the lead in presenting their demands and expectations. The integration of international human rights instruments such as the Convention on the Elimination of all Forms of Discrimination Against Women (CEDAW) into national post-conflict legal systems is key to ensuring sustainability and should thus be considered. A living example is what happened in the Great Lakes region in Africa (Arostegui, 2013). International women's and human rights organizations should support local organizations to monitor the state's enforcement of laws.

Meanwhile, it should be recognized that one simple national model of women's inclusion will not fit all Yemeni women. Innovative models will need to be developed to respond to such diversity. Intersectionality of gender with class, ethnicity, age, social status, regional, and tribal and political affiliation should be considered. Raising people's awareness of their rights at different levels and enforcing constitutional articles[5] are the minimum starting steps. Preexisting regional diversity has been exacerbated by political fragmentation and the isolation of Yemen's regions from one another. Local women should be involved at the outset from initial planning to final implementation—and then in monitoring and evaluation of these models. Experience from similar regional or global contexts could be helpful in enhancing the quality of programs and projects. One of the initial steps that will have to be taken is to conduct situation and risk analyses for different regions to capture the political, socioeconomic, and sociocultural changes that shaped gender and power relations at the household and at the community level. The few studies conducted over the past three years have focused on certain geographical areas or certain issues such as women's role in peace building or economic opportunities for women during the war but only in areas that were accessible to researchers. Local research efforts should be more comprehensive to enable the state to develop more inclusive and appropriate gender policies.

Legal reform should address gender gaps in the current laws such as legalizing the age of eighteen years to be the minimum age for marriage for both sexes as agreed in the NDC outcomes and Yemen's commitments under CEDAW. Further, women need clearly stated laws that enable them to enjoy the right to work, to inherit, own land, and access resources, and be treated as eligible citizens before the law with no need to resort to a male guardian. Lifting male guardianship and the existence of a supportive legal environment and laws would enhance women's capacity to control their life choices, to get education, to move and work, to decide on marriage, divorce, and custody issues, and to handle their reproductive health rights and well-being.

A practical priority for Yemeni women is the employment of more women in the military, police, and security apparatus (Heinze, & Ahmed, 2013; Cook, 2015) provided they are adequately trained, and equipped with decision-making power and adequate tools to exercise their functions with professionalism. The military and security institutions involved should be reformed and held accountable for their actions. They must respond to the needs of women; the local context of the vulnerable women in terms of GBV requires special attention to protection modalities.

Most importantly, the state must conduct social security reforms fairly, and ensure the inclusiveness of various social categories such as women, the disabled, IDPs, and the marginalized, in terms of pension and health care systems. This will enable these groups to enjoy the right to live with dignity.

Socioeconomic Perspectives

One of the urgent requirements to assist the recovery of the socioeconomic situation of the country is to accelerate lifting the embargo on airports[6] and sea ports to enable the flow of basic foodstuff, medications, and fuel. Hunger, deterioration of health and living conditions, and the gradual erosion and destruction of infrastructure have worsened poverty rates among Yemeni people. Reconstruction is meant to bring both women and men out of the poverty trap. This section will discuss some socioeconomic perspectives that need to be prioritized in the reconstruction phase.

One of these key priorities is ensuring good education for girls and women through formal and informal paths. In rural areas, women are not educated or are less educated than women in urban areas. Equal access of girls to formal education (general and vocational) can be ensured by eradicating barriers which hinder enrollment and continuation in schools. More girls' schools need to be built and equipped with sufficient teaching equipment, staff, and proper sanitary facilities. Ways will need to be found to enable girls to travel to and from school without any harassment. With the help of local authorities, local women should be motivated to become trained as teachers by providing incentives (financial, housing, etc.). For this to happen, awareness of the importance of educating girls must be raised among men and women alike. Religious leaders should assert the value of education in Islam for all men and women.

Women should no longer be suffering from health problems because of a lack of quickly available medication, in particular in rural areas. A fundamental change in access to adequate health services must be generated by the Ministry of Health and Population, eventually in cooperation with local councils and the private sector. They should spare no efforts to educate and train more rural female doctors, midwives, and nurses, raise the awareness of men and women, and establish an effective referral system in rural areas.

It is also vital to find more innovative approaches to empowering women in the economy through, for example, promoting female entrepreneurship and appointing women to leadership positions at the Chamber of Commerce. A host of other measures should be considered: for example, facilitating access of women to micro-credit, particularly in rural areas, and training women on how to submit project proposals, and how to start, implement, and sustain successful projects— and learning from the lessons of previous attempts to take such action in Yemen and elsewhere in the world.

Agricultural extension and veterinary services should ensure the provision of technical and material support to rural women to strengthen the quality and quantity of their production, and to facilitate their access to local markets to be part of local supply chains. Similarly, public and private fishery institutions, and local associations, should work on activating women's engagement in fishery. One of the applicable solutions is to reactivate the role of the Rural Women's Development Directorate in the Ministry of Agriculture and Fisheries, which has maintained a well-trained network and branches in all governorates for twenty years.

Since women are more likely to care about solving potential threats they should be equipped with proper tools and mechanisms to report these threats. Women, for example, are more likely to report identified public health risks, weaknesses in the sewage and neighborhood garbage disposal systems, etc. Hotlines or other systems which facilitate their access to reporting to specific relevant authorities can contribute to public health risk management.

With so many women engaging in the informal sector as a result of the collapse of the economy during the war, there is a need to regulate this sector to protect women from exploitation due to the lack of knowledge and experience.

New Levels of Networking Among Women

It is important to establish different forums or platforms to facilitate networking among women. When women had the chance to meet, discuss, plan, advocate, and work together during the 2011 uprising and in the NDC, they made tangible gains. Such platforms contributed to unifying women's vision, strengthening their strategies, and creating advocates in society. The establishment of women's peace forums that gather activist women and women members of political parties is a good first step to work on women's inclusion in peace negotiations. The setting up of the Yemeni Women's Pact for Peace and Security (PACT, *Tawafuq*) by UN Women and the Office of the Special Envoy of the Secretary General is a good example, although it bypassed existing women's networks and organizations. Further, no tangible results have been achieved so far.

As noted earlier, it is crucial to include women at the local level and in different regions to ensure the capture of the diversity of Yemeni women and their needs and challenges. Online networking and tools need to be part of the capacity-building and skills packages provided to women at the local level, which could enhance their opportunities of networking and utilization of these networks to improve their lives. Even illiterate women (e.g., women farmers) at the community level could benefit from easy-to-use mobile phone applications to network among themselves, to access and share information, to market their products, to find nearby services, etc. Therefore, women's economic empowerment projects need to adopt more innovative design approaches.

How the International Community can Enhance Women's Inclusion

International organizations can play a key role in women's economic empowerment through developing and financing programs responding to their specific needs and by improving access to basic services. The international community can continue supporting the government to enhance its performance regarding international rights commitments such as the National Action Plan for 1325 (2019) and its obligations to CEDAW. The government should develop national gender sensitive/responsive (inclusive) legal frameworks and good governance practices and link them to local cultural practices. For successful outcomes, monitoring, evaluation, and the inclusion of women, including the illiterate and the disadvantaged, in all project stages are essential. INGOs should build on local knowledge and good practices to ensure sustainability. More importantly, reaching women and men in remote places should be prioritized regardless of the extra cost involved.

Media and Advocacy

Much more will need to be done to enhance the role of women in Yemeni media. If significant independent and gender-responsive and -sensitive press and media coverage is to exist in post-war Yemen, institutional reforms will be needed to allow women to shape media policy: women must have a say in what and how information about them is published. One example is the recognition of Hadeel al-Yamani's outstanding media coverage of war-torn Ta´izz city with the Journalism Courage Award from the International Women's Media Foundation, which should inspire Yemenis to acknowledge the value of such work.

To enable women to work in media professionally, more investment should be allocated for on-the-job training in leadership skills, audio production, storytelling, documentary production, job safety, language skills, and much more (Farhan,

2017; GDRSC, 2018; UNESCO, 2017). Yemeni media needs to widen its coverage of the diverse roles and contributions of women to local development (GDRSC, 2018), enhancing social cohesion and their potential roles in reconstructing the new Yemen.

To be active community members, women will have to learn how to advocate for their right to participate in building a new Yemen. Training workshops on advocacy are a first step. There will be a need to advocate for the specific needs of women, rural and urban, literate and illiterate, IDPs, *Muhamasheen (Akhdam),*[7] and the disabled. More importantly, men must be encouraged to campaign for women's rights and oppose the deep-rooted discrimination against women and girls.

Conclusion

In this chapter, we have tried to address Yemeni women's most emergent concerns along the time line from the past to the future by looking at enduring features of women's status and roles, the impact of the uprising and transition period between 2011 and 2014 and the impact and implications of the still continuing war.

As mentioned earlier, the devastating war has left more than twenty-five million people in need of some form of humanitarian aid, and this situation will impose itself as an urgent priority in the post-war reconstruction phase. So there should be a greater focus on introducing income-generation projects and on improving local production to enable self-reliance and sustained means of livelihood, especially among women at the community level. Equally important is empowering a broad spectrum of women at various levels.

At the community level, track 3 of the peace processes, where the largest population of women exists, women must be targeted with diverse capacity-building programs to alleviate their socioeconomic status. They should also be equipped with the tools and skills to reach local authorities at the district and governorate level to contribute to enhancing peace, social cohesion, and coexistence. Further, it is vital to understand how to identify opportunities where women can have access to influence circles and decision-making levels and contribute to discussing priorities and finding ways to overcome community challenges.

Complementary to that, women must also play a more active role in peace negotiation talks through lobbying with influential networks at the diplomatic level, track 1 of the peace processes. However, this trajectory needs to be accompanied by a unified vision of women's demands, priorities, and their potential roles in Yemen's reconstruction phase.

Peace building efforts, Yemen's governing structures, and development programs should fully recognize women as vibrant social actors with a considerable stake in shaping the new Yemen, and not merely as war victims. Recognizing women's contributions in supporting their families and strengthening cohesion in their communities during the war will pave the road toward a more meaningful inclusion in post-war Yemen. The rebuilding of Yemen after the war provides a unique opportunity to build a system that fully involves "half of society" and it is one that must be seized.

Notes

1 In 2019, the number of displaced women who may be heading their families was estimated at 30 percent compared with 9 percent before the conflict.
2 In southern cities such as Aden, men mainly took over this responsibility.
3 Pictures and videos of women armed with various weapons have repeatedly appeared in the media of the *de facto* authorities in Sana'a and in Ta'izz.
4 The UN Yemen Special Envoy has appointed a number of women as his advisers.
5 Article 41 of the 1994 Yemen's constitution and article 75 of the 2015 newly drafted constitution.
6 The successful reopening of Mukalla airport came after the intervention and lobbying of women in Hadhramaut, Taiz, and Marib governorates.
7 The Akhdam are a marginalized group in Yemen. In fact, though their name means "servant," they prefer to call themselves "al-Muhamasheen"—"the marginalized ones."

References

Abirafeh, L. (2009), *Gender and International aid in Afghanistan: The Politics and Effects of intervention*, London: McFarland.

Aboueldahab, N. (2019), Reclaiming Yemen: The Role of the Yemeni Professional Diaspora, Brookings Doha Center Analysis Paper No. 26, April. Available online: https://www.brookings.edu/wp-content/uploads/2019/04/Reclaiming-Yemen-The-role -of-the-Yemeni-professional-diaspora_English_Web.pdf (accessed on March 6, 2020).

Adra, N. (2006), "Social exclusion analysis- Yemen." Unpublished report prepared for DFID and the World Bank. Available on line: https://d1wqtxts1xzle7.cloudfront.net /31454781/YemenSEFINAL-21Jan06.pdf (accessed February 12, 2020).

Adra, N. (2016), "Tribal Mediation and Empowered Women: Potential Contributions of Heritage to National Development in Yemen," *International Journal of Islamic Architecture* 5(2): 301–37.

al-Ammar, F. , Patchett, H., and Shamsan, S. (2019), A Gendered Crisis: understanding the experiences of Yemen's war., Sana'a Center for Strategic Studies . Available online: https://sanaacenter.org/publications/main-publications/8480 (accessed on February 4, 2020).

al-Ashtal, A. N. (2012), "A Long, Quiet, and Steady Struggle: The Women's Movement in Yemen," *Mapping Arab Women's Movements: A Century of Transformations from Within*, 197–252.

Al-Dawsari, N. (2012), *Tribal Governance and Stability in Yemen* (Vol. 24). Washington: Carnegie Endowment for International Peace. https://www.jstor.org/stable/pdf/ resrep13057.pdf

al-Dawsari, N., D. Kolarova and J. Pedersen (2011). Conflicts and Tensions in Tribal Areas in Yemen." Available online: https://partnersbg.org/wp-content/uploads/2018/12/2011 -Yemen-Conflict-Assessment-.pdf (accessed on March 10, 2020).

al-Gawfi, I., B. Zabara and S. P. Yadav (2020). "The Role of Women in Peacebuilding in Yemen," CARPO Brief 14. Available online: https://carpo-bonn.org/en/portfolio/carpo

-brief-14-the-role-of-women-in-peacebuilding-in-yemen/ (accessed on March 6, 2020).

Al-Naami, A. and S. Moodley (2017), We Won't Wait: As War Ravages Yemen, Its Women Strive to Build Peace. OXFAM. Available online: https://oxfamilibrary.openrepository .com/handle/10546/620182 (accessed on February 28, 2020).

al-Sakkaf, N. (2012), Yemen's Women and the Quest for Change. *Political Participation after the Arab Revolution*. Available online: https://library.fes.de/pdf-files/iez/09434.pdf (accessed February 26, 2020).

Alwazir, A., N. Al-Dawsari, W. Picard, and Al-Shami, M. (2016), "We Will Survive: Women's Rights and Civic Activism in Yemen's Endless War (WHAT THE WOMEN SAY Brief 14)." ICAN. Available online: http://peacewomen.org/sites/default/files/ What-the-Women-Say-Yemen-Winter-2016.pdf (accessed on February 9, 2020).

al-Zwaini, L. (2006), "State and Non-State Justice in Yemen," in *Paper for the conference on the Relationship between State and Non-State Justice Systems in Afghanistan*, Kabul, pp. 10–14.

Alley, A. (2010), "The Rules of the Game: Unpacking Patronage Politics in Yemen." *Middle East Journal* 64(3): 385–409. Retrieved March 18, 2021, from http://www.jstor.org/ stable/40783106.

Arostegui, J. (2013), "Gender, Conflict, and Peace-building: How Conflict Can Catalyze Positive Change for Women," *Gender & Development* 21 (3): 533–49.

Aulaqi, A. (2014), "On the Edge: The Challenges of Yemen's Healthcare System," in Lackner, H. (ed.). *Why Yemen Matters: A Society in Transition*. Saqi. London: SAQI books.

Awadh, M. and N. Shuja'adeen (2019), "Women In Conflict Resolution and Peacebuilding In Yemen," research paper, edited by Edited By Al- Refaei, S. and supported by UNWOMEN. Available at https://yemen.un.org/sites/default/files/2019-09/WomenIn ConflictResolutionAndPeacebuildingInYemenFIN.PDF.

Carapico, S. (2003), "How Yemen's Ruling Party Secured an Electoral Landslide." *Middle East Report Online, 16*.

Carapico, S. and A. Würth (2000). "Passports and Passages: Tests of Yemeni Women's Citizenship Rights," in S. Joseph (ed.), *Gender and Citizenship in the Middle East*, 261–71. Syracuse, NY: Syracuse University Press.

CARE (2015). *Rapid Gender Analysis of Yemen*. Available online: https://interagencystan dingcommittee.org/system/files/care_rapid_gender_analysis_yemen.pdf, (accessed on March 15, 2020).

Cook, J. (2015). "Our Main Concern Is Security: Women's Political Participation, Engagement in the Security Sector, and Public Safety in Yemen," in S. Al-Sarhan and Brehony (eds.), *Rebuilding Yemen: Political, Economic and Social Challenges*, 149–66. Berlin: Gerlach Press.

Cornwall, A. (2007). "Buzzwords and Fuzzwords: Deconstructing Development Discourse." *Development in practice* 17 (4–5): 471–84.

Dahlgren, S. (2013). "Revisiting the Issue of Women's Rights in Southern Yemen: Statutory Law, Sharia and Customs." *Arabian Humanities. Revue internationale d'archéologie et de sciences sociales sur la péninsule Arabique/International Journal of Archaeology and Social Sciences in the Arabian Peninsula, Volume* (1). Available online: https://journals .openedition.org/cy/2039 (accessed March, 2020).

Dahlgren, S. (2018). "Popular Revolution Advances Towards State Building in Southern Yemen," in *Politics, Governance, and Reconstruction in Yemen*. Washington, DC. The Project on Middle East Political Science. https://pomeps.org/popular-revolution -advances-towards-state-building-in-southern-yemen (accessed on March 5, 2020).

Dresch, P. and B. Haykel (1995), "Stereotypes and Political Styles: Islamists and Tribesfolk in Yemen," *International Journal of Middle East Studies* 27 (2): 405–31.

FAO (2019), *Famine Prevention Plan*. http://www.fao.org/3/CA3134EN/ca3134en.pdf

Farhan, M. (2017), "The Current Status of Yemeni Women Journalists: Challenges in Peace and War," Studies and Economic Media Center (SEMC). Available online: http://economicmedia.net/EN/wp-content/uploads/2017/11/Yemeni-women-journalists -study-English.pdf (accessed on March 5, 2020).

Freedom House (2005), *Women's Rights in the Middle East and North Africa—Yemen*. Available online: https://www.refworld.org/docid/47387b712f.html (accessed on February 6, 2020).

GDRSC (2018), "Including Women's Issues in Yemeni Media," A Survey Study on communicators in Radios and electronic websites 2018, The Gender Development Research and Studies Center (GDRSC), Sana´a University.

Ghanem, A. (2019), "Addressing Social Fragmentation in Yemen. Sana'a Center for Strategic Studies." https://sanaacenter.org/publications/analysis/7137 (accessed March 10, 2020).

Gressmann, W. (2016), "From the Ground Up: Gender and Conflict Analysis in Yemen." Oxfam.

Gulf Center for Human Rights (2015), "Special Report: Yemeni Journalists and Human Rights Defenders at Risk during Wartime," GC4HR. Available online: http://www .gc4hr.org/report/view/36

Harb, T. (2019). "Yemen: One of the Worst Places in the World to be a Woman – Yemen," Available online: https://www.amnesty.org/en/latest/campaigns/2019/12/yemen-one-of -the-worst-places-in-the-world-to-be-a-woman (accessed on February 28, 2020).

Heinze, M. (2016), "Literature Review: Women's Role in Peace and Security in Yemen." Saferworld, CARPO and YPC. Available online: http://carpo-bonn.org/wp-content/ uploads/2016/12/HeinzeWomens-role-in-peace-and-security-in-Yemen-Literature -review.pdf (accessed on March 1, 2020).

Heinze, M. C. and Ahmed, S. (2013), *Integrating Women's Security Interests into Police Reform in Yemen*. Sanaa: Yemen Polling Center.

Heinze, M. and S. Stevens (2018), "Women as Peacebuilders in Yemen." Social Development Direct and Yemen Polling Center. Available online: http://www.sddirect .org.uk/media/1571/sdd_yemenreport_full_v5.pdf (accessed on March 1, 2020).

Human Rights Watch (2015), "World Report 2015: Yemen." https://www.hrw.org/world -report/2015/country-chapters/yemen (accessed January 15, 2020).

IOM (2020), Yemen | Situation Report – Covid-19 Response | 06–19 September 2020 Available online: https://www.iom.int/sitreps/yemen-situation-report-covid19 -response-06-19-september-2020 (accessed on October 25, 2020).

Kangas, A and S. Stevens (2018), "Women, Peace and Security in Yemen – Yemen." VAWG Helpdesk Research Report No. 158. UKaid. Available online: https://reliefweb.int/ report/yemen/women-peace-and-security-yemen, (accessed on March 10, 2020).

Krause, J., W. Krause, and P. Bränfors (2018), "Women's Participation in Peace Negotiations and the Durability of Peace," *International Interactions*, 44 (6): 985–1016. Available online: https://doi.org/10.1080/03050629.2018.1492386 (accessed March 20, 2021).

Krishnan, N. (2014), "The Status of Yemeni Women: From Aspiration to Opportunity." MENA Knowledge and Learning Quick Note Series. World Bank.

Lackner, H. (1995), "Women and Development in the Republic of Yemen," in Khoury, N. and Moghadam, V. (eds.), *Gender and Development in the Arab World – Women's Economic Participation: Patterns and Policies*, 71–96, London: Zed Books

Longley, A. (2007), "The High-Water Mark of Islamist Politics? The Case of Yemen," *Middle East Journal* 61 (2): 240–60.

Ministry of Public Health and Population (2013), "Yemen National Health and Demographic Survey 2013, 2015," Central Statistical Organization, Pan Arab Program for Family Health and ICF International, Available online: https://dhsprogram.com/pubs/pdf/FR296/FR296.pdf (accessed on February 1, 2020).

Mundy, M. (2017), "Empire of Information: The War on Yemen and Its Agricultural Sector." Available online: https://blogs.lse.ac.uk/mec/2017/06/19/empire-of-information-the-war-on-yemen-and-its-agricultural-sector/ (accessed on October 6, 2020).

NDI (2019), Women Peacebuilders in Yemen Advocate for the Re-Opening of Al-Riyyan Airport. Www.ndi.org. https://www.ndi.org/our-stories/women-peacebuilders-yemen-advocate-re-opening-al-riyyan-airport (accessed on January 25, 2021).

OHCHR (2018), Report of the Group of Eminent International and Regional Experts as submitted to the United Nations High Commissioner for Human Rights (A/HRC/42/17). https://www.ohchr.org/Documents/HRBodies/HRCouncil/GEE-Yemen/A_HRC_42_CRP_1.PDF

Oxfam (2019a), Women in conflict zones. Oxfam Intermón report number 51. Available online: https://oxfamilibrary.openrepository.com/bitstream/handle/10546/620690/bp-women-in-conflict-zones-290319-en.pdf (accessed on October 20, 2020).

Pandya, S. (2015), "From Arab Spring to War in Yemen: Challenges to Women's Activism (Rethink Brief 06)." Rethink Institute. Retrieved from: http://www.rethinkinstitute.org/wpcontent/uploads/2015/08/Pandya-Yemeni-Women-Activism.pdf

Pandya, S. (2018), "The War Took Us Backwards: Yemeni Families and Dialectical Patriarchal Reordering." *hawwa*, 16(1–3): 266–308.

Rageh, M., A. Nasser and F. Al-Muslimi (2016), „Yemen Without a Functioning Central Bank: The Loss of Basic Economic Stabilization and Accelerating Famine." Sana'a Center for Strategic Studies. https://sanaacenter.org/publications/main-publications/55.

Rohwerder, B. (2017), "Conflict and Gender Dynamics in Yemen, K4D Helpdesk Report." Available online: http://www.gsdrc.org/wp-content/uploads/2017/07/068_Conflict-and-Gender-dynamics-in-Yemen.pdf (accessed on January 20, 2020).

Strzelecka, E. (2013), "Gender and Islam in development policy and practice in Yemen." *Arabian Humanities. Revue internationale d'archéologie et de sciences sociales sur la péninsule Arabique/International Journal of Archaeology and Social Sciences in the Arabian Peninsula* (1). https://journals.openedition.org/cy/2062?lang=en (accessed January 15, 2020).

The Conversation (2018), "How Yemeni Women Are Fighting the War." Available online: https://theconversation.com/how-yemeni-women-are-fighting-the-war-89951 (accessed on January 12, 2020).

The New Arab (2015), "Yemeni Women Armed and Dangerous." Available online: https://www.alaraby.co.uk/english/society/2015/12/21/yemeni-women-armed-and-dangerous (accessed on January 20, 2020).

UNHCR (2018), "Yemen Operational Update, 5–30 April 2018." Available online: https://reliefweb.int/sites/reliefweb.int/files/resources/Yemen%20Update%2015-30%20April%202018%20%28Final%29.pdf (accessed on January 20, 2020).

UNDP (2019), "Human Development Report." Yemen Country report. Available online; http://hdr.undp.org/sites/all/themes/hdr_theme/country-notes/YEM.pdf (accessed on January 5, 2020).

UNDP (2020), "Human Development Report." Available online: http://hdr.undp.org/sites/default/files/hdro_statistical_data_table5.pdf (accessed on October 20, 2020).

UNDP (2020), "Yemeni Women Take the Lead in the Fight Against COVID-19." Available online: https://www.ye.undp.org/content/yemen/en/home/stories/yemeni-women-take-the-lead-in-the-fight-against-COVID-19.html (accessed on October 20, 2020).

UNESCO (2017), "Empowering Yemeni Women Journalists in Mukalla." Available online: http://www.unesco.org/new/en/media-services/single-view/news/empowering_yemeni_women_journalists_in_mukalla/ (accessed on January 26, 2020).

UNFPA (2017, April 26), "Women and Girls among the most Vulnerable in Yemen." Available online: http://yemen.unfpa.org/en/news/women-and-girls-among-most-vulnerable-yemen (accessed on January 10, 2020).

UNFPA (2019), "Meet the Woman Protecting Women in Yemen." Available online: https://www.unfpa.org/news/meet-woman-protecting-women-yemen (accessed on February 20, 2020).

UNOCHA (2018), "Humanitarian Response Plan." Available online: https://www.unocha.org/sites/unocha/files/dms/20180120_HRP_YEMEN_Final.pdf (accessed on February 20, 2020).

World Bank (2009), *The Status & Progress of Women in the Middle East & North Africa.* Available online: http://siteresources.worldbank.org/INTMENA/Resources/MENA_Gender_Compendium-2009-1.pdf (accessed on February 2, 2020).

World Bank (2019), "Yemen's Economic Update - April 2019". http://pubdocs.worldbank.org/en/365711553672401737/Yemen-MEU-April-2019-Eng.pdf (accessed March 11, 2020).

Würth, A. (2003), "Stalled Reform: Family Law in Post-unification Yemen." *Islamic Law and Society* 10(1): 12–33.

Yadav, S. P. and Clark, J. A. (2010), "Disappointments and New Directions: Women, Partisanship, and the Regime in Yemen," *Hawwa* 8 (1): 55–95.

World Bank (2014), "Republic of Yemen. The Status of Yemeni Women: From Aspiration to Opportunity." Available online: http://documents.worldbank.org/curated/en/640151468334820965/pdf/878200REVISED00Box0385200B00PUBLIC0.pdf (accessed on February 17, 2020).

Yadav, S. P. (2010), "Segmented publics and Islamist women in Yemen: Rethinking Space and Activism." *Journal of Middle East Women's Studies* 6(2): 1–30.

Zabara B. (2018), "Enhancing Women's Role in Water Management in Yemen, Brief 09." CARPO, https://carpo-bonn.org/wp-content/uploads/2018/03/09_carpo_brief_final.pdf

Chapter 6

A PARASITICAL POLITICAL ECONOMY

Charles Schmitz

Introduction

Yemen's economic future depends upon investment from not only existing investors domestic and foreign, but also new investors, ordinary Yemenis who pool new savings to gain education, improve their crops, develop local businesses and small enterprises, or construct buildings. In a conducive environment, ordinary Yemenis from all walks of life will feel secure investing in their long-term futures. But such an environment requires a supportive state and politics. States not only provide social and physical infrastructure essential to a market economy, but also coordinate, facilitate, and guide growth in new sectors of the economy or improve the productivity of existing sectors. States provide the long-term guidance and coordination that a country like Yemen needs to transition to a more productive economy based upon domestic labor and resources. To achieve growth, states must maintain social peace by avoiding social cleavages that damage state legitimacy and foster social cohesion by helping those whose livelihoods are threatened as the economy changes or global markets shift. Such a state needs to maintain itself, to have the capacity to raise sufficient revenue while maintaining its legitimacy.

A review of Yemen's recent political economy shows that Yemen's rulers use the economy to consolidate their political position rather than to foster broad economic growth. Rulers reward political allies with economic assets in a way that inhibits investment, spreads distrust, and stunts growth. If politics is the road to wealth, then those without political protection cautiously shield their investments or simply refrain from investing in the domestic economy. In fact, even the powerful send their assets abroad as we saw with far-flung investments of the Saleh family or the Bishr brothers (see later).

Today we see new rulers reshaping the economy in their favor. Marib, Hadhramaut, and Aden benefit from the military payrolls of the coalition forces and the commerce and construction that supports them, not to mention the smugglers profiting from the coalition's blockade and the destruction of infrastructure that crippled former commercial routes. Aden is seeing another iteration of what seems like an eternal game of property confiscation first initiated by successive socialist regimes in the 1970s and 1980s but carried further by the

Saleh regime after the 1994 war, and now by the warring southern factions that vie not only for key properties but also for control of tariffs and taxes (Sana'a Center for Strategic Studies 2020). The anti-Huthi coalition is politically incoherent and cannot even formulate policy, much less implement it. Factionalism has undermined any semblance of a state. In Huthi- controlled territory, Huthi leaders use their power to control markets, tax heavily, and consolidate key assets in the hands of supporters. In contrast to the anti-Huthi coalition, the Huthi state is unified and can implement policy; however, its resources are so meager that its efforts to raise revenue are oppressive to the extent that they stifle incentives for investment. In Yemen, the economy is a prize in a political contest, the spoils of the victor. Economic growth is a distant second to security and consolidation of power in the minds of Yemen's rulers.

Macroeconomic Security and Investment

Rather than any particular prescription for trade policy, the keys to economic growth in the post-war period in the developing world have been macroeconomic stability and social peace (Rodrik 1999: p 77). Rodrik tested the common wisdom of the 1990s that open, export-oriented economies performed best and that import substitution strategies focused on the domestic economy were failures (see Lackner in this volume). Rodrik's empirical data revealed that import substitution was sometimes a very successful strategy and that openness did not correspond to growth, as in the case of Yemen.[1] Rodrik found that trade policy prescriptions were driven more by ideology than empirical results. Instead, the evidence pointed to a strong relationship between growth and macroeconomic stability. Economies that performed best were able to manage their integration into the global economy such that trade and fiscal balances did not interfere with the state's capacity to provide basic social and physical infrastructure and allowed the state sufficient resources to maintain domestic social peace. In a capitalist economy, states provide social services such as basic health infrastructure and education, which develops the capacity of the labor force as well as the physical infrastructure of a national economy such as roads, electricity, and communications. In addition, states provide the legal foundation for dispute resolution as well as a national currency and banking system. But states are also tasked with coordinating public and private investment for long-term development specific to an economy's circumstances (Rodrik 1999: p 15) and maintaining social peace among labor, various fractions of the private sector, and society at large. Economic development can be disruptive, and states must manage the potential fallout from swings in commodity prices or the dislocations caused by competitive pressures or changes in international economic circumstances. Disruptions require compensation for losers and political bargains that prevent social cleavages from becoming political ruptures that destroy the state's capacity to manage the economy. In order to carry out these essential tasks, states must be capable of raising necessary revenue. Managing states' budgets and fiscal health is a central challenge. Those states that are successful find funds to staff the competent and effective bureaucracies of a capable state while retaining the social legitimacy necessary for sustainable taxation.

In a best-case scenario, Yemen's post-war economy would focus on promoting domestic investment—the return of Yemeni investors from overseas and the enabling of new investment from local savings—that would employ domestic labor, Yemen's untapped resource: "The major factor of production of an economy is its supply of labour" (ILO 2004: p 34). Employing Yemen's labor in the domestic economy would provide increased productivity, output, and income—increase domestic resources for the Yemeni economy. Natural resources are a challenge, but the key challenge is cultivating an economic environment that allows a domestic "investment transition," (Rodrik 1999) moving the Yemeni economy onto a more productive basis. Yemen's water is scarce, but most agree that water challenges can be overcome by effectively regulating withdrawals, something the Yemeni state has yet to achieve (Ward 2014).

Talk of natural resource scarcity always raises the specter of overpopulation. Since Malthus' simple but false equation of population growth with resource scarcity, population growth is faulted whenever resources appear scarce or overexploited. In contrast, economists generally welcome population growth because more people means more labor, income, consumption, investment, and growth. However, population growth can become an obstacle to economic expansion when an economy cannot educate and employ new young laborers as they reach working age. Thus, for economists, the key is employment and the productivity of labor (an appropriately trained labor force), which is why the overarching focus of Yemen's economic policies must be on productively employing its workforce. Yemen's future depends not only on increasing investment—domestic and foreign—but also on increasing the productivity of labor stuck in low productivity sectors, where labor redundancy essentially divides minimal returns between many underemployed workers, as well as training new entrants into the labor force with the skills—literacy to start with—they need to contribute productively to the economy. Policies that emphasize foreign investment, for example, in capital-intensive mineral resource extraction do not address the key issue of raising the productivity and income of the mass of Yemeni workers. Foreign investment, in fact any investment, is more than welcome in Yemen, but without an accompanying focus on the labor force, the mass of Yemenis will not share in the benefits of investment, and growth will not contribute to the improvement of most Yemenis' lives.

Still, Yemen's population growth poses significant challenges. As Alsoswa shows in Chapter 8, from a population of about four million in the 1950s, Yemen's population has grown rapidly to about thirty million today and will likely peak at forty-five million within three decades. With income stretched thin already, an addition of fifteen million more people threatens to reduce further the thin slice of income of the average Yemeni. However, in the past, Yemen was able to achieve substantial improvement in average standards of living despite its rapid population growth: from 1962 until 2012, each year Yemenis were better educated, lived longer, and earned more even while the number of Yemenis increased at unprecedented rates. And while Yemen may have had the highest fertility rates in the world for a time—in the 1980s, Yemen's fertility rate remained close to nine children per woman—its fertility rate collapsed at an equally spectacular rate. From its high of close to nine in the late 1980s, Yemen's fertility rate is now less than four and will continue its rapid decline. Yemen's fertility collapse parallels the dramatic declines demographers have traced across the world and upon which prediction of the world's peak population has recently been revised significantly downward. The world's population is now expected to peak at nine billion at mid-century and then begin to decline rapidly. Many of the world's countries will see their populations reduce by half (Gallagher 2020). Because of Yemen's population momentum—the number of women reaching childbearing age continues to increase though at current trends, Yemen's fertility rate will soon fall below the replacement level of two—Yemen will continue to see population growth for a time before reduced fertility will translate into falling population numbers. In short, population increase will exacerbate Yemen's development challenge in the medium term. Given that other countries will see population decreases sooner than Yemen, the obvious short-term remedy is migration, but at the moment, the political climate does not encourage global or regional migration.

That population increase is a challenge does not alter the need for policy to focus on employing Yemeni labor. Without a focus on Yemeni labor, the dividends of any growth in Yemen will not contribute to the improvement of the mass of the Yemeni population.

However, the largest challenge Yemen faces is not scarce natural resources or population but cultivating the social contract necessary to focus on long-term economic development. Yemen has always struggled to produce sufficient domestic resources, even when its population was much smaller—drought caused famine as recently as the 1940s—and the Yemeni economy has always relied upon trade, remittances, and external resources. Even in the pre-Islamic period, familiar problems of scarce resources, economic collapse, emigration, and remittances were part of the Yemeni economy—al-Attar points to the economic failures related to the decline of the incense trade and the two collapses of the Marib dam that caused large-scale emigration and consequent remittances (al-Attar 1965: p 29). Scarcities have always been a challenge; what Yemen has lacked in the modern period is a supportive domestic environment for investment.

A Focus on the Domestic Economy

Yemen has suffered long wars in its past. In the 1960s the conflict between republicans and royalists lasted eight years and was more destructive than today's conflict. Yet at the war's conclusion in 1970, Yemen faced a very favorable economic environment. The windfall oil revenues in neighboring oil states spilled into Yemen by way of worker remittances. In the decades following the war's conclusion, Yemen not only recovered from the war but also achieved significant increases in incomes, education, and health despite rapid population growth. In the 1990s when worker remittances declined as a proportion of GDP, oil replaced emigres as the engine of Yemeni growth. Oil revenue funded an expansion of public employment, kept debt low and incomes rising, and supplied hard currency for imports, while allowing for substantial infrastructure development.

Unfortunately, Yemen today faces a hostile economic environment. In the 2000s, Yemen's oil production fell precipitously even before the war punctuated the end of Yemen's oil-driven economy. Revenues from oil exports still reached $6.7 billion in 2014 but fell to $248 million in 2016. The Hadi government revived oil exports in 2017 and 2018 by trucking oil in Marib and Shabwah to the pipeline that leads to al-Nushayma port west of Bir Ali to add to the oil produced in the Masila block in the Hadhramaut exported at al-Shihr, east of Mukalla. Revenues rose to $894 million in 2018 (World Bank 2019), but this pales in comparison with the past and in the face of the cost to rebuild Yemen.

While the post-conflict resumption of LNG gas exports and small amounts of oil exports will supply some revenue (see Al-Akhali in this volume), those revenues will be only a fraction of the oil revenue during Yemen's flush years. Unlike the production-sharing agreements in oil production, the Yemeni government owns an investment share in the LNG plant (sixteen percent plus five percent for the Social Welfare Fund), so revenues are dependent upon distributions of profit once investment costs are paid. The Yemeni government will also receive taxes of about $100 million per year when the plant is in full production. However, estimates prior to the war put average annual revenue to the Yemeni government at only $500,000 over a twenty-five-year estimated production life, a relatively small amount compared to the $2,700 million the Yemeni government averaged in oil revenues over the period between 2000 and 2012 (Schmitz 2012). And the resumption of LNG production is dependent not only upon security—the attack on the pipeline in June 2019 is cited by Total, the largest shareholder, as an indicator of the continued security risk (Total 2019)—but also on new market conditions. LNG markets have slumped due to new production in the United States and Australia and lack of demand since the global COVID-19 contraction (Connelly 2020), though market forecasters expect a rebound over the long term due to increased demand from countries substituting cheaper LNG for dirty coal (Sekiguchi 2020). Despite the constant push by political leaders for the resumption of gas exports and their blaming of delays on Emirati-backed forces, the decision is an economic one in the hands of private-sector actors and outside the control of the Yemeni government.

Similarly, though remittances today offer a threadbare lifeline in a severe economic crisis, they will not play the central role in the economy that they did in the 1970s. Neighboring oil economies facing their own challenges today have embarked on dramatic workforce nationalization policies that reduce opportunities for Yemeni emigres, particularly in Saudi Arabia where a majority of Yemeni emigrants live (Ministry of Planning and International Cooperation 2018). The value of worker remittances remained steady in the 2000s, averaging about $1.2 billion (International Monetary Fund 2009: p 25), but their relative contribution to total output declined as the economy grew. One billion dollars is only a small fraction of a thirty-billion-dollar economy. When the political crisis began in 2011, remittances increased to about $3.8 billion (World Bank 2020)[2] but their importance increased significantly because the economy had collapsed, losing almost half its value. Remittances contributed almost a quarter of GDP in 2017, but the COVID-19 crisis in 2020 hit Yemeni workers in Saudi Arabia hard. The dramatic reduction in demand for oil shrank the Saudi economy and Yemeni workers at the bottom rung of the Saudi labor force bore the brunt of the economic contraction. Anecdotal evidence suggests that remittances sent home to Yemen fell precipitously, but the real dimensions of the change in remittances is difficult to determine given Yemen's extremely poor statistical capacity (Sana´a Center Economic Unit 2020a: p. 14). World Bank economists suggest that overall flows of remittances from the Gulf States have recovered and are quite robust (World Bank 2020a: p. 3). Still, if the fighting ever subsides and the economy begins to recover, the value of remittances will at best remain constant and probably decline due to changes in the host country demand for Yemeni workers, but the relative contribution of remittances to the total economy will fall to below pre-crisis levels. Whereas remittances were the heart of the economy in the 1970s and 1980s, today remittances are only a lifeline that keeps Yemenis alive. The oil and worker remittances that drove Yemeni growth in the past can no longer do so.

Finally, foreign aid has propped up the Yemeni economy significantly during the war. In the three years prior to the war, aid accounted for about $350 million on average but jumped to a billion dollars in 2016, then to two billion in 2017 and was just short of four billion in 2019. Four billion dollars is a significant portion of the economy valued at fifteen billion dollars (Republic of Yemen 2020: p. 2). Foreign aid in all its forms plus worker remittances accounted for about half the Yemeni economy. In the last donor conference in June 2020 in Saudi Arabia, commitments fell far short of needs: commitments reached only slightly over a billion dollars, and Yemen is facing serious donor fatigue.

If the conflict resolves, Yemen will be forced to rely upon its main domestic resource—the ingenuity of its labor. While observers often deplore Yemen's lack of natural resources, the heart of economic growth is not natural resources but labor productivity (International Labour Organization 2004). Yemen's economic future depends upon its ability to productively harness its domestic labor—putting Yemenis to work. Whereas during the remittance era of the 1970s and early 1980s, Yemeni labor worked in Saudi Arabia, in the late 1990s and 2000s, the state passed on domestic oil revenues to Yemeni public employees, consumer subsidies, and cash transfers. Some 1.25 million civilian and military employees were paid by the state before 2015, constituting a little more than a third of state expenditures (al-Bashiri 2019). A slightly larger proportion of the budget was spent on transfers: subsidies to consumers (mostly fuel), cash transfers to tribes, and social welfare payments. This meant that more than two-thirds of the state budget effectively transferred oil revenue to common Yemenis (IMF 2014: p. 31; Republic of Yemen 2012; Sanaa Center for Strategic Studies 2019). Oil revenues raised individual income and provided significant domestic consumer demand for the economy. State expenditure constituted thirty percent of GDP, so public-sector salaries, cash transfers, and consumer subsidies contributed about a fifth of the value of the total economy. Given that oil revenue was the lion's share of state income, and oil production was rapidly falling even before the war, the state's payroll and welfare transfers were unsustainable. The war certainly exacerbated the fiscal crisis of the state, but it was not the cause of the crisis. The real cause of the fiscal crisis was clear for all to see before the outbreak of the war.

Nevertheless, payment of the civil service bill remains an acrimonious topic in Yemen that serves the wartime propaganda of all sides. The Huthis demand that the Hadi government pay civil servant salaries in the territory that the Huthis control. In the Stockholm agreement, the Hadi government forced the Huthis to place tax revenue on imported oil in Hodeida in a special account to pay for civil servants in Huthi-controlled territory. But the reality is that even before the war, the decline in oil revenues would have made state support for such a large proportion of the workforce and consumer demand impossible. Al-Bashiri (2019) argues that an important confidence-building measure toward ending the war is the payment of the civil servant wage bill in all Yemeni territory, and since neither the Huthis nor the Hadi government has the revenue to pay the wage bill, international donors should foot the bill. Given the reluctance of international donors to give to relief efforts evidenced in the failure of the donor conference in Riyadh in the summer of 2020, the suggestion is simply a fantasy: in the future, the Yemeni state will not rely upon windfall resource revenues but will be dependent upon taxation. Domestic consumption will be driven more from private-sector wages than state wages. Yemen will need to focus on putting Yemeni labor to work productively in the domestic economy. Barring unforeseen developments, no single sector of the economy will dominate the Yemeni economy as in the past. Instead, development strategies will focus on increasing employment, earnings, and investment across all sectors of the economy, but particularly those that can increase employment opportunities. Broad growth across all sectors creates a more diversified economy more immune from the vicissitudes of commodity fluctuations and distributes income more evenly.

Yemen will have to focus on not only employing its labor at home but also producing foreign currency to pay for imports. Yemen imports its staple food of rice and wheat, and while given Yemen's scarce agricultural resources, it makes sense to use Yemen's agricultural resources for higher value-added products such as vegetables, fruit, fodder for livestock, and of course *qat*; the need for hard currency to import basic food staples means that Yemen's economy must export to earn foreign currency. As the cost of imported food increases, principally a result of the dramatic depreciation of the Yemeni riyal, farmers may be induced to shift crops into domestic grains such as sorghum for local consumption. Anecdotal evidence supports some shift in consumption patterns: *Asid,* the traditional sorghum dish in Yemen, is experiencing a renaissance in restaurants. In theory, a dollar's worth of value created on the domestic market is the same as a dollar earned in exports to international markets, but in Yemen's case the export dollar is important because of the import bill. Thus, future development strategies must focus not only on increasing employment but also on generating export earnings, a dual challenge.

One obvious strategy is to reintroduce coffee exports. Agriculture employs a large portion of the labor force (still forty percent), and coffee is a high value-added crop that earns hard currency. Even during the war, efforts have succeeded in introducing international quality controls in portions of Yemen's coffee production that raise the value of Yemeni coffee and returns to farmers (Khan 2018). However, the big challenge is to shift cultivation from *qat* to coffee on a broader scale. Such an effort will take extensive state management and support to induce Yemeni farmers to switch from *qat* to coffee and adopt cultivation methods that would make Yemeni coffee competitive on international markets.

Similarly, Yemeni industry exhibits what used to be called a dual economy—a sea of inefficient micro-enterprises, single owner-worker shops, mostly fabricators of metal doors, wood windows, and water tanks, amid a small number of large firms (Republic of Yemen 2010), mostly import substitution industries in Ta'izz and Hodeida, that use imported capital-intensive technology to produce food items that enjoy natural protection such as juice boxes and yogurt.[3] The mass of small and medium enterprises are fertile ground for diversification and improved productivity (International Labour Organization 2004).

Increasing the productivity in manufacturing and stimulating competitive coffee exports, not to mention implementing a coherent water strategy, require not only investment but also state coordination and support. Yemen needs a capable state that has the resources to help develop the economy and can provide a sense of security that allows Yemenis to feel secure in investing in their future. The real key to successful rebuilding of the Yemeni economy is not only attracting investments from existing Yemeni capital abroad but also cultivating new investment from small savings of the mass of Yemenis by making ordinary Yemenis feel they are secure in making long-term investments in their own futures. Given a secure environment and an appropriate institutional structure, Yemenis will jump on the opportunity to invest their labor in their children's future—the kind of long-term, sustained investment needed to move the economy toward a more productive basis.

Unfortunately, Yemen's track record is not good, and nothing in the present indicates that Yemen will change course. At issue is the capacity of the Yemeni state to mobilize resources—public and private—for development. The logic of Yemen's political economy subjugates the long-term interests of the economy to the short-term interests of the many competing political factions. Today Yemen is at war, and logically the economy serves as a tool in the war, but unfortunately subordination of the economy to political aims is the norm in times of peace as well as war. Rather than staking their political careers on mobilizing Yemen's social and physical resources to achieve economic growth, policymakers in Yemen use the economy for short-term political interests. Subjecting the economy to political considerations per se is not the problem—economics is always imbibed with political calculations, populist public-sector wage increases during election years, or military spending in a representative's district, for example—rather, it is the short-term calculus of the Yemeni leaders' interventions in the economy that is problematic. Instead of promoting the broad capacities of the economy,

Yemeni leaders are concerned foremost with the immediate political implications of policy—the politics of dividing the pie—and hardly consider larger economic implications—the politics of increasing the pie. As a result, Yemeni capital—even politically favored capital—prefers safe harbours abroad rather than investing in the domestic economy.[4]

Foundations of the Current Crisis—the Curse of Oil

Oil allowed the Yemeni regime to avoid building a state capable of managing sustainable economic growth and taxing society to fund state expenditure. Throughout the 2000s, the regime negotiated corporate tax legislation and implementation with the Yemeni Chamber of Commerce, but the negotiations were inconsequential because the issue was driven not by financial need but by the desire to show foreign development agencies such as the IMF that Yemen was, indeed, serious about planning for the post-hydrocarbon economy. Oil sufficed as both a source of state revenue that kept the state solvent and an export that balanced the country's external accounts. In the 2000s, oil constituted ninety percent of merchandise exports, seventy-five percent of state revenue, and thirty percent of GDP. Customs and sales taxes made up an additional ten percent of state revenue and taxes on income, profit, and capital gains were between ten and twenty percent (Ministry of Finance 2013: p Table 11 - 11). At the same time, military assistance from the United States solidified the central role of the military forces and security in the Saleh regime and allowed Saleh to concentrate power in his son's hands. Scholars of Yemen began talking about the patronage system (Alley 2010) and the patrimonial state (Phillips 2011). As Phillips put it,

> The informal, though implicitly understood extraction and delivery mechanisms of the patronage system constitute the "rules of the game" for Yemen's elites. These principles have also metastasized into a more predatory and collusive form since oil revenues began to dominate the country's GDP and the regime's incentives to bargain with society were reduced. (Phillips 2011: p loc 1113)

There emerged a group of wealthy people connected to the Saleh regime who made fortunes from licenses and concessions granted from the state. Among the names revealed in the Panama Papers were the Bishr brothers, Shaher Abd al-Haqq and Abd al-Jalil, who were close to Saleh and were rewarded with, among other things, the rights to Coca Cola in Yemen, thus earning the nickname "the sugar kings" (Schmitz and Burrowes 2018: p 93). Shaher also owned the telecommunications network MTN, the Mercedes Benz distribution in Yemen, and the famous Taj Sheba Hotel in downtown Sana'a. Another key actor was Hamid al-Ahmar who had interests in Sabaphone, the Saba Islamic Bank, and oil production services and who was the local representative for foreign fast food chains such as Kentucky Fried Chicken and Baskin-Robbins as well as the German Siemens Corporation. What distinguishes these men is their political access to the Saleh regime that granted them concessions and licenses for communications companies, for example. Their closeness to the regime also reassured foreign businesses that their investments in Yemen were secure, or at least more secure than without these connections.

Saleh's patronage system worked to tie all important actors to his regime, but it had the negative effect of discouraging other investors. People who lacked a connection to the regime felt marginalized and that they lacked opportunity in the Yemeni economy. Worse, even these well-connected people were risk-adverse, responding rationally to the environment they understood well. They invested in Yemen only in businesses that could be liquidated quickly and maintained the bulk of their businesses and assets outside of Yemen. The Panama Papers showed that Shaher held much of his money in offshore bank accounts in the Virgin Islands as well as in businesses outside of Yemen (al-Mahdi 2016). Risk adverse behavior is understandable in Yemen. The case of Hamid al-Ahmar is exemplary of the dangers of investing in Yemen. Hamid and his late father Shaikh Abdullah al-Ahmar, were key members of the Islah Party in Yemen which the Huthi militias targeted in their advance south from Sa'ada in 2014. When the Huthis overran Sana'a, Hamid deftly liquidated much of his assets, moved overseas, and continued his business activity outside the country. His recent investments in what he called Saba Housing Development in Djibouti caused a stir in Yemen from those who asked why he did not invest in Aden (al-Omana 2018). From an investor's perspective, the answer is obvious: investments in Yemen are dangerous, need political protection (which Hamid lacked in Aden), and should be as liquid as possible.

Assessment of Yemen's Prospect

If economic growth is, indeed, dependent upon a stable and effective state, one that can support itself and maintain social peace, and that can generate a broad transition to a more productive economy, then what are Yemen's prospects given the records of the current governments? In short, the Huthi state is more capable, it can effectively tax, but lacks an economic vision and steers assets toward the war effort and political supporters. On the anti-Huthi side, the state lacks legitimacy and capacity, in fact it barely exists. Local powers organize military efforts and society to some degree, and though the Hadi side has more resources, it has no capability of using those resources effectively.

All sides of the conflict recognize that economic growth grants legitimacy. In the modern era, the capacity of the state to promote economic growth and improve the livelihoods of its citizens is a mark of a strong state. When the Huthis took power in 2014, the technocratic government it helped install aimed primarily to address the deteriorating economy and security situation. The Hadi government had brashly withdrawn all subsidies to fuel against the advice of economists who counselled a gradual lifting of subsidies. The new Huthi-backed government rescinded that order to gain the support of the street. When the behavior of the Huthi supervisors became unsupportable and Hadi and his government resigned in December 2014, the Huthis immediately announced the establishment of regular flights between Sana'a and Tehran on Iranian airlines and a five-billion-dollar economic package. The Huthis calculated that the shock of an abrupt turnabout in Yemen's international relations would be tempered by the promise of significant economic gain.

Five years later, on the fifty-eighth anniversary of the republican revolution, Huthi media carried stories of upbeat economic plans. The deputy minister of development and services, Hussein Maqbuli, declared that improving livestock production was an urgent need. The head of the presidential office, Ahmad Hamid, hoped that the second stage of the Nation Vision 2021–25 would meet the needs and desires of the people of Hajjah Governorate. The governor of Dhamar met to discuss projects funded with local funds in the governorate. The deputy minister of agriculture inaugurated a new joint agricultural cooperative office in Al-Jawf. These projects give the appearance of concern for the livelihoods of citizens, many of whom lack sufficient food, and project a sense of normalcy and stability in government, something the Huthis want to reinforce after five years of continuous calls for sacrifice in the war effort.

On the side of the fractured coalition against the Huthis, the sponsors of the coalition, the Saudis and the Emiratis, contribute substantially to infrastructure, food security, the Central Bank, and small development projects to improve the livelihoods of ordinary Yemenis. More than simply symbolic, especially the deposits in the Central Bank, the Saudi and Emirati investments in electrical generation, transportation, and relief efforts are designed to show that the coalition supports the Yemeni people despite the hardship and destruction their forces have wrought. They are also an attempt to show that citizens are better off in the coalition territories than in Huthi territories. Both sides know that economic performance is an important popular measure of a regime's success.

In neither side are these attempts at economic improvement effective. MOPIC estimates the economy has contracted fifty percent from 2015 (Republic of Yemen 2020a: p. 2). On the Huthi side, the projects are a desperate attempt to stimulate economic activity under very difficult circumstances. In contrast to the anti-Huthi coalition, the Huthi state is capable of organizing society. The Huthi leadership has internal policy disputes but is united and controls a cadre of bureaucrats capable of effectively implementing its policies. The Huthis collect taxes on lucrative fuel markets (International Crisis Group 2020; Sanaa Center for Strategic Studies 2018). The Huthis collect taxes on goods imported into Huthi-held territory, they collect taxes from commercial stores in cities, and even on a myriad of services like praying in mosques or medical operations. The Huthis also control black markets and real estate. While critics decry Huthi taxes as oppressive and social media activists make fun of Huthi fees for use of the mosque, the reality is that the Huthis have no windfall funds from foreign backers or from the sale of oil like the Hadi government. The Huthi economy does benefit from international humanitarian assistance which Huthi officials manipulate and even attempted to tax, but the Huthi state must balance its budget with domestic resources, a reality modern Yemeni states have not faced before.

The Huthi state's capacity to regulate was demonstrated in their effective control of monetary policy. In a now familiar story, the Hadi government nominally moved the Central Bank to Aden to attempt to wrest control of monetary policy and state revenues from the Huthis in Sana´a. State revenues from tariffs and taxes in territory controlled by Hadi's forces were redirected to Aden preventing the Huthis from using funds collected in Hadi territory for their war effort. In 2017, the Central Bank in Aden issued new bills in new denominations in the normal process of maintaining the money supply and replacing old worn bills, an important function as the Yemeni economy is a cash economy, and very little money is held in accounts or credit. Initially, the Huthis forbade the use of the new bills but did not strictly enforce the ban in all Huthi-controlled territories. However, when the Hadi government began covering its rapidly growing fiscal deficits by printing money along with domestic borrowing (World Bank 2019), the Huthis demonstrated their capacity to regulate by effectively negating the Hadi government's monetary policy. Huthi authorities forced people holding the new bills to purchase the old currency, or sometimes confiscated the new currency, and used the new currency to purchase supplies from Marib (Biswell 2020). The Huthis essentially created a new currency zone in their territory and treated the new bills from Aden as foreign currency. The result was to undermine the value of the riyal in Hadi territory because the bulk of economic activity was in Huthi territory. The much smaller Hadi economy was forced to absorb all the new currency that was printed for the much larger economy of the whole of Yemen. As a result, Yemen is split into two currency zones. In Huthi-controlled territory, the (old) riyal is stable, in part because the lack of replacement of the normal loss of bills in circulation keeps the money supply tight. Outside the Huthi territories, the riyal deteriorated dramatically having to absorb a huge increase in bills. The ability of the Huthis to stop the circulation of the new bills demonstrates their capacity to implement policy.

But while the Huthis can tax, organize markets, and prosecute a successful war, they lack legitimacy. The Huthi state ruthlessly oppresses its opponents with arbitrary detentions and disappearances and lacks any semblance of rule of law (despite the Huthi "National Vision" document of 2019). Huthi courts approved the confiscation of opponents' property (Sanaa Center Economic Unit 2020). Investors fear not only war, but also the abusive behavior of Huthi officials/militias.

On the Hadi side, the Saudis and Emiratis foot much of the bill for the military and the government (Sanaa Center for Strategic Studies 2018), which provides income for the economy, though not consistently. The coalition pays military salaries and makes critical contributions of hard currency to the Central Bank in Aden. The Saudis and Emiratis also contribute infrastructure such as the new power generation plant in Aden and their respective relief agencies contribute significant aid to the poor. In contrast to the Huthi side, there are resources on the Hadi side, but unlike the Huthis, the Hadi side lacks an effective state. The Hadi side is racked by internal political divisions that have hampered even the war effort. Battles between competing factions prevent restoration of order and efforts to rebuild the economy.

The war transformed the southern and eastern governorates. While Marib was always fiercely independent, the southern governorates found themselves with *de facto* independence, long a popular political demand. Though backed by the resources of Saudi Arabia and the Emirates, the Hadi government was unable to bind the disparate political elements of the eastern and southern governorates into a coherent bloc; worse, Hadi exacerbated the divisions.

Marib became a gathering place for refugees from Huthi-controlled territories and home to the northern Yemeni forces fighting the Huthis. Marib benefited from the influx of support from Saudi Arabia for the forces of Ali Mohsen, Mohammed al-Maghdashi, Abd al-Aziz al-Sughayr, and Hashem al-Ahmar. Marib also benefited from the trade between Saudi Arabia and Huthi-held Sana'a, and Marib hosts oil and gas fields, a refinery, and an electric power plant. But Marib's powerful governor holds Hadi at arm's distance. The tribes of the eastern desert have always fiercely defended their independence, for the most part successfully. The rapid transformation of Marib City at the onset of the war did nothing to abate distrust of Yemen's central government, though Marib and Hadi shared an animosity toward the Huthis. Marib's strategic importance and Hadi's lack of legitimacy in Marib forced Hadi to concede a percentage of tax revenues to Marib. Whether revenues are even being sent from the Central Bank branch in Marib to its headquarters in Aden is always a contested question.

Similarly, the governor of Hadhramaut negotiated a deal with Hadi to guarantee that a portion of revenues collected stayed in the Hadhramaut. Governor Faraj al-Bahsani presides over a politically and militarily divided governorate. The interior is the first military zone and includes the important border crossing at Wadia through which trade, people, and armies transit the desert from Saudi Arabia. The interior is controlled by those in Marib close to Ali Mohsen, Mohammad al-Maghdishi, and Abd al-Aziz al-Sughayr. The coastal portion of Hadhramaut constitutes the second military zone, which the governor commands, contains the lion's share of Yemen's remaining oil and the ports for its export, and is less aligned politically with northern Marib than with Aden and the cause of southern independence. But while carrying resentments toward northerners because of abuse under the Saleh regime, many Hadhramis also distrust the southerners from Aden, Lahej, and Dhala who dominated the south during the last years of the PDRY. Governor al-Bahsani balances these conflicting Hadhrami political currents by emphasizing Hadhrami independence: Hadhramaut for Hadhramis. As a result of both his political stance and Hadhramaut's strategic significance, the Hadhrami governor draws considerable concessions from the Hadi government, usually by threatening to cut off oil supplies (Debriefer 2020; Debriefer 2018).

However, the most serious challenge to Hadi's government comes from the Southern Transitional Council that controls Aden and its environs as well as Lahej and Dhala. The STC was created when Hadi fired four governors he himself had appointed because of their popularity in the south. However, Hadi was threatened by their political popularity and their relationship with the Emirati-backed forces that liberated the south, which gave the STC considerable independent power. In August 2019, STC forces ousted Yemeni government forces from Aden. Though the STC still negotiates with the Hadi government, it is a *de facto* government in Aden that collects government revenue for deposit in its own accounts (Abdulrab 2020).

Hadi's response to these challenges is typical of Yemeni leaders. Having little legitimacy anywhere in the south or east, Hadi surrounded himself with close family relatives, people from his home region of Abyan, and others dramatically opposed to the STC and southern independence in general. Rather than negotiating the regional political tensions in the territory nominally under the government of Yemen, Hadi exacerbated them. For example, in mid-2020 Hadi's powerful interior minister (domestic security), Ahmad al-Maysari, the head of the Central Bank, Ahmad Ubayd al-Fadhli, the wealthy oil importer and presidential adviser, Ahmad al-Eisei, were from Abyan, Hadi's home. His son Jalal ran his presidential office. His prime minister was from Ta'izz, his defense minister was from Dhamar in the north, and his military chief of staff, al-Sughayr, was a famous tribal sheikh from the far north. The Riyadh agreement of 2019 to end the standoff in Abyan between Hadi supporters and the STC stipulated a compromise government in which none of the protagonists of the Hadi war on the STC could participate. Although a new government was formed in December 2020, the Riyadh agreement remained unimplemented; the protagonists were more interested in continued squabbling over control of the south than uniting against the Huthis in the north.

Neither strategy is sustainable. The Huthis depend upon the war to justify their extreme austerity, heavy taxation, and manipulation of markets. Without the war, the Huthis would undoubtedly face much greater opposition to their policies. And after a political settlement, the Saudis and Emiratis are not going to subsidize the Yemeni economy to the extent that they do now—they must attend to their own fiscal pressures.

What Yemen needs for the future is a capable state that can tax and organize society, but one that is inclusive and cultivates a sense of security among all Yemenis—powerful and ordinary—that long-term investments in their own future are achievable. The Huthis can tax and organize, but their lack of rule of law and arbitrary repression against political opponents spreads a sense of insecurity amongst Yemenis. The Hadi side is reliant on Saudi largess, hopelessly divided, and cannot agree upon a common social contract that would enable a stable and capable state to emerge.

Corrosive Logic of Power

In short, Yemeni politics is a deadly game that forces competitors to throw all available resources into survival. Security is more urgent than economic coordination and building social capital and physical infrastructure. Staking political careers on the long-term outcome of a five- or ten-year economic plan is not possible in the Yemeni environment. If Yemeni politics remain a dangerous competition, Yemenis will look outside the country for places to invest or will invest in relatively safe, liquid sectors such as commerce and transportation. Only investors with political protection will invest in Yemen and even these investors will keep one foot outside of Yemen. Without investment in the domestic economy, Yemenis will have no source of income—unless another external source of revenue appears. In contrast to the civil war in the 1960s, Yemen's prospects in this post-war period appear bleak indeed.

Notes

1 Yemen's experience with IMF liberalization policies in the 1990s confirms Rodrik's findings. Yemen was praised by the IMF and World Bank for its thorough implementation of liberalizing reforms in the late 1990s, but in the words of the International Labour Organization, "although these reforms have contributed to the stabilization of the economy, especially in eventually producing a more stable exchange rate, their translation into growth and development has remained very limited" (ILO 2004: p 14).

2 Given the Bank's own estimation that the statistical capacity of the Yemeni government is very low, its estimation of Yemen's remittances also should be taken with a large grain of salt.

3 Food dominates the gross value of industrial production in Yemen, accounting for about half of output, followed by non-metal construction materials, metal fabrication, and plastic products (Republic of Yemen 2010).

4 The siphoning off of oil for politically important people during the Saleh regime is symptomatic. The country's main resource, oil, was delivered to smugglers who took the oil over the border to Saudi Arabia to make a fortune. While Saleh always said that he would die in Yemen, he made sure that his wealth was tucked away safely in the Gulf or elsewhere outside the country. Private-sector actors whose connections to Saleh allowed them to profit also took their money abroad.

References

Abdulrab, Rageb (2020), "STC's Aden Takeover Cripples Central Bank and Fragments Public Finances," *Sanaa Center Economic Unit*, June 17. Available online https://sanaacenter.org/publications/analysis/10219 (accessed on December 10, 2020).

al-Attar, M.S. (1965), *al-Takhaluf al-Iqtiṣādi wa al-Ijtimāʿi fi al-Yaman*, al-Maṭbūʿāt al Waṭaniyya al-Jazāʾriyya.

al- Bashiri, Mansour Ali (2019), "Economic Confidence Building Measures – Civil Servant Salaries," *Development Champions Policy Brief*, No. 11, March 18, 2019. Available online: https://devchampions.org/uploads/publications/files/Rethinking %20Yemen%E2%80%99s%20Economy%20-%20policy%20brief%2011.pdf (accessed on December 10, 2020).

al-Mahdi, M. (2016), Taqrir Muhim Yakshef Wathaʿq Khaṭīr ʿan Fasād Shāher ʿAbd al-Ḥaqq wa ʿAlāqat Shirkātihi al-18 binidhām Ṣāleḥ. *BūYemen*.

al-Omana (2018), Ḥamīd al-Aḥmar Yastathmir Amwāl al-Ḥarb fi Afrīqiyya wa Isṭanbūl. *al-Omanāʿ*.

Alley, A. L. (2010), "The Rules of the Game: Unpacking Patronage Politics in Yemen," *Middle East Journal* 64(3): 385–409.

Biswell, Anthony (2020), "The War for Monetary Control Enters a Dangerous New Phase," *Sanaa Center for Strategic Studies*, January 21. Available online: http://sanaacenter.org/files/The_War_for_Monetary_Control_en.pdf (accessed on December 10, 2020).

Connelly, Colby (2020), "Will Yemen Be a Gas Exporter Again?" March 10. The Arab Gulf States Institute in Washington. Available online: https://agsiw.org/will-yemen-be-a-gas-exporter-again/ (accessed on December 10, 2020).

Debriefer (2018), "Hadramout Governor Threatens to Halt Oil Exports Amid Escalating Yemen Protests," *Debriefer*, September 6. Available online: https://debriefer.net/en/news-3157.html (accessed on December 10, 2020).

Debriefer (2020), "Hadramout Governor Threatens to Halt Oil Exports Amid Escalating Protests." *Debriefer*, September 22. Available online: https://debriefer.net/en/news-20036.html (accessed on December 10, 2020).

Gallagher, J. (2020), "Fertility Rate: 'Jaw-dropping' Global Crash in Children Being Born." *BBC News*. July 14. Available online https://www.bbc.com/news/health-53409521 (accessed on December 10, 2020).

International Crisis Group (2020), "Rethinking Peace in Yemen," Middle East Report No. 216, July 2.

International Labour Organization (2004), A National Employment Agenda for Yemen, Paper for the National Tripartite Symposium on Employment, Sana'a, September 29th–30th & October 2nd, 2004. *National Tripartite Symposium on Employment*. Sanaa: ILO.

International Monetary Fund (2009), *IMF Country Report 09/100*. Washington, DC: International Monetary Fund.

International Monetary Fund (2014), *Republic of Yemen: IMF Country Report No. 14/276*. Washington, DC: International Monetary Fund.

Khan, A. (2018), "Yemen's Epic Coffee Revival: From War to Hipster New York Cafes." *Al-Jazeera*. Qatar, Al-Jazeera.

Ministry of Finance (2013), Bulletin of Government Finance Statistics 2013. M. o. Finance. Sanaa, Republic of Yemen.

Ministry of Planning and International Cooperation (2018), "Yemeni Expatriate Remittances . . . Last Resource Under Threat." *Yemen Socio Economic Update* (32).

Phillips, S. (2011), *Yemen and the Politics of Permanent Crisis*. New York: Routledge for the International Institute for Strategic Studies.

Republic of Yemen (2010), Statistical Yearbook. C. S. Organization. Sanaa, Republic of Yemen.

Republic of Yemen (2012), "Finances and Banking," *Statistical Yearbook 2011*. Sana´a. Central Statistical Organization.

Republic of Yemen (2020), "Socio-Economic Developments," Ministry of Planning and International Cooperation. June 2020. Available online: https://reliefweb.int/sites/reliefweb.int/files/resources/YSEU50_Arabic_Corr..pdf (accessed on December 10, 2020).

Rodrik, D. (1999), *The New Global Economy and Developing Countries: Making Openness Work*. Washington, DC: Overseas Development Council.

Sana´a Center Economic Unit (2020), "Tax and Rule: Houthis Move to Institutionalize Hashemite Elite with 'One-Fifth' Levy," September 2020. Available online :https://sanaacenter.org/publications/analysis/11628 (accessed on December 10, 2020).

Sana´a Center Economic Unit (2020a), "Yemen's Accelerating Economic Woes During the COVID-19 Pandemic," October 2020. Available online: https://devchampions.org

/uploads/publications/files/Rethinking_Yemens_Economy_No7_En.pdf (accessed on December 10, 2020).

Sana'a Center for Strategic Studies (2018), "Combatting Corruption in Yemen," September 2018. Available online: https://sanaacenter.org/publications/main -publications/6614 (accessed on December 10, 2020).

Sanaa Center for Strategic Studies (2019), "Inflated Beyond Fiscal Capacity: The Need to Reform the Public Sector Wage Bill," Policy Brief No. 16, September 23. Available online :https://devchampions.org/publications/policy-brief/Inflated_Beyond_Fiscal _Capacity (accessed on December 10, 2020).

Sanaa Center for Strategic Studies (2020), "STC's Aden Takeover Cripples Central Bank and Fragments Public Finances," June 17. Available online https://sanaacenter.org/ publications/analysis/10219 (accessed on December 10, 2020).

Schmitz, Charles (2012), "Building a Better Yemen," Carnegie Endowment for International Peace. April 3, 2012. Available online https://carnegieendowment.org /2012/04/03/building-better-yemen-pub-47708 (accessed on December 10, 2020).

Schmitz, C. and R. D. Burrowes (2018), *Historical Dictionary of Yemen*. Lanham, MD: Rowman & Littlefield.

Sekiguchi, Mina (2020), "LNG Market Outlook post-COVID-19," *KPMG Global Energy Institute*. June 12, 2020. Available online :https://institutes.kpmg.us/content/dam/ institutes/en/global-energy/pdfs/2020/drilling-down-lng-market.pdf (accessed on December 10, 2020).

Total (2019), "Yemen LNG Update," July 11, 2019. Available online : https://www.total.com /media/news/press-releases/yemen-lng-update (accessed on December 10, 2020).

Ward, C. (2014), *The Water Crisis in Yemen: Managing Extreme Water Scarcity in the Middle East*, New York: I.B. Tauris.

World Bank (2019), "Yemen Economic Monitoring Brief." Winter 2019. p. 7.

World Bank (2020), "Personal Remittances – Yemen, Rep." Available online: https:// data.worldbank.org/indicator/BX.TRF.PWKR.CD.DT?locations=YE (accessed on December 10, 2020).

World Bank (2020a), "Yemen Monthly Economic Update," June 2020. Available online: http://pubdocs.worldbank.org/en/933471597048500989/Yemen-Monthly-Economic -Update-June-2020-eng.pdf (accessed on December 10, 2020).

Chapter 7

POST-CONFLICT ECONOMIC RECOVERY AND DEVELOPMENT IN YEMEN

Rafat Al-Akhali

Introduction

Even before the current conflict in Yemen began, the country suffered from recurring cycles of conflict and instability, poor governance, underdevelopment, economic decline, and widespread poverty. The share of the population living in extreme poverty[1] increased from 7.4 percent in 1998 to 18.8 percent in 2014. The overall poverty headcount ratio at national poverty lines increased from 34.8 percent in 2005 to 48.6 percent in 2014 (World Bank 2020). The World Bank estimates that extreme poverty reached 51.9 percent in 2018, with the overall poverty rate reaching 80.6 percent (World Bank 2019a).

In the first two decades following the country's unification in 1990, Yemen made modest improvements on the United Nations (UN) Human Development Index (HDI), a summary measure for assessing long-term progress in three basic dimensions of human development: a long and healthy life, access to knowledge, and a decent standard of living. Yemen's score improved from 0.399 in 1990 to 0.498 in 2010. However, those improvements began to deteriorate after 2010, and by 2015, Yemen's HDI score had dropped to 0.483. In 2017, Yemen was ranked 178 out of 189 countries on the Human Development Index with a score of 0.452, placing Yemen below the average of 0.504 for countries in the low human development group and below the average of 0.699 for countries in Arab states (UNDP, 2019).

In this chapter, an overview of the labor force and the main economic activities in Yemen prior to the conflict are presented. This is followed by an analysis of the impact the conflict has had on jobs, economic industries, infrastructure, and macroeconomic indicators. Finally, the priorities and key considerations that should be taken into account when planning for post-conflict economic recovery and development are presented, together with an overall framework and the main pillars of a feasible post-conflict recovery vision.

Yemeni Economy Before the Conflict

Structure of the Labor Force

According to the Labour Force Survey 2013–14 (ILO, 2014), Yemen's working age population (aged fifteen plus) was 13.4 million. Of those, 4.85 million were employed, while 653,000 remained unemployed (a 13.5 percent unemployment rate). The youth unemployment rate of 24.5 percent was almost twice the national average. About thirty percent of the labor force worked in the public sector, while employment in the agriculture sector represented over 29 percent of available jobs (not including subsistence farmers) (Figure 7.1). It should be noted that the vast majority of employment (73.2 percent) was in the informal sector (ILO 2014).

Structure of Economic Activities

Hydrocarbons contribute significantly to the Yemeni economy (Figure 7.2). Mining and quarrying (which is dominated by oil and gas production) represented

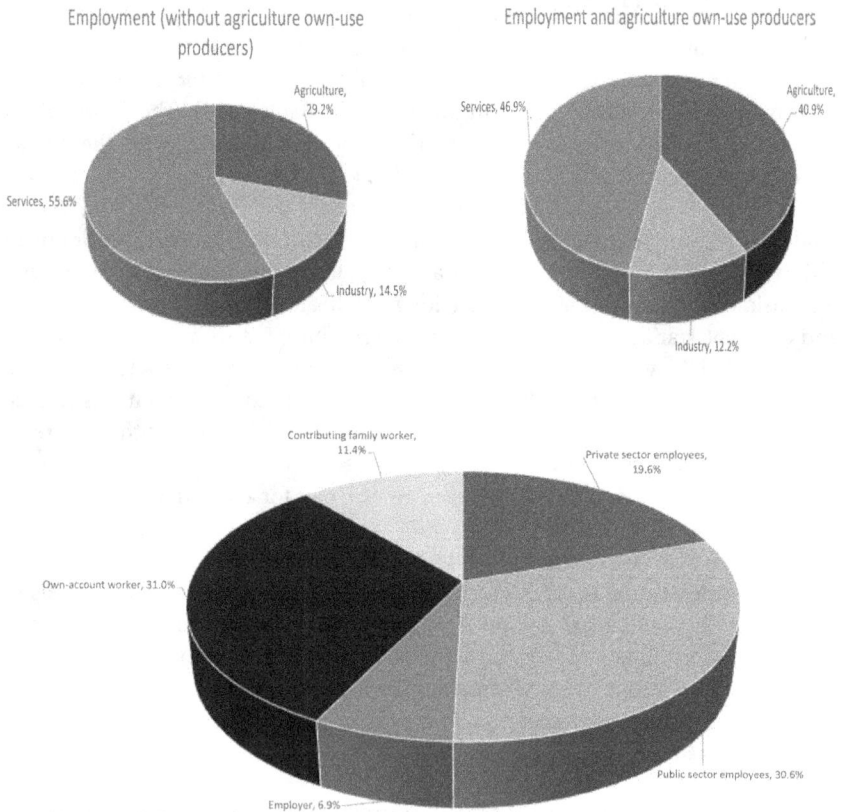

Figure 7.1 Yemen Employment by Sector (ILO 2014).

GDP by Economic Activity 2014 (In percent of total GDP)

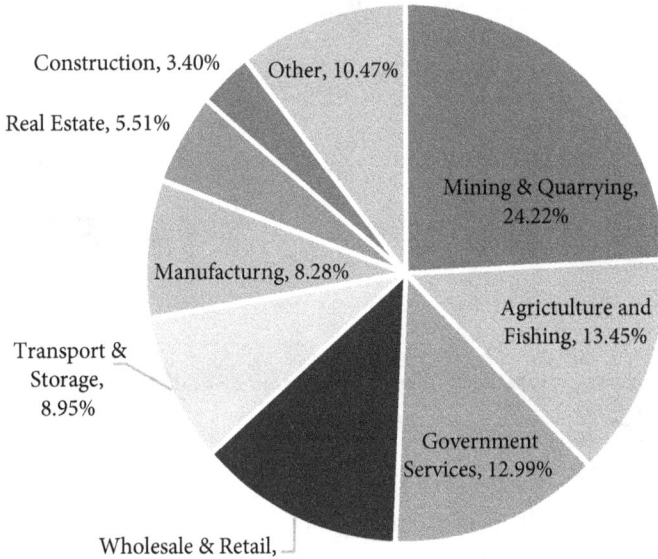

Figure 7.2 GDP by Economic Activity (Yemen Central Statistical Organization 2016).

24.22 percent of Yemen's GDP (by current prices) in 2014. Yemen's second largest economic activity is agriculture, forestry and fishing which represented 13.45 percent of the country's GDP (by current prices) in 2014. This is followed by production of government services (12.99 percent), wholesale and retail trade services (12.73 percent), transport and storage services (8.95 percent), manufacturing (8.28 percent), real estate and business services (5.51 percent), and construction services (3.4 percent) (Yemen Central Statistical Organization 2016).

Hydrocarbons are important not only because of their contribution to the country's GDP, but they also constitute a significant portion of government revenue and Yemen's total share of exports as shown later (IMF, 2014) (Figure 7.3).

Impact of the Conflict

Over five years of armed conflict have almost completely collapsed Yemen's already feeble economy. From 2000 to 2010, Yemen's average growth rate in real per capita GDP was sluggish at less than 1.5 percent a year (IMF 2014) (Figure 7.4). However, from 2011 to 2018, the real per capita GDP in Yemen dropped on average to 8 percent per year (World Bank 2019c). This effectively means Yemen lost half of its GDP per capita in nominal terms. It plummeted from a high of $1,334[2] in 2010 to an estimated $667 in 2018.

Hydrocarbon Receipts
(percentage shares)

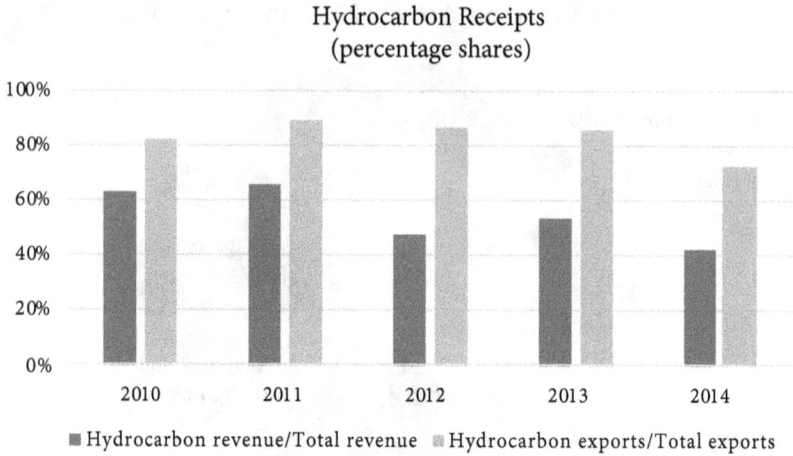

■ Hydrocarbon revenue/Total revenue ■ Hydrocarbon exports/Total exports

Figure 7.3 Share of hydrocarbon of total revenues and exports (IMF 2014).

GDP per capita growth (annual %)

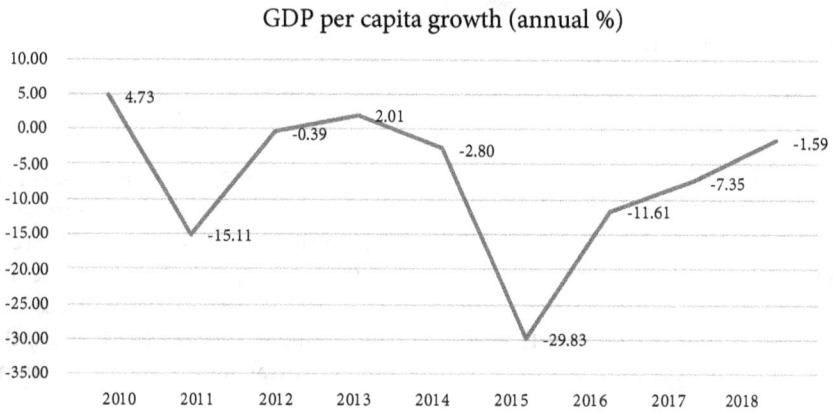

Figure 7.4 GDP per capita growth, 2010–2018 (World Bank 2019c).

While the conflict has impacted almost every aspect of daily life in Yemen—ranging from demographic factors such as mortality, fertility, and migration rates to human development determinants such as health, education, and poverty—this section focuses on the impact the war has had on specific economic development indicators such as job numbers, purchasing power, public revenue, infrastructure, and production.

For the average Yemeni citizen, the conflict has significantly impacted the population's purchasing power in two major ways. The first is the way stunted economic activity has disrupted even simple forms of income generation such as agriculture. The second way citizens have notably reeled under the deteriorating economy is the inflationary pressure on prices of everyday and basic consumer goods. These two factors have pushed hundreds of thousands of Yemenis to the brink of famine and contributed to what international aid organizations consider the world's worst humanitarian crisis. As of June 2020, the UN estimated that 24.3 million people—close to 80 percent of the population in Yemen—were in need of some sort of assistance and protection, with about ten million people classified as having acute needs for food (OCHA 2020a).

Impact on Income Opportunities

To understand the impact of the conflict on employment and income opportunities, the following section analyzes, specifically, the war's effect on public-sector employees, private-sector jobs, and jobs in agriculture.

In 2014, the Government of Yemen employed roughly 1.25 million people, according to data from the Ministry of Civil Service and Pensions. In September 2016, public-sector employees' salaries were suspended amid a liquidity crisis. Salary payments to civil service employees and military personnel in areas controlled by the Internationally Recognized Yemeni Government (IRG) resumed in early 2017 (Al-Bashiri, 2019). At the end of 2018, the Ministry of Civil Service and Pensions reported that 246,963 civil service employees were regularly receiving their salaries that year, while the remaining 225,390 civil service employees (largely teachers and health workers) were outside the government's reach. With an average of 6.7 people per household in Yemen (Ministry of Public Health, 2013), this loss-of-income shortage has impacted at least 1.5 million people.

Apart from the civil service employees, there were roughly 650,000 military and security personnel listed on the payroll in 2014. The IRG has continued paying the salaries of military and security personnel who are located in government-controlled areas or are part of its military units, and is expected to have added a significant number to the 2014 payroll, though there are no official numbers publicly available. The IRG stopped paying salaries of military and security personnel in Ansar Allah-controlled areas. Military personnel who joined Ansar Allah, as well as new hires by Ansar Allah since the conflict started, are known to be receiving salaries directly from Ansar Allah, though no official numbers are published. It is also reported that there is a large number of military personnel who chose to stay at home and did not join the war effort. This group reportedly has not received a regular salary since September 2016. In addition, multiple security and paramilitary units have been established and trained in the south with funding from the UAE and Saudi Arabia. It is yet to be seen if and how the salaries of these large units can be sustainably included in the government's budget.

Yemen's dire moribund economy has been equally catastrophic for private-sector employees. A survey conducted by the Small and Micro Enterprise Promotion Services agency (SMEPS) and United Nations Development Programme (UNDP) not long after the conflict began (August–September 2015) showed that over a quarter (26 percent) of all businesses had closed since March 2015 (SMEPS & UNDP, 2015). In January 2016, the International Labour Organization (ILO) published a rapid assessment report on the crisis' impact on employment and the labor market in three of Yemen's major cities (Sana'a, Hodeida, and Aden) (ILO, 2016a). The assessment found a 12.8 percent reduction in overall employment across sectors, or the equivalent loss of 130,000 jobs. Again, with an average household size of 6.7 people, this income loss impacted some 870,000 people. A 2017 study from the Studies and Economic Media Center shows that 83 percent of private-sector enterprises have suffered direct or indirect damages from the war. The World Bank conducted an assessment of the war's impact on private enterprises, releasing its report in July 2019. This assessment finds that 25 percent of firms closed as a result of the conflict, 80 percent experienced a drastic decline in sales, and over 50 percent had to downsize their operations. Many went from large to medium size or small to micro. Of the businesses that have been able to stay open, 20 percent have lost (at least some) their full-time employees and 27 percent of businesses have lost at least some part-time employees (Sofan, 2019). A business climate survey published by SMEPS in October 2020 shows a continuing negative trend: 42.2 percent of survey respondents noted that their capital had declined between 2017 and 2019, compared to 28 percent noting positive changes in their capital, and 27.2 percent reporting no change. Profitability trends closely mirrored those of capital, with almost 45 percent of firms reporting decreased profits in 2019 compared to 2017, while 30.3 percent and 25.3 percent reporting positive and no changes, respectively (SMEPS, 2020).

As stated earlier in the chapter, prior to the war, about a third of the Yemeni labor force was employed in the field of agriculture (including the forestry and fishing industries), according to the ILO (ILO, 2016b). The conflict has significantly disrupted the agriculture sector in Yemen. According to the Food and Agriculture Organization of the United Nations (FAO), the agriculture sector was the primary source of livelihood for two-thirds of the Yemeni population prior to the conflict. The conflict has had the largest impact on this sector with almost 50 percent of the sector's workers losing their jobs (FAO, 2017). For example, a study by the Flood-based Livelihoods Network Foundation concluded that farmers in Yemen's western Tihama region have seen a 40 to 80 percent drop in their monthly household income (Flood-based Livelihoods Network Foundation 2017).

Impact on Public Revenue and Inflation

Public revenue has dropped precipitously since the war broke out. This rapid decline was mostly a result of the collapse of Yemen's hydrocarbon exports. The majority of international oil and gas companies have yet to resume their operations after suspending them when fighting broke out. Moreover, the government's tenuous authority in sections of the country that are nominally under its control has inhibited its ability to collect tax revenues. Public revenues have declined from nearly 24 percent of GDP prior to the conflict, to an estimated 8 percent of GDP in 2018, with non-hydrocarbon tax collection being the key source for revenues, amounting to around 5 percent of a much-reduced GDP (World Bank 2018c).

This downturn for government revenue has resulted in a severe budget deficit, given that the government expenditures on the public wage bill continued and even increased in the case of the expanding military and security sector. The Central Bank of Yemen has compensated for the majority of this fiscal deficit by printing money, spurring spiralling inflation as will be further explained later. It should be noted that the aforementioned figures only represent revenues from areas controlled by the IRG. Although large tax-payers (large businesses, telecommunication companies, banks) continue to be headquartered in Sanaʹa and Ansar Allah-controlled areas and paying taxes there, and while Ansar Allah have been reported to have significantly improved tax collection in their areas, data on tax revenues from these areas is not available publicly.

The drop in hydrocarbon exports has also caused acute shortages of foreign currency needed to import essential items such as food, fuel, and medicine. This imbalance has been complicated by the fragmentation of the Central Bank of Yemen which was relocated by the Government of Yemen to Aden in September 2016 while the de-facto authorities in Sanaʹa maintained their own central bank there. As a result of all of these factors, Yemen has had a highly volatile foreign exchange rate (Figure 7.5). The Yemeni Riyal has depreciated from 215 YER/USD in 2014 to 570 YER/USD in January 2019 (Ministry of Planning 2018). By December 2019, the rivalry between the two administrations of the central bank reached a new peak, when the Sanaʹa authorities announced a ban on all new banknotes issued by the central bank in Aden citing concerns over inflationary pressures from excessive printing of new banknotes. The effect of this split, combined with the impact of Covid-19 and declining global oil prices, has pushed the average unofficial market exchange rate of the Yemeni Riyal against the US dollar in Aden to a historic low of YER800/USD recorded on August 30, 2020—an increase of 19 percent compared with January 2020, when the rate stood at YER651/USD (OCHA, 2020b). The exchange rate in Sanaʹa and areas controlled by Ansar Allah was better by roughly 33 percent, standing at YER605/USD by the end of August 2020 (Sanaʹa Center Economic Unit, 2020).

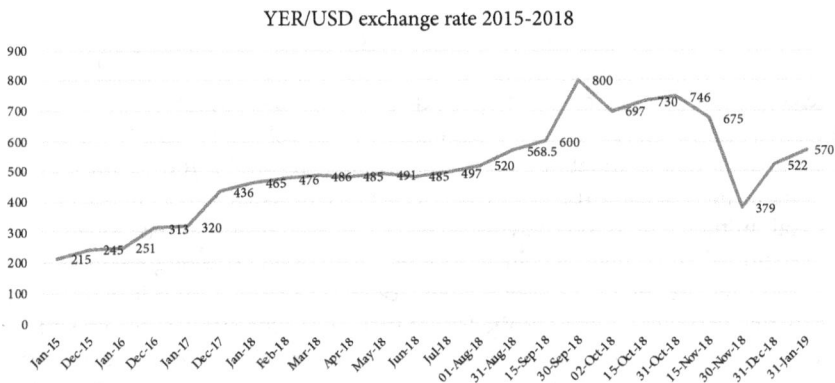

Figure 7.5 YER/USD exchange rate, 2015–2018 (Ministry of Planning 2018).

The depreciation in the exchange rate has been reflected in the inflated prices for the vast majority of goods and especially food items. In September 2020, the World Food Programme (WFP) data shows that the prices of wheat flour, red beans, sugar, and vegetable oil increased by 148 percent, 199 percent, 97 percent, and 109 percent, respectively, compared to January 2015. The cost of a food basket had risen by 127 percent. Additionally, as of September 2020, the average prices of petrol and diesel rose up by 168 percent and 196 per cent, respectively (WFP, 2020).

Impact on Infrastructure

Ongoing fighting has decimated infrastructure across Yemen. Assessing the monetary impact of the destruction is difficult while front lines remain active, but the World Bank produced a "Dynamic Damage and Needs Assessment" (DNA) report in May 2018, providing a snapshot of the cost of the war on Yemen's physical infrastructure.

The DNA report estimates the cost of physical damage in sixteen cities to be between $6 billion to $7.5 billion. The housing sector represented more than 72 percent of these costs, totaling between $4.5 billion to $5.4 billion. Damage to the health sector (hospitals, medical centers etc.) was estimated to be as high as $665 million and costs to the energy sector (power stations, electricity transport lines etc.) could have been as high as $640 million (World Bank, 2018a).

According to a 2018 Emergency Employment and Community Rehabilitation Cluster (EECR) survey based on 2000 respondents from twenty different districts across Yemen, the water supply infrastructure was the most commonly cited damage. Electricity infrastructure was the second most common followed by health, education, and roads (Lambert and Afcar, 2018).

Impact on State Institutions

The current conflict in Yemen is the country's longest and most devastating war since the formation of the modern Yemeni state in 1990. Its far-reaching destruction has left state institutions reeling at multiple levels.

One of the most sweeping effects the war has had on the central government is the fracturing of central state institutions historically located in Sana´a. Following the concerted effort to centralize political and administrative power since 1990, the majority of the state's ministries, independent authorities, and the country's central bank operated out of Sana´a. Shortly after the Huthis took control of the capital at the end of 2014, the IRG government declared Aden the temporary capital. Initially, there were few projections that conflict would last long, and it was assumed that Sana´a would shortly return to be the seat of government. As a result, the IRG operated only a "shell" cabinet in Riyadh, and later in Aden, consisting of ministers and a limited set of staff. As the conflict dragged on and the IRG increasingly came under pressure to deliver services and exercise authority in areas under its control, there was a snowballing emergence of duplicative state institutions between Sana´a and Aden.

The most visible and studied example of an institution that had undergone fragmentation is the case of the Central Bank of Yemen (CBY). In September 2016, President Abdu Rabu Mansour Hadi ordered the CBY to be relocated to Aden and appointed a new governor of the bank. This move marked the beginning of the banking sector crisis in Yemen that is still unfolding, and established competing monetary policies dictated out of Sana´a and Aden (al-Muslimi, 2019).

In addition to the CBY, all other central state institutions have also been effectively duplicated in Sana´a and Aden. This includes the Ministry of Finance, the Tax Authority, Customs Authority, Central Organization for Control and Audit, and the Supreme National Authority for Combating Corruption, among others.

In addition to the split of state institutions along IRG and Huthi conflict lines, there has also been a further impact on institutions within territories under the control of each party. Within areas controlled by the IRG, there has been an additional fracturing between central and local authorities. Largely due to the central government's enfeebled state, the balance of power has tilted toward local authority leaders, namely governors. This effect is especially pronounced in natural resource-rich governorates such as Marib, Hadhramaut, and Shabwah or governorates with control over border revenues such as Al-Mahrah. Governors have gained significant control of their respective areas' sources of revenue and in turn have the autonomy to use the revenue as they see fit, with less than adequate checks and balances. In some cases, this increased level of local authority is in line with the pre-conflict legal framework that existed during the thirty-three-year rule of President Ali Abdullah Saleh and the transitional period that followed after his toppling, from 2012 to 2014. But in many other cases this seizure of local power violates the current legal framework. For example, in order to appease residents in Hadhramaut and resume oil production and export operations, the central government reached a deal with local leaders to allocate 20 percent of international oil sales to development projects in the governorate. There is no legal basis for this agreement, but it is maintained through a special "development account" specifically created to allocate this share of oil sales to Hadhramaut. A similar agreement was reached in the Shabwah region when oil exporting capabilities resumed there.

In areas under Huthi control, an informal shadow system referred to as "*mushrifeen*" (supervisors) is practiced at both the central level in Sana´a and at the governorate level (see Chapter 3 in this volume). These supervisors parallel the formal structure of state institutions on each administrative level and establish a symbiotic relationship with state officials at all levels (Nevola 2019). They do not hold a formal state position but, rather, act on behalf of the Huthi movement, "relieving existing authorities of their duties or rendering them redundant" (UNHCR, 2018). This has led to an overall weakening of the state's institutions and further eroded transparency and accountability in these areas.

The change in the balance of power between central and local authorities in government-controlled areas has shaped, and in many cases has been in response to, local public opinion in these governorates. This more diffused power structure has created a very different reality, state structure, and processes in government-controlled areas compared to the governing systems in areas under Huthi control. In these areas, the pre-conflict power structure that revolves around a central command is still dominant while also molding to fit the Huthi implemented "parallel supervisory" order.

The human resources running state institutions have also been impacted. As mentioned in previous sections, at least half of the civil servants in Yemen have not received their salaries since 2017 (al-Bashiri, 2019) and the ones who did receive their salaries have seen its value decrease over time with the rampant inflation. Although there are not exact numbers or studies capturing the details, it can be expected that the civil service lost many of its qualified cadre who either left the country or moved to the International Non-Government Organizations sector which is currently the only active employer in the country.

Post-Conflict Economic Recovery

As described in the previous section, the impact of the conflict has been devastating across all aspects of life in Yemen: from loss of lives to loss of livelihoods, and from damage to infrastructure to fragmentation of state institutions. This makes post-conflict recovery planning a daunting challenge, albeit an absolute necessity to ensure quicker action when the conflict ends and to lower the chances of a return to violence. Needless to say that developing a grand plan for post-conflict recovery is beyond the scope of this chapter, but the following sections will attempt to outline key considerations that need to inform post-conflict recovery planning based on the structure of the Yemeni economy, the impact of the current conflict, lessons learned from previous post-conflict and post-disaster recovery efforts in Yemen, and lessons learned from international post-conflict recovery efforts.

Prioritizing Economic Growth

The traditional approach to post-conflict recovery tends to follow a phased, discrete, and largely non-overlapping sequence: starting with relief and humanitarian assistance, then reintegration of fighters, refugees and internally displaced persons, followed by rebuilding of physical infrastructure, and finally interventions geared to facilitate economic growth (USAID, 2009). While there has been an increasing shift away from this "relief to development continuum" approach, it is still deeply ingrained in the international relief and development communities. As a matter of fact, this exact prioritization of humanitarian relief and assistance while neglecting economic growth has been witnessed in Yemen during the current conflict, including in areas of the country that have effectively transitioned into a "post-conflict" period yet lack any economic growth intervention, increasing the risk of return to conflict. There is a danger that given Yemen's desperate humanitarian situation (classified as the world's worst humanitarian crisis), focus will continue to be on the humanitarian response even in a post-conflict scenario, to the detriment of economic growth.

There is a simple reason to prioritize economic growth in post-conflict periods: research shows that the typical post-conflict country faces a 40 percent risk of reversion to conflict during the first decade (Collier and Hoeffer, 2002). Given the significant consequences of returning to violent conflict, the top priority should be to reduce this risk of reversion to conflict. Evidence shows that early attention to the fundamentals of economic growth increases the likelihood of successfully preventing a return to conflict and moving forward with renewed growth (USAID, 2009). Economic growth mainly affects the risk of violence through addressing youth unemployment. Young unemployed men are typically the target for recruitment by armed groups and constitute the fuel for armed conflicts. This is also true in the case of Yemen. Addressing this challenge through absorbing large numbers into the military and security forces is extremely expensive and waste of a large pool of labor. Attempting to address it through social spending is unlikely to directly reach young men as they are not heavy users of social services (Collier, 2009). Therefore, creating job opportunities for unskilled young men is probably the most effective strategy to counter youth unemployment, and these opportunities can be created only by focusing on economic growth as early as possible in the post-conflict period.

Adopting an Integrated Approach

A major dilemma in post-conflict situations is how much attention should be devoted to economic policies relative to security priorities and political arrangements of the post-conflict period. Research shows that economic recovery substantially contributes to the reduction of risk of reversing the conflict (Collier, Hoeffler and Soderbom 2008). In Yemen's post-2011 transitional period, there is a consensus that too much emphasis was placed on the political process (power-sharing arrangements, the national dialogue conference, and the subsequent constitution drafting process) at the expense of economic growth and service delivery, possibly contributing to the collapse of that transitional period and sparking the current conflict (Salisbury, 2019).

In reality economics, politics, and security of post-conflict situations are closely linked, and little can be achieved in any of these tracks without advancing in the other two tracks (Brinkerhoff, 2005) (Figure 7.6). Economic recovery cannot take place without an enabling political environment, and both economic and political reforms require a minimum threshold of security, which in itself can be achieved only through an acceptable political settlement and an adequate level of economic growth providing jobs and stability. Therefore, an integrated approach to post-conflict recovery needs to be adopted that takes into account, and balances attention across, economic, political, and security priorities.

Reforms on the political front help restore state legitimacy in the post-conflict period. These would include expanding participation and inclusiveness initially through power-sharing, then moving into addressing inequities while

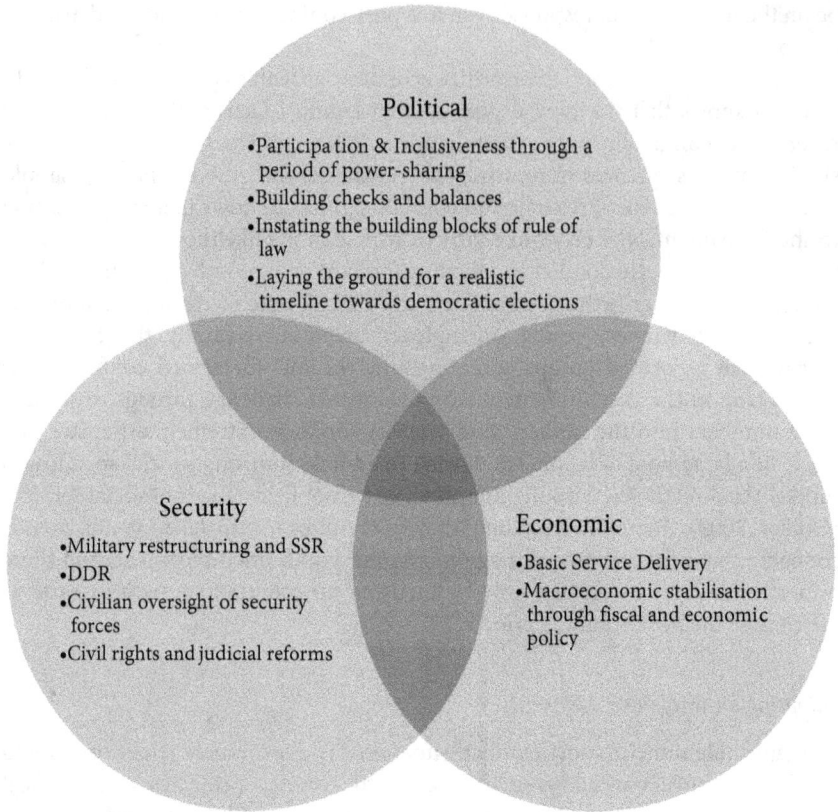

Figure 7.6 Yemen post-conflict recovery priorities (adapted from Brinkerhoff 2005).

building checks and balances and the rule of law, and finally building a plan to consolidate these reforms and start the journey toward democratic elections, which should be seen as the end point of restoring state legitimacy post-conflict rather than the beginning point (Collier, Besley and Khan, 2018). Yemen went through some of these reforms in the post-2011 transitional period but, with the benefit of hindsight, many mistakes were made. Perhaps the most significant of those mistakes was the unrealistic time line enforced to complete the envisioned transition (two years to go through a national dialogue, reshape the state structure, go through a constitution drafting and referendum process, and prepare for and conduct elections).

On the security front, issues of military restructuring and security sector reform (SSR), as well as disarmament, demobilization, and reintegration (DDR) are typically expected to dominate the agenda. Again, this was seen in the post-2011 transition which prioritized military structuring as one of the early steps of the transitional period. But this should not take away from the critical functions of civilian oversight of security forces, and critical reforms to the judiciary system. In addition, an important area of the security agenda post-conflict, which Yemen did not have previous experience with, is international peacekeeping. The nature of the current conflict, including the role of regional actors, might require some level of international peacekeeping as part of the peace settlement. This can already be seen in the establishment of the United Nations Mission in Support of the Hodeida Agreement (UNMHA), which includes international monitors.

On the economic front, the priority is to restore a level of functioning service delivery capacity across Yemen, especially when it comes to core services such as health, education, water, sanitation, and electricity. In parallel with restoring service provision, the government will need to focus on macroeconomic stabilization through efficient fiscal and monetary policy implementation. The following sections will further explore key considerations on the economic front.

Addressing the Delivery Dilemma

The challenges and tasks facing any post-conflict government in Yemen are daunting, to say the least. Figure 7.7 presents a summary of the main priorities that will need to be addressed. Yemen has always scored low on government effectiveness even before the conflict, as shown in Figure 7.8 (World Bank 2019b), and from that low base it is critical to take into account the deep structural impact of the conflict on state institutions presented earlier in this chapter when planning for the post-conflict period.

With fragmented institutions, empowered local leadership at the governorate level, weakened civil service, and militarily powerful non-state actors across the country, it is not expected that any central government formed following a

Yemen Government Effectiveness (Percentile Rank)

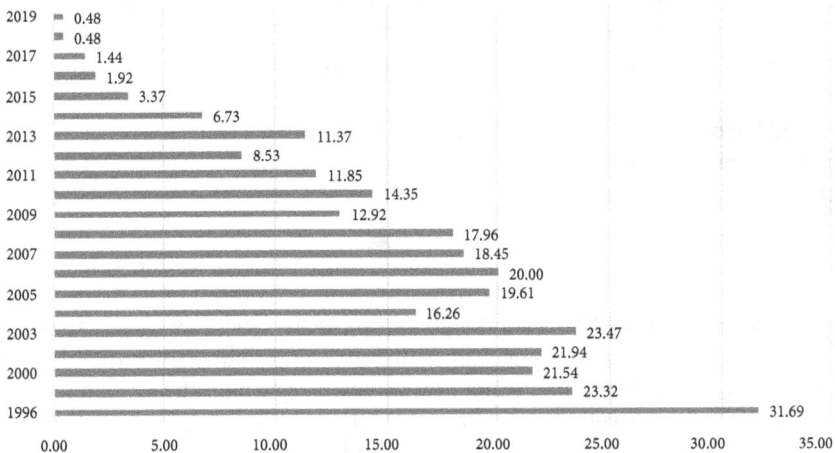

Figure 7.7 Yemen Government Effectiveness percentile rank (1996-2019) (World Bank 2019b).

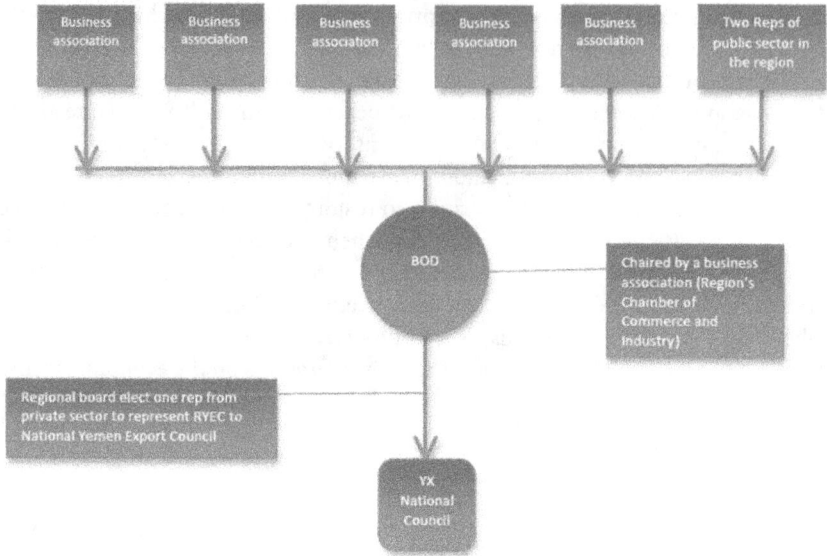

Figure 7.8 Proposed structure of regional export councils (ADE and Lambard 2013).

political settlement will be able to reestablish and operate the same governance system that prevailed before the conflict, even with all the weaknesses of that system. Therefore, there is a need to seriously address the dilemma of how any post-conflict government will be able to deliver the much-needed restoration of basic services and achieve the economic stabilization and growth needed to secure peace with such pervasive needs, inherent weaknesses, and severe constraints it will inevitably find itself facing.

To address this dilemma, the post-conflict government will need to reconceptualize the traditional role and modus operandi of previous governments in Yemen. It will need to have a laser focus on developing the private economy to achieve a sustained increase in productive jobs, and empowering local authorities to lead the delivery of basic services effectively. Through an enabled private sector and empowered local authorities, the post-conflict government might have a chance to achieve success.

Developing the Private Economy

As presented in previous sections, preserving peace and preventing a return to conflict requires generating and sustaining new job opportunities. It is inconceivable that the public sector will be able to generate the needed jobs in post-conflict Yemen, and therefore the key is in developing the private economy.

Given the structure of economic activities and the labor force in Yemen outlined in earlier sectors of this chapter, economic policies aimed at developing the private economy need to have a dual focus: one on supporting rural economies which will inevitably center on the agricultural sector, and one on developing urban economies which will cover multiple services and manufacturing sectors.

While approximately 40 percent of the labor force in Yemen is working in the agricultural sector (including own-use producers), and agriculture represents 13 percent of GDP, the productivity of the agricultural sector is very low in Yemen. The sector suffers from insufficient availability of inputs, post-harvest losses, inadequate value addition and marketing systems, low human resource capacity, and poor infrastructure (World Bank 2018b). The agri-food export sector contributes only 11 percent of Yemen's exports. Water scarcity and limited arable land (less than 3 percent of the total land in Yemen is arable) are two major challenges in the agricultural sector (World Bank 2019b).

However, technological improvements have been greatly boosting output and bringing down costs in the agricultural sector around the world. Advances in water-saving technologies, as well as renewable energy, could greatly help in improving the productivity of the agricultural sector in Yemen. In addition, many countries with similar agricultural sectors to Yemen (such as sub-Saharan countries in Africa) were able to capitalize on advances in mobile phone technologies, big data, drones, and satellite imaging to vastly improve extension services to farmers, helping them boost their yields (Pathways 2018).

While increasing yields is a necessary step, it will not be sufficient without ensuring that farmers (including fishers) are not efficiently connected to national and international markets. Investments along value chains of key products such as fish, honey, and coffee in Yemen can go a long way in unleashing agriculture's full potential for growth.

Developing the agricultural sector, and the rural economy that is strongly intertwined with it, will require the government to adopt innovative policies and institutional structures that are able to respond to the need for modernization in this sector as well as to the diversity of landscape and resources across Yemen.

As for the urban private economy, post-conflict recovery will require rapid and critical reforms and improvements in three key areas: critical urban infrastructure, regulatory services and contract enforcement, and tax collection. Firms need a reliable supply of energy and this is a key requirement in supporting firm growth. Investing in grid-based supply of energy to firms should be prioritized in the immediate term. In addition to energy, firms require effective road networks and functioning water and sewerage infrastructure. Naturally, any post-conflict government will not be able to supply these critical infrastructure across the whole country. Therefore, prioritizing a few urban areas in which to improve these urban infrastructures will be required in order to achieve impact.

In addition to efficient infrastructure, firms need key public institutions that provide them with secure property rights (Collier, Besley, and Khan 2018). Implementing targeted and rapid reforms to establish a public register for urban land, and to improve the functioning of commercial courts in order to provide rapid processing of commercial disputes would go a long way in improving the business environment. Again, it would not be realistic to expect the government to implement reforms across the whole judicial system and across the country, but targeting specifically commercial courts and possibly prioritizing reforms in key commercial cities would form a more feasible agenda for the post-conflict government.

Restoring tax collection capacity and targeted reforms to the tax collection process will have the dual effect of increasing government revenues, enabling it to make the required infrastructure investments, and providing a more stable and certain business environment for private firms to invest in.

Where both rural economy and urban economy intersect is in the exports sector. With weak domestic demand expected to continue for a number of years after the conflict, Yemen needs to focus on export-led economic growth. Given that Yemen can no longer rely upon its depleting hydrocarbon sector as a source of sustainable economic development, the country will need to position export expansion as a primary tool to achieve economic development in the post-conflict period. This means diversifying export income to include a range of existing sectors such as agriculture, fisheries, and processed food as well as new sectors such as value-adding semi-finished and finished products manufactured using Yemen's extensive non-hydrocarbon minerals, as well as services including tourism (ADE and Lambard 2013).

To achieve this export diversification and growth, the current institutional framework will have to be revisited. The Supreme Council for Export Development (SCED) has been the main institution envisioned to carry the mandate of export development since its formation in 1997. The SCED is an overly public-sector dominated institution with very centralized and bureaucratic processes, which prevented it from achieving any significant impact in its field. The draft National Export Strategy formulated in 2013 (but never officially adopted) suggested a more decentralized and private sector-led institutional framework through the establishment of five or six Regional Yemen Export Councils and a National Yemen Export Council to replace the SCED. Figure 7.9 presents the proposed structure of the regional councils and the national council. Such structures would better fit the need to address the de-facto decentralization explained in previous sections and the need to rely on private-sector leadership in developing the private economy.

Empowering Local Authorities

The second pillar of a successful post-conflict governance system in Yemen are empowered local authorities capable of leading the development process and the delivery of basic services at the governorate level effectively. The National Dialogue Conference Outcomes envisioned an orderly transition into a federal state in Yemen. However, the current conflict has led to a more rapid and chaotic transition into de-facto decentralized authorities at the governorate level. Given this deep structural change that cut across not only the institutional structures but also people's expectations in the different governorates where it has become politically unfeasible to return to either the pre-conflict centralized system of governance or to a longer-term structured transition to federalism.

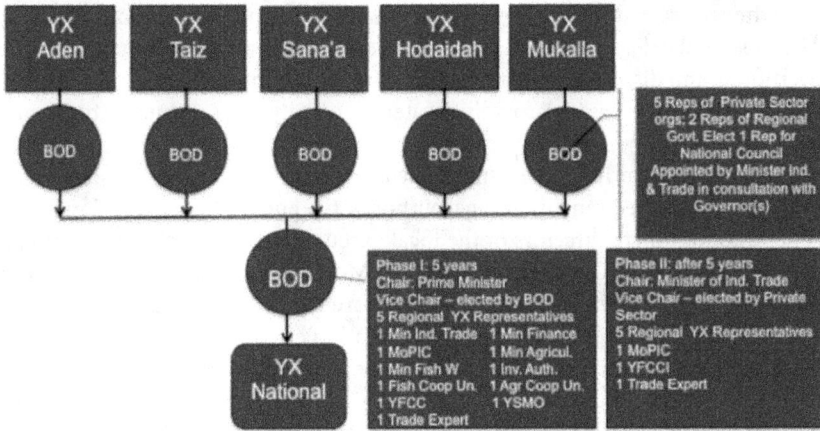

Figure 7.9 Proposed structure of national export council (ADE and Lambard 2013).

Therefore, any post-conflict government will need to take rapid actions to deal with this de-facto reality and make something positive out of it. The goal should be to maintain a thread of national coherence and coordination across the different governorates, while providing them with the resources and capacity to take a leading role in the development process and service delivery in their areas.

The major criticism of the current legal framework for local administration in Yemen (Local Authority Law No. 4 for the year 2000 and its amendment Law No. 18 for year 2008) is that, beyond the fact that practice (prior to the conflict) never conformed to the law, there are contradictions and ambiguities in the law itself (Rogers, 2019). In addition, there have been many criticisms of the way central authorities transferred functions and activities to local authorities without the needed resources.

> Staff, resources and equipment were not transferred to the local level, financial allocations were insufficient, central organization branches were not provided the databases and information necessary, and localities received no training in their new functions. All this undermined the local authority objectives, rendering it incapable to provide efficient and quality services or realize the interests of citizens in their services.
>
> (Basalmah, 2018)

The post-conflict government needs to move quickly to address these issues and create an enabling environment for local authorities to function effectively. This would include granting additional revenue-raising powers to the local authorities and giving them the right to set development priorities in the governorates and sign contracts for local projects, and in addition, enabling local authorities to access assistance and grants directly from international donors and international development agencies.

On the services side, supervisory powers on local security institutions such as the police need to be delegated to the local executive, as well as supervisory powers on governorate and district branches of institutions providing local services including publicly owned companies providing water, electricity, telecommunications, and other services.

To enable local authorities to effectively manage and administer these services, governors should be granted the legal authority to appoint, transfer, and mandate staff and to nominate directors of the local executive offices, as stipulated in Law 4/2000 but never implemented in practice. More importantly, it is well known that the capacity challenges and lack of transparency and accountability measures at the central level is present, sometimes to a larger extent, at the local level as well. Therefore, ensuring that adequate transparency and accountability measures are in place at the local level, and implementing rapid steps to address capacity constraints in local authority will also be a key priority in this pillar.

Conclusion

Yemen was one of the poorest and least developed countries in the region prior to the current war. The ongoing conflict has had a significant impact on Yemen's economy, causing loss of jobs, closure of businesses, damage to infrastructure, fragmentation of state institutions, and bringing economic activity in the country to almost a standstill. Post-conflict recovery will require a sustained focus on economic growth, while balancing economic policies, security priorities, and political arrangements in the post-conflict period. The post-conflict challenges are daunting, but a post-conflict government can achieve success through empowered local authorities and an enabled private sector, focusing on both rural and urban economies and adopting an export-led economic growth model.

Notes

1 Defined as living with per capita household consumption below $1.90 per day (based on prices in 2011)
2 Constant 2010 US$

References

al- Bashiri, M. (2019), "Economic Confidence Building Measures – Civil Servant Salaries," Deep Root Consulting, Sanaa Center for Strategic Studies and CARPO, Sanaa, March. Available online: https://devchampions.org/uploads/publications/files/Rethinking%20Yemen's%20Economy%20-%20policy%20brief%2011.pdf (accessed September 3, 2019).
al-Muslimi, F. (2019), "Revitalizing Yemen's Banking Sector: Necessary Steps for Restarting Formal Financial Cycles and Basic Economic Stabilization," The Sanaa

Centre for Strategic Studies, Sanaa, February). Available online: http://sanaacenter.org/publications/analysis/7049 (accessed April 17, 2020).

Analysis for Economic Decisions (ADE) and Lambard Management Consultants Ltd. (2013), *Technical Assistance report on Formulation of National Export Strategy in Yemen*, October.

Basalmah, B. (2018), "Local Governance: Engine for Stability in Yemen," Berghof Foundation. Berlin, 2018. Available online: https://www.berghof-foundation.org/fileadmin/redaktion/Publications/Other_Resources/Berghof_Foundation_Yemen_locgov_Paper02LocalGovernance_WEB.pdf (accessed January 28, 2020).

Brinkerhoff, D. (2005), "Rebuilding Governance in Failed States and Post-Conflict Societies: Core Concepts and Cross-Cutting Themes," *Public Administration and Development* 25: 3–14, Wiley InterScience. Available online: http://citeseerx.ist.psu.edu/viewdoc/download?doi=10.1.1.390.2714&rep=rep1&type=pdf (accessed January 28, 2020).

Collier, P. (2009), "Post-conflict Recovery: How Should Strategies Be Distinctive?" *Journal of African Economies* 18 (suppl_1): i99–i131, Oxford. Available online: https://academic.oup.com/jae/article/18/suppl_1/i99/783894 (accessed January 28, 2020).

Collier, P., T. Besley and A. Khan (2018), *Escaping the Fragility Trap*. London: International Growth Centre. Available online: https://www.theigc.org/publication/escaping-fragility-trap/ (accessed January 28, 2020).

Collier, P. and A. Hoeffler (2002), "On the Incidence of Civil War in Africa," *Journal of Conflict Resolution* 46 (1): 13–28 (accessed January 28, 2020).

Collier, P., A. Hoeffler and M. Söderbom (2008),"Post-Conflict Risks," *Journal of Peace Research* 45(4): 461–78. Oslo. Available online: https://journals.sagepub.com/doi/abs/10.1177/0022343308091356 (accessed January 28, 2020).

FAO (2017), *Smallholder Agricultural Production Restoration and Enhancement Project*. Sana´a, June. Available online: http://www.fao.org/3/a-bt085e.pdf (accessed April 17, 2020).

Flood-based Livelihoods Network Foundation (2017), *Food Production, Irrigation Marketing, and Agricultural Coping Mechanisms*. Available online: http://spate-irrigation.org/wp-content/uploads/2018/02/Briefing-Note-2-%E2%80%93-Food-Security-Copy.pdf (accessed September 3, 2019).

ILO (2016a), *Yemen Labour Force Survey, 2013–2014*. Beirut. Available online: https://www.ilo.org/wcmsp5/groups/public/---arabstates/---ro-beirut/documents/publication/wcms_419016 (accessed September 3, 2019).

ILO (2016b), *Yemen Damage and Needs Assessment*. Beirut. Available online: https://www.ilo.org/wcmsp5/groups/public/---arabstates/---ro-beirut/documents/publication/wcms_501929.pdf (accessed September 3, 2019).

IMF (2014), *Yemen 2014 Article IV Consultation*. Washington. Available online: https://www.imf.org/en/Publications/CR/Issues/2016/12/31/Republic-of-Yemen-2014-Article-IV-Consultation-and-Request-for-a-Three-Year-Arrangement-41901 (accessed April 17, 2020).

Lambert, T. and Afcar Consulting (2018), *Yemen Multi-Sector Early Recovery Assessment*. United Nations Emergency Employment and Community Rehabilitation Cluster. UNDP. Available online: http://earlyrecovery.global/sites/default/files/yemen-multisector-earlyrecoveryassessment.pdf (accessed April 17, 2020).

Ministry of Planning and International Cooperation (2018), *Yemen Social and Economic Updates*. Sana´a, December.

Ministry of Public Health and Population (2013), "Central Statistical Organization, Pan Arab program for Family Health and ICF International." *2013 Key Findings: Yemen National Health and Demographic Survey*. Available online: https://dhsprogram.com/pubs/pdf/SR220/SR220English.pdf (accessed April 17, 2020).

Nevola, L. (2019), *From Periphery to the Core: A Social Network Analysis of the Ḥūthī Local Governance System*, VERSUS Working Paper, University of Sussex.

OCHA (2020a), United Nations Office for the Coordination of Humanitarian Affairs. Humanitarian Response Plan. June. Available online: https://reliefweb.int/sites/reliefweb.int/files/resources/Extension%20Yemen%20HRP%202020_Final%20%281%29.pdf (accessed October 28, 2020).

OCHA (2020b), "United Nations Office for the Coordination of Humanitarian Affairs." Yemen Situation Report. United Nations Office for the Coordination of Humanitarian Affairs, September 2020. Available online: https://reliefweb.int/report/yemen/yemen-situation-report-7-oct-2020-enar (accessed October 1, 2020).

Pathways for Prosperity Commission (2018), *Charting Pathways for Inclusive Growth: From Paralysis to Preparation*. Oxford. Available online https://pathwayscommission.bsg.ox.ac.uk/sites/default/files/2018-11/inclusive-growth-report.pdf (accessed January 28, 2020).

Rogers, J. (2019), *Local Governance in Yemen: Theory, Practice, and Future Options*, Berghof Foundation, Berlin. Available online: https://www.berghof-foundation.org/fileadmin/redaktion/Publications/Other_Resources/Berghof_Foundation_Yemen_locgov_Paper02LocalGovernance_WEB.pdf (accessed 28 January, 2020).

Salisbury, P. (2019), *Yemen: Stemming the Rise of a Chaos State*. London: Chatham House.

Sanaa Center Economic Unit (2020), *Yemen Economic Bulletin: Widening Exchange Rate Disparity Between New and Old Banknotes*, Sanaa Center for Strategic Studies, Saana, July/August. Available online: https://sanaacenter.org/publications/analysis/11562 (accessed 1 October 2020).

Small and Micro Enterprise Promotion Service (2020), *Yemen Business Climate Survey Report, 2020*. Sana´a, 2020. Available online: https://smeps.org.ye/testnewweb/upfiles/posts/SMEPS_File_17-12-2020-8842.pdf (accessed January 28, 2020).

Sofan, S. (2019), *Yemen - Bringing Back Business Project: Risky Business – Impact of Conflict on Private Enterprises* (English). Washington, 2019. Available online: http://documents.worldbank.org/curated/en/205781562185537178/Yemen-Bringing-Back-Business-Project-Risky-Business-Impact-of-Conflict-on-Private-Enterprises (accessed January 28, 2020).

UNDP (2019), *Human Development Report, 2019: Inequalities in Human Development in the 21st Century*. New York. Available online: http://hdr.undp.org/sites/all/themes/hdr_theme/country-notes/YEM.pdf (accessed 29 January 2020).

UNDP and Small and Micro Enterprise Promotion Service (2015), *Rapid Business Survey: Impact of the Yemen Crisis on Private Sector*. November 2015. Available online: https://www.ye.undp.org/content/yemen/en/home/library/crisis_prevention_and_recovery/undp-smeps-rapid-business-survey.html (accessed September 3, 2019).

UNHCR (2018), *Situation of Human Rights in Yemen, including Violations and Abuses since September 2014*. Geneva. Available online: https://www.ohchr.org/EN/NewsEvents/Pages/DisplayNews.aspx?NewsID=23479&LangID=E (accessed September 3, 2019).

USAID (2009), *A Guide to Economic Growth in Post-conflict Countries*. Washington, January, p. 1. Available online: https://pdf.usaid.gov/pdf_docs/PNADO408.pdf (accessed January 28, 2020).

WFP (2020), "World Food Programme's Vulnerability Analysis and Mapping unit." *Yemen Economic Explorer*. Available online https://dataviz.vam.wfp.org/economic_explorer/ prices?adm0=269 (accessed October 1, 2020).

World Bank (2018a). *Yemen Dynamic Damage and Needs Assessment – Phase III*. (May 2018a). Internal document (accessed September 3, 2019).

World Bank (2018b). *Improving Food Availability and Access for Rural Households in Yemen and Djibouti*. Washington. Available online: documents.worldbank.org/curated /en/181081539873944469/pdf/Summary-slides-on-food-availability-and-access-for -rural-households-in-Yemen-and-Djibouti.pdf (accessed January 28, 2020).

World Bank (2018c), Economic Monitoring Brief, Fall 2018. Washington. Available online: http://documents1.worldbank.org/curated/en/508301539801659212/pdf/130967 -REVISED-BRI-PUBLIC-Disclosed-10-19-2018.pdf (accessed January 28, 2020).

World Bank (2019a), *Yemen's Economic Update – April 2019*. Washington. Available online: http://pubdocs.worldbank.org/en/365711553672401737/Yemen-MEU-April -2019-Eng.pdf (accessed September 23, 2019).

World Bank (2019b), *World Governance Indicators*. Washington. Available online: http:// info.worldbank.org/governance/wgi/index.aspx#reports (accessed January 28, 2020).

World Bank (2019c), *GDP per capita growth in Yemen*. Washington. Available online: https://data.worldbank.org/indicator/NY.GDP.PCAP.KD.ZG?locations=YE (accessed September 23, 2019).

World Bank (2020), *Poverty Data on Yemen*. Washington. Available online: https://data .worldbank.org/topic/poverty?locations=YE (accessed September 23, 2019).

Yemen Central Statistical Organization (2016), *Gross Domestic Product estimates, 2000– 2014*. Sana´a. Available online: http://www.cso-yemen.com/content.php?lng=arabic &id=683 (accessed September 23, 2019).

Chapter 8

THE ROLE OF THE INTERNATIONAL COMMUNITY AND THE GCC COUNTRIES IN THE ECONOMIC DEVELOPMENT OF YEMEN

Amat Alsoswa

In this chapter I discuss the future role of external economic cooperation and support in Yemen, taking into account the achievements, failures, and obstacles encountered in the period leading up to the current war and the resulting humanitarian crisis. Effective means and tools will be required to develop economic cooperation between Yemen and the donors who have pledged to help rebuild the country. There are many challenges, including limited government capacity to absorb donor pledges, the lack of qualified officials at high levels, and the complex procedures and excessive bureaucracy that accompany the implementation of donor-funded projects. The way forward has many obstacles due to the prolonged civil conflict and reflective of the vast humanitarian crisis. Ultimately, Yemen must restore its security and stability in a way that remains true to the aspirations of the Yemeni people while simultaneously fostering effective regional and international cooperation for reconstruction and good relations with its neighbors in the future.

The major priority is rebuilding national institutions that are able to mediate between private, public, and informal sectors as well as addressing the diverse needs of women, men, and children. This can succeed only with concentrated local effort to foster a sense of shared national identity that can take the country forward. The skills of Yemeni men and women are valuable for all phases of reconstruction. They are well aware of the potential impacts of new infrastructure on their work and communities. For example, will a new road cut off their water supply, or make it more difficult to access their agricultural fields? How will it impact access to schools or health centers? Will a thoroughfare too close to villages impede their mobility and freedom to frequent local markets, or will it improve their access to employment opportunities? Will planned infrastructure construction require displacement and resettlement? If so, will women and men be fairly compensated for lost land and property, or only men?

Yemeni citizens currently on the ground can assess needs, distribute supplies, and monitor the effectiveness of interventions. They can teach, work in health care, and apply their marketable skills. It is important to address the fact that donors are often excited and motivated at the beginning of the post-conflict period and pledge high amounts of aid funding. However, state capacity at such a point is almost always very weak and unable to absorb the assistance efficiently. As state capacity becomes stronger over the years, the donors tend to lose interest and funding drops. Without dealing with these contradicting trends the mistakes of the past will be repeated. Thus, nation building, if it is to succeed, will require the concerted efforts of women and men from the diverse sectors of the Yemeni population. If adequate institutional mechanisms to deliver aid on the ground are absent in Yemen, even the best designed plans will have little value.

Far too often the potential roles of women and marginalized groups for designing and implementing policies are ignored and they are only treated as victims. Throughout the country's long history Yemeni women have made major contributions to informal labor, especially in agriculture and livestock raising, yet donors and foreign agencies have consistently failed to utilize their assistance and empower them in the overall development process. The recent conflict has created several million IDPs; many are women who have lost their husbands. There has also been a continual stream of refugees crossing over from the African coast. The range of skills possessed by IDPs and refugees in host communities or in camps can also be utilized during and after the conflict. Their participation in planning, implementation, and monitoring would not only reduce overhead costs but also enhance the agency of beneficiaries and reduce aid-dependence.

The Role of Foreign Aid in Supporting Development in Yemen

The earliest international support for Yemen's north dates to the period after the Second World War, with assistance from both sides of the Cold War. In South Arabia efforts by the British focused on the strategic port of Aden, which in the 1950s was one of the busiest in the world. After the revolution of 1962, development arrived slowly to Yemen's north, due to a civil war that lasted until 1968. Throughout the 1970s and 1980s, international aid poured into Yemen from both bilateral and multilateral donors. Agriculture was a priority for the state throughout this period, with several small dams built along the major wadis (valleys) in the coastal Tihama region. A new network of roads was initiated by the United States in the early 1970s and expanded by China in the 1980s (El Mallakh, 2014). From the start, all areas of development needed support, particularly for education, health care, legal institutions, urban planning, electricity, sewage, and industry. However, there was little regulation of development activities. This was especially true in the water sector, where the drilling of tube wells led to drastic reductions in the water table and the creation of an environmental crisis with devastating consequences for present and future Yemeni generations (Ward, 2014).

Kuwait has been a generous donor to Yemen since the early 1970s, establishing Sana´a University and building agricultural facilities, roads, schools, hospitals, and government offices in the north and the south. Loans granted by Kuwait for north and south Yemen between 1968 and 1989 amounted to a total of 91 million

Kuwaiti dinars. Saudi Arabia provided 300 million dollars of aid from 1969 to 1987, at least half of which was granted directly to the government budget (Smith and Poole, 2011). The United Arab Emirates (UAE) has also been a substantial donor to Yemen over the years. In 2009, the UAE gave Yemen 134 million dollars in aid, which amounted to 32 percent of total government contributions to Yemen that year. These countries thus have a long experience of development spending in Yemen and will be expected to provide the main part of international assistance in the future. The need for workers in the oil fields in Saudi Arabia and the Gulf in the 1970s led to large numbers of Yemeni labor migrants to the Gulf, and their resulting remittances financed much of the local development in Yemen. These remittances were immediately put to use in rural areas for local development that the government was not able to provide. The boom in housing construction created jobs at home, but the influx of new wealth also increased the demand for the cash crop *qat* and a rapid inflation in the traditional bride wealth, which had risen to about YER50,000 ($12,000 at 1970's exchange rates) in the late 1970s (Varisco and Adra 1984:142). The full cost of a wedding could almost double that figure. Remittance recipients created the cooperative Local Development Associations that the government eventually took over (Cohen, Hébert, Lewis and Swanson, 1981).

In 1990 Yemen, which held the Presidency of the United Nations Security Council as a non-permanent member, voiced its opposition to the intervention of foreign powers in Iraq in response to Saddam's invasion of Kuwait. Yemen's refusal to support the intervention resulted in the suspension of aid from both the United States and the Gulf Cooperation Council (GCC) (Carapico, 1998). Yemeni workers were expelled from the Gulf, causing the GDP per capita in Yemen to shrink from $686 to $261 between 1990 and 1996, which had a devastating effect on the economy (al-Mutawakel, 2007). The forced return of an estimated 800,000–1,000,000 Yemeni workers from Saudi Arabia and the Gulf States to Yemen deprived thousands of families of critical remittances, swelling the labor force and creating an unemployment crisis. GCC, US, and European aid to Yemen remained suspended until 1994, when it was resumed following the short civil war that ousted Vice President al-Beidh.

While there have been limited development gains, this has been hindered in both the former YAR and PDRY, as well as the ROY after unification, by chronic domestic volatility and weak government institutions. After the bombing of the USS Cole in Aden's harbor in 2000, Yemen became associated with al-Qaeda and a front line in the United States' War on Terror, as US drones targeted terrorists from the skies above Yemeni territory. In 2004, the northern city of Sa´ada and surrounding areas were devastated by a series of six wars between the government and the Huthis, a Zaydi-Shi´a revivalist armed movement (Brandt 2017). The eventual removal of President Ali Abdullah Saleh during the Arab Spring uprising and the Huthi takeover of the capital in 2014 led to the Saudi-led intervention in 2015 (Lackner 2018). The resulting civil war has killed thousands and created a humanitarian crisis in the country. As a result of this cumulative damage to essential infrastructure, previous developmental gains have been reversed throughout Yemen.

For more than six decades, international support for Yemen developed through bilateral relations and the multilateral and bilateral contributions of the GCC states, the European Union, United Nations organizations, the United States, and regional and international financial institutions and banks. This assistance has been used to support the public budget and the national currency. In addition, infrastructure including factories, main roads, bridges, airports, hospitals, public and technical education institutions, public health and water development projects, as well as sanitation facilities, were externally funded. One of the major areas for development has been agriculture, despite unsustainable results. Although Yemen remains primarily an agricultural economy, production has declined as the population has increased (Varisco, 2018). Yemen has also received assistance and loans to strengthen and develop security and military institutions to protect the ruling regime and combat terrorism. The success of state-strengthening projects has been limited due to a long and disturbing history of corruption among public officials. Most Yemenis undoubtedly feel as though very little development has reached them personally, especially in recent years. Without gaining public confidence in the rebuilding process, there is no guarantee for future security and improvement of people's lives.

The need for humanitarian assistance predates the current crisis. In the 1980s, an earthquake caused major damage in the Dhamar region, and several development agencies provided emergency relief. Periodic floods, especially in the Hadhramaut valley, have also overwhelmed the ability of the government to provide support. The 1991 civil war in Somalia resulted in over a million refugees entering Yemen. In 2018 alone it is estimated that more than 160,000 individuals arrived in Yemen, mostly from Ethiopia. Currently, Yemen has almost 280,000 refugees, many of whom are supported through aid provided by the UN High Commissioner for Refugees. Internal displacement has also been a major issue since the beginning of the current conflict. As of March 2019, over 3.5 million Internally Displaced Persons (IDPs) were registered in Yemen (UNHCR, 2019).

The new Yemen will have to deal with some major endemic problems. Post-Saleh the donors faced difficulties in dealing with their Yemeni counterparts due to insecurity throughout Yemen. Contributing factors were the absence of vision in the government, competition between ministries to attract foreign aid, the lack of competent cadres of professionals, poor management in the government apparatus, and poor coordination between the central and local authorities. Compounding the problem, the Yemeni government was unable to provide its contributions to the budgets of some of the joint projects. Principles of transparency and effectiveness were compromised by delays in reform of the civil service system and the failure to implement an efficient and reliable national identification system. On the part of the Yemeni government there was corruption, a lack of accountability of officials in default, and insufficient transparency in the recruitment and use of donor funds. Yemen also faced difficulties in convincing donors to align their support to the country's perceived development priorities, commit to cash donor pledges on agreed-upon dates, facilitate allocation procedures and sign financing agreements (Executive Bureau, 2014).

Why Did the Development Experiment Fail in Yemen?

There is never a single cause of failure in the design and implementation of the wide range of development programs needed by a developing country. Rather than starting from the early development scenarios, it is best to begin with the failures that precipitated the current political and economic crisis. The recent efforts at economic reform and structural adjustment took place under an internal situation that, according to Sheila Carapico (2007), was "an inflamed mixture of bad governance and economic stagnation." Poor governance had plagued the YAR from its creation, with military coups driving the succession of rulers. Even then, the legitimacy of the ruling regimes declined because of their strong tendencies to monopolize power in Yemen within specific tribal or regional groups, as well as within established parties. Although the political rhetoric addressed democracy, power never left the hands of the military. Consequently, a strong administrative structure did not evolve. This often led to a collective absence of rational decision-making that would have benefited the entire country.

The dominance of the presidency as an institution came at the expense of the legislative and executive authorities. The security and military sectors, which were more essential to regime preservation than the country's general development, were prioritized by both the Yemeni government and its Western partners, especially as the War on Terrorism evolved. Not surprisingly, there was corruption within and across governmental and military institutions, especially given the poor state of the economy. Appointments in government were more often based on personal and political loyalty or regional affiliation rather than competence and merit. Given the endemic nature of this corruption it will present a major challenge to any new Yemeni government.

The potential for economic growth in the YAR was limited from the start, and after the mid-1980s it relied heavily on newly discovered oil wealth. Due to the scarcity of private- sector jobs, the most promising employment opportunities have been limited to the security, military, and administrative institutions of the government. Employment policies, however, have been neither open nor transparent, leading to an over-abundance of staff in these institutions that quickly became a burden on the national budget. Between 1990, when unification created the Republic of Yemen (ROY), and 2000, the number of employees in the government's administrative system increased from 191,000 to 428,000 (Al-Shami, 2013). One of the endemic negative features of this overloaded system is the attendant creation of a "ghost" workforce that receive salaries for nonexistent jobs; and "double dippers" who receive wages from multiple authorities. The expansion of the government payroll must be reduced by working with the private sector, especially in the vital sectors of agriculture, fishery, and reconstruction, including informal labor as partners in revitalizing the economy.

During the current conflict many young people and those who had to earn their living after losing their jobs joined the military and militia groups for the salary. A major question haunting the future of Yemeni labor is the willingness of GCC countries to absorb a higher number of Yemeni migrant workers and to make some exceptions in the policies to localize the vast majority of jobs traditionally occupied by Yemenis. The post-Covid realities in Yemen and its neighborhood should have room for Yemeni migrant workers to receive remittances from GCC countries to Yemen, a lifeline to households and to the economy. There must be no return to the huge level of military spending, which doubled after the achievement of Yemeni unity, and was not subject to any form of accountability and monitoring. This denied Yemeni society the opportunity to use these financial and labor resources in the essential development. In 1990 Yemen's military budget was $2.257 billion, decreasing to $1.511 billion in 1996 but rising to $3.439 billion in 2009 (SIPRI, 2019). In 2006 defense spending accounted for 40 percent of Yemen's budget (Library of Congress, 2008:2). The United States military aid to Yemen after the rise of al-Qaeda in Yemen was $176 million in 2010, but much of this was used by President Saleh to expand his personal security forces and weaponry, reducing the effectiveness of this counterterrorism policy in the eyes of the US Government. More funds were spent for Yemen to acquire military aircraft, so the full amount of aid exceeded official statistics. The money spent on military weapons could be spent on creating jobs that would reintegrate the many combatants, formal and informal, into the rebuilding process and boosting future economic growth.

There must also be no return to the way that for many years the military profited from the import of basic commodities. For instance, the Yemeni Economic Corporation (YECO) was established to provide army personnel with economic commodities. In 1979, the army became the sole importer of basic goods such as wheat, sugar, rice, meat, and clothes for non-military staff. Thus, the army not only competed with the private sector, but also almost monopolized large businesses, mainly due to its exemption from taxes (Al-Istithmar net, 2007). YECO, representing its military stakeholders, confiscated many of the assets and former state-owned enterprises seized by Saleh in the 1994 war (Phillips 2011:110). By 2017 YECO had 7,000 employees.

It is vital to note that reform plans that were formulated by donors and external players had limited impact because they were mainly piecemeal and failed to address the dire need for systemic comprehensive reform. In order to be successful, reforms in any society require farsighted political, economic, and social visions and a social contract that establishes a system based on respect for the constitution, law and order, the regular peaceful transfer of power through ballot boxes, equal citizenship, broadening political participation, protecting the rights and culture of local communities, and clarifying the general foundations of political, economic, and cultural reform. Admittedly, this is a tall order, especially for a country that is currently undergoing such a major humanitarian disaster, but it is important to learn from the failures of the past in order to pursue a way forward.

A major cause of the crisis in Yemen is the population boom, which began in the 1970s. In 1962 there were an estimated 4.3 million people in the former Imamate and an additional 910,000 in Aden and the Hadhramaut region (Tarsisi, 1962:210). In 1973, the census of the PDRY noted a population of 1.6 million. In 1990 at the point of unification, Yemen's population had reached twelve million and in 2019 it was estimated to be above twenty-nine million. Some estimates suggest that by the year 2050, the population of Yemen could reach forty-seven million. Several factors have led to the rapid population increase. Although Yemeni families traditionally have many children, limited access to medicine and health care as well as insufficient hygiene led to high infant mortality rates in the past. In 1979 the infant mortality rate of the Yemen Arab Republic was estimated at 161.5/1,000 with an overall under-five mortality rate of 236.5, one of the highest in the world at that time (Chidambaram et al., 1985:18). According to World Bank figures, the infant mortality rate in the newly formed Yemen Arab Republic was 267.5/1000, decreasing to 179.6/1,000 at the time of the first official census, 88.5/1,000 at unification in 1990 and estimated at about 43.2/1,000 in 2010 (Federal Reserve Economic Data, 2018). It is not entirely clear how the current crisis is affecting this rate, but in May 2019, Save the Children reported that as many as two and a half million pregnant or breastfeeding women in Yemen "are in urgent need of nutrition and counseling services to treat or prevent malnutrition" (ReliefWeb, 2019b). UNICEF reports that two million Yemeni children under the age of five are suffering from acute malnutrition (ReliefWeb, 2019a). By the end of 2018, it was estimated that as many as 85,000 Yemeni children under five years had died from extreme hunger or disease since 2015, the start of the war. It is difficult to assess the current population growth, although it is estimated by the UN that the current fertility rate for Yemen in 2020 is 3.673 births per woman, a 2.18 percent decline from 2019 (Macrotrends 2020).

The 1970s population boom coincided with massive migration from the countryside to the cities, coupled with the later return in 1990 of 800,000–1,000,000 Yemeni workers from Saudi Arabia and the Gulf. Under the influence of globalization, consumption of imported items increased dramatically even as import rates for food and luxury items exceeded domestic financial capacities. Yemen became increasingly reliant on imported food as productive agricultural production was unable to meet demand and continued to suffer from the water crisis. Additionally, the government policy of subsidizing oil derivatives and basic consumer goods such as wheat, rice, and sugar contributed to widening the budget deficit and depleted a large part of its foreign exchange resources. When the government took the unpopular but necessary decision to abolish this support, it was unable to assist the people who could no longer afford these items.

By the end of the first decade of this century, the internal situation reached a high degree of crisis and led to the youth revolution (Arab Spring) on February 11, 2011, which demanded the overthrow of the regime of President Saleh. Yemeni elites of various ideological groups were unable to read the public reaction correctly and remained under the influence of a fragmented military establishment that legitimized the use of violence to settle disputes with rivals and adversaries within the party or group. Such militarization fuels the continuation of contemporary civil and sectarian strife. In this process, national, religious, and humanitarian values continue to be sacrificed. However, given the historical focus in Yemen on mediation and reconciliation, peace building can be attained.

Developing Yemen's Future

As one of the poorest countries in the world prewar, now in the midst of a crippling, six year-long humanitarian crisis, Yemen will require significant development aid and peaceful relations with its neighbors on the Arabian Peninsula and the international community in order to rebuild. Before the conflict that began in 2015, Yemen was one of the neediest countries in the world, ranking 153 on the UN Human Development Index (HDI) in 1990. Today, Yemen is ranked at 179 out of 189 countries on this index (UNDP, 2020). At the time of writing, Yemen is considered the worst man-made humanitarian crisis in the world, with hundreds of thousands killed and many more maimed or wounded. The massive scale of the destruction of infrastructure and businesses has led to inadequate access to potable water, the threat of famine, and an outbreak of over one million cholera cases. Were the war to end today, these development needs would be unprecedented in Yemen's long history. A recent study commissioned by UNDP suggests that the conflict has already set back human development in Yemen by some twenty-one years (Moyer et al., 2019:6). If the war lasts until 2022 the setback for development would be twenty-six years, forty years if it persists until 2030. While it is impossible to predict the future, it is obvious that several decades of development gains have been almost totally erased.

Yemen's Ministry of Planning and International Cooperation has offered three scenarios for the future of development (Relief Web, 2019c). The first was optimistic in the event of a comprehensive political settlement during 2020. For this to be realized, ongoing negotiations would have to have taken successful steps to build political and economic confidence on all sides. The second possibility assumed the continuation of the war at a sporadic pace and slow consultations during 2019 and 2020. The third, most pessimistic scenario, envisioned a deadlock in the negotiations for peaceful resolution of the war and the expansion of the military conflict. Each of these scenarios assumed that Yemen will remain united, although given what has been happening on the ground, the preservation of the union between north and south is looking less achievable. Given the reality created by the war and the multiple rivals, Yemen's post-war options remain open to two *de facto* states or a continued stalemate as well as eventual reunification. Yemen's non-state actors will play a pivotal role in any future state development (Varisco 2019b: 159).

A future for Yemen dictated from the top down with undue influence by external actors is flawed from the start and bound to fail. Despite their ultimate failure in improving life in Yemen, the protests that led to the fall of President Saleh in 2011 highlight the desire of Yemeni citizens to define their own future. The National Dialogue Conference (NDC), lasting about a year in 2013/2014, brought together most of Yemen's political parties and factions and provided some 1,200 specific proposals for Yemen's future. These remain a useful starting point for future donor support of Yemen. Unfortunately, the momentum of the NDC outcome was compromised by the later addition of a proposal to create six new federal regions in Yemen without full consultation with the parties involved. This was rejected by multiple groups, such as the southern separatists and the Huthis who used this decision to exploit the Yemeni public's reaction and the government's decision to lift its subsidies (as required by the IMF) as a pretext to overthrow the government in Sana'a. Despite its flaws, Yemen is the only democracy experiment in the Arabian Peninsula, and there is little desire among Yemen's people to return to corrupt authoritarian rule or allow Yemen's foreign policy to be determined by parties outside of Yemen (Salisbury, 2018).

The critical role of women is often overlooked in the analysis of the conflict in Yemen. Yemeni women have participated in the political process, government offices, civil society, and local mediation and they should take part in the economic recovery and post- conflict reconstruction. Women—and youth—have been excluded from political decision-making for too long. Although the mandated quota of 30 percent women members for the NDC was only partially achieved, Yemeni women played an important role in the process. The major achievements of the female members included guaranteeing equality under the law through the new draft constitution and a ban on discrimination on the basis of gender. Major issues such as protection against child marriage, trafficking, domestic violence, and genital mutilation were also addressed. Despite facing many challenges during the current conflict, Yemeni women have been a crucial element in maintaining the resilience of the society during the humanitarian crisis.

Only when a suitable settlement is reached will it be possible to talk about economic recovery and create security and political stability in the various regions of Yemen. Some estimates indicate that during the first year alone, the development aid needed will be as high as $14 billion (Bayoumy, 2016). An ever-present danger is that following the cessation of hostilities, regional powers with a continuing interest in influencing Yemen's affairs will attach unwanted strings to development aid. Another major problem will be Yemen's ability to absorb the vast amount of development aid and coordinate its effective use in all sectors. Following the GCC-sponsored agreement to secure Saleh's peaceful departure, the government of Yemen received $7.9 billion to fund Yemen's Transitional Program for Stability and Development (TPSD) in the Riyadh and New York Conferences of September 2012. Moreover, additional pledges and support of $3.1 billion were given to Yemen in 2013 and 2014. US humanitarian aid pledged to Yemen in the fiscal year of 2018/19 reached almost $721 million (USAID, 2019). An Executive Bureau was set up in November 2013 to implement a mutual accountability framework between Yemen and the donors structured around the concepts of good governance (Executive Bureau, 2014). Prior to the military conflict in 2015, there was no national aid policy in place, nor specific national indicators established for measuring aid effectiveness and its impact in accordance with the Paris Declaration on Aid Effectiveness (2005). Donors also had different rules for the disbursement of funds, implementation of projects, and evaluation with little information shared between them. The relevant ministries in Yemen were not able to effectively implement and monitor the aid programs.

After 2015, most aid to the areas controlled by the Huthis, that is, the territory representing the majority of Yemen's population, was stopped, while the GCC members of the coalition provided some development assistance to areas under the control of the Internationally Recognized Government of Yemen. Among the regional bodies that have overseen support for Yemen since 2015 are the Saudi Development and Reconstruction Program for Yemen, the King Salman Center for Comprehensive Humanitarian Relief, and the UAE, especially the UAE's Red Crescent Society. Western donors, such as the United States, the European Union and the United Kingdom, have also given humanitarian relief aid. However, by June 2020, pledged donor aid for Yemen's crisis fell far short of what was needed, prompting one UN official to ask if the world was willing to watch Yemen "fall off the cliff" (Yee 2020). Unfortunately, throughout the conflict much of the humanitarian aid has not reached those who desperately need it (Michael 2018). All sides have politicized aid delivery, with parts of Yemen not receiving any needed aid.

After Yemen was labeled the worst humanitarian crisis in the world, it was hit by the COVID-19 pandemic. This follows the worst cholera outbreak in the world. Yemen's health system was totally broken with many hospitals and clinics destroyed, and lacking suppliers and qualified doctors and nurses. Even Médecins sans Frontières had recently been forced to close some of its field clinics due to the fighting. A study at the Imperial College in London estimated that COVID-19 could affect half of Yemen's population and kill an estimated 30,000–40,000 Yemenis (Stone 2020). Yemen's crisis has continued to deteriorate, with few signs of relief in the near future.

Priorities for Yemen's Future Development

After six years of war, the extent of the humanitarian disaster on all levels will require literally rebuilding Yemen from the bottom up. Establishing priorities when there are so many important needs will not be easy. There are obviously significant short-term needs, but in the long run no sustainable development can occur without a return to stability, with the protection of civilians and the ability for aid to be distributed efficiently, transparently and fairly to those in need. The road to recovery will be difficult, especially given the regional political context. This is due not only to the level of destruction but also to the trauma that such partisan fighting and personal tragedies bring. Reconciling differences will not be easy to achieve after the prolonged power struggles and sectarian conflict, fueled by external players, that began prior to the war. However, Yemenis in the north came together in the late 1960s after a long civil war, so there is a precedent for overcoming political and sectarian differences.

Throughout Yemen's long history, stretching back several millennia, there has never been a strong central state in total control of the area now encompassed by the Republic of Yemen. Historically, Yemen has a long tradition of negotiating peace agreements between tribes and with other regional powers. The skills of Yemenis in mediation at all levels provide the strongest argument for eventual reconciliation between the many factions involved in and created by the conflict

(Adra 2011). It is important that the international community, including Yemen's neighbors on the peninsula, build on the mediation skills of Yemenis rather than trying to dictate as outsiders. This will not only ensure more acceptance of donor assistance, but also empower Yemeni citizens to determine their own destiny.

Important lessons from past development policies in Yemen, as documented in this chapter, provide guidance on the best way to move forward in rebuilding Yemen. There are important critiques of past development in Yemen from the World Bank and other assessments (e.g., Boucek 2009, World Bank 2006). These need to be examined so that the same mistakes are not made, no matter what the nature of the future government. The experience of development groups currently working in the war zone, such as various UN agencies, Médecins sans Frontières, the Yemen Red Crescent Society, and local community self-help groups, also provides a window on the ways to channel aid to the areas most badly hit by the conflict.

The long-term development of Yemen requires thinking beyond its immediate needs, important as they are. It will be necessary to repair the great imbalance in the economic system, where certain individuals were able to amass large fortunes and land at the expense of others. Yemen has always had pockets of poverty, but throughout most of its history there were social safety nets. Even in the current crisis, there are numerous cases of local humanitarian assistance. In Sana´a a number of local restaurants have provided free food to those in need. "It is a crime to see hungry people and not help them. God commands us to help needy people," said one restaurant owner (al-Sakkaf, 2018).

As a result of the war, many government officials have not been paid for several years and the savings of many Yemeni families have been lost. Businesses and homes have been destroyed or damaged, and repair will often be too expensive for those affected. While the influx of foreign development aid is needed, it is not sufficient in itself to rebuild the country. Without viable sources of income for Yemeni citizens, foreign development assistance will simply be a band-aid to try and stop the bleeding from an open wound. Economic growth is essential, but the options are limited. Yemen at present does not have sufficient oil and gas resources to become a rentier state.

There will be no success without the creation of a governmental administration that is both efficient and fair to its citizens. Past corruption by government officials has created a sense among the population that government cannot be trusted. Economic reform must be a top priority to lift Yemen out of its historically entrenched poverty, exacerbated by the 2015 war. The process of rebuilding the economy requires reconstruction and rehabilitation of the damaged infrastructure, estimated at hundreds of billions of dollars (World Bank, 2017b). This high cost far exceeds the capabilities of Yemen and may not be fully supported by donor institutions and the international community. The renewed flow of financial assistance from the Arab Gulf countries and other donors will be needed to support reconstruction, but it is also important to renew opportunities for Yemeni workers in neighboring countries. This can take place at the same time as investment is made by GCC countries in assisting private-sector job growth within Yemen. All this must happen simultaneously with the resumption of critical health services, a response to human development needs in education, and building confidence among citizens. Other essential measures are the return of the many displaced persons to their home regions and, finally, providing monetary compensation for those severely impacted by the war (Henderson et al., 2017).

Economic revitalization cannot be accomplished without addressing the major environmental crisis facing Yemen, one that predates the current conflict. Yemen's population has far outstripped the available water supply resulting in a drastic decline in water tables. Desalination is too expensive, at least in the near future, to remedy the problem. The lack of potable water is especially acute in the two major cities of Sana'a and Ta'izz, where many citizens are forced to depend on trucked-in water due to the inadequacy of public water supply. While Yemen's water crisis resulting from the excess pumping of groundwater was known in the late 1970s, there was no single authority to assume a leadership position on this and other critical environmental issues. Regulation of well-drilling, rules for irrigation, hydrological research on groundwater availability, and urban water supply were scattered across different ministries and/or authorities. The fact that much of the irrigation water from tube wells has been used for the cash crop *qat* (*Catha edulis*) rather than food crops contributes to the inability of Yemen to best utilize the fertile land that has sustained it for centuries (Mounassar 2014). Given that Yemen's population is still at least two-thirds rural, the role of sustainable agricultural production must be pursued as a way to both reduce dependence on imported food and create employment in production and marketing. While irrigation from groundwater cannot be expanded, dry farming and other measures can be effective methods to increase production in the fertile areas of the country (Varisco, 2018).

Concluding Remarks

At the time of writing it is difficult to predict when the conflict will end and what new priorities for reconciliation and rebuilding might arise. The most urgent need is for an end to the fighting and the blockade that make life so hard for the bulk of Yemen's population. The warring parties must deal seriously with the peace negotiations rather than using the process to build up their next offensive. No single party should be allowed to obstruct or stall the implementation of signed agreements. There must be no resort to military escalation in any location, nor any attack by any armed group on residential and civil sites including businesses, factories, agricultural structures, roads, and bridges. Only with the cessation of violence can the desperately needed flow of goods and services be facilitated safely to and from Yemen, including foodstuffs, medicines, agricultural materials, and construction and industrial supplies.

When an agreement is reached there are many things that will need to be done simultaneously. First is the immediate repair and opening of the major civilian airports and main ports such as Sana'a, Hodeida, Ta'izz, and Riyan (Mukalla) so that Yemeni citizens can travel freely to and from their country. This is also vital to restoring the import and export of commodities and the expected arrival of assistance from donors. At the same time, the freedom of movement of Yemeni citizens inside and outside Yemen must be returned, with assistance provided to Internally Displaced Persons (IPDs) in returning and rebuilding their homes. Some cities in Yemen, especially Sa´ada and, Ta´izz will require major rebuilding due to the level of destruction from the bombing and internal fighting. Restoring roads and bridges will also require high priority on the development agenda.

The economic burden on Yemen's citizens has been devastating in all parts of the country. Although a few individuals have profited from the wartime economy, most people have suffered major losses and have no savings left. Government employees, and civil and military personnel need to be paid, no matter where they are working, and many should be compensated for past unpaid work. This will help circulate money in the economy and preserve the humanity and dignity of the recipients. One of the hardest economic problems to address will be that of reparations for illegitimate land grabbing, which has plagued Yemen for almost three decades. Southern Yemenis have vociferously complained for many years about the illegal appropriation of land and at times brutal treatment they received from the government of Saleh after the 1994 civil war. During his period in office many rural Yemenis throughout Yemen lost their land due to poverty and corrupt actions by some members of the elite and military. The elites can no longer be allowed to hold a monopoly over the financial market and land ownership— though the difficulties of achieving this should not be underestimated.

The influx of development assistance will have a direct impact on the Yemeni riyal. Between 2015 and 2018, the riyal lost 75 percent of its value (Joplin 2018). In order for Yemeni citizens to regain trust in their own currency there must be a halt to illegal speculation and manipulation of currency prices. Until oil and gas revenues start to flow again—limited as these are—the government will have to depend on direct foreign aid and loans. Restoring Yemen's oil and gas production will be a difficult task after the current crisis in which only a trickle has been produced and insecurity has prevented proper maintenance of the system (Wang 2020). The collapse of the country's tax system has further limited the resources available to the government. The freedom of internal and external trade within the private sector needs to be guaranteed to prevent monopoly and manipulation of the prices of oil derivatives and other commodities (World Bank, 2017a).

Economic development cannot be achieved simply through donor assistance and revitalization of government revenues. The future of Yemen is necessarily the future of its people, who now number over twenty-nine million. In a real sense the future belongs to Yemen's youth, the dominant age group in the country. They need an educational system that will prepare them to act as rational citizens, preserve their health, and provide them with the needed skills for the workplace in Yemen and abroad. It is imperative that Yemen's women be brought into the peace-making process, given the importance of their participation in mediation and promoting peace in the past (Adra, 2013). Moreover, their role is pertinent to the economic growth of Yemen, as they make up more than half of the potential human capital. Development policy must not be solely from the top down, a major failure in the past, but involve the active participation of local communities and the thriving indigenous civil society. The rich knowledge they possess, honed by survival through a difficult time of conflict, is crucial to the reconstruction phase in Yemen. The skills and experience of many Yemenis living abroad, some of whom fled during the recent conflict, will be needed. The path forward is not easy, and certainly not assured, but the hopes of the vast majority of Yemeni citizens are for a free country where life can be lived peacefully, and war wounds can finally begin to heal.

References

Adra, N. (2011), *Tribal Mediation in Yemen and Its Implications to Development, AAS Working Papers in Social Anthropology*. Vienna: Austrian Academy of Sciences.

Adra, N. (2013), *Women and Peacebuilding in Yemen: Challenges and Opportunities*. Oslo: Norwegian Peacebuilding Resource Center, November 2013.

al-Isthmar Net. (2007), *Al-Mou'asasah al-iqtisadyiah al-yemeniah*. Available online: http://www.alestethmar.net/news.php?id=7188 (accessed May 23, 2019).

al-Mutawakel, Y. (2007), "The Republic of Yemen: The Economic Situation and the Manufacturing Sector," in K. Mahdi, A. Würth and H. Lackner (eds.), *Yemen into the 21st Century: Continuity and Change*. Ithaca, NY: Ithaca Press.

Bayoumy, Y. (2016), "Exclusive: *Civil War Costs Yemen $14 Billion in Damage and Economic Losses.*" *Reuters*. August 17. Available online: https://www.reuters.com/article /us-yemen-security-damages/exclusive-civil-war-costs-yemen-14-billion-in-damage -and-economic-losses-report-idUSKCN10R2B7 (accessed May 23, 2019).

Boucek, C. (2009), *Yemen: Avoiding a Downward Spiral*. Washington, DC: Carnegie Endowment for International Peace, Carnegie Papers, No. 102.

Brandt, M. (2017), *Tribes and Politics in Yemen: A History of the Houthi Conflict*. London: Hurst.

Carapico, S. (1998), *Civil Society in Yemen: The Political Economy of Activism in Modern Arabia*. Cambridge: Cambridge University Press.

Carapico, S. (2007), "No Quick Fix," in L. Binder (ed.), *Rebuilding Devastated Economies in the Middle East*. New York: Palgrave Macmillan.

Chidambaram, V., J. McDonald and M. Bracher (1985), "Infant and Child Mortality in the Developing World: Information from the World Fertility Survey," *International Family Planning Perspectives* 11 (1): 18.

Cohen, J., M. Hébert, D. Lewis, and J. Swanson (1981), "Development from Below: Local Development Associations in the Yemen Arab Republic," *World Development* 11–12 (11–12): 1039–61.

El Mallakh, R. (2014), *The Economic Development of the Yemen Arab Republic* (RLE Economy of Middle East). London: Routledge.

Executive Bureau (2014), "Status report: Mutual Accountability Framework (Pledgeds and Reforms)," *Executive Bureau for the Acceleration of Aid Absorption and Support for Policy Reforms*. December 20, 2014. Sana´a.

Federal Reserve Economic Data (2019), *Infant Mortality Rate for the Republic of Yemen*. September 27, 2018. Available online: https://fred.stlouisfed.org/series/ SPDYNIMRTINYEM (accessed May 22, 2019).

Henderson, D., et al. (2017), "Emerging from the Rubble: Rebuilding a Unified Yemen," in *Institute for the Study of Diplomacy*, 1–29, Georgetown University. Available online: https://georgetown.app.box.com/s/922dsp9yelnl5s9b4uk0bqfjb74qf60y (accessed 19, March 2021).

Joplin, T. (2018), "Yemen's Escalating Currency Collapse and the Slow Death of Its People." *Albawaba News*, October 3. Available online: https://www.albawaba.com/news/yemen%E2%80%99s-escalating-currency-collapse-and-slow-death-its-people-1194832 (accessed April 20, 2020).

Lackner, H. (2018), *Yemen in Crisis: Autocracy, Neo-Liberalism and the Disintegration of a State*. London: Saqi.

Library of Congress (2008), *Country Profile: Yemen*, p. 22. Available online: https://www.loc.gov/rr/frd/cs/profiles/Yemen.pdf (accessed April 20, 2020).

Macrotrends (2020). *Yemen Fertility Rate, 1950–2020*. Available online: https://www.macrotrends.net/countries/YEM/yemen/fertility-rate (accessed April 20, 2020).

Michael, M. (2018), "'The Poor Get Nothing': In Yemen Corruption Keeps Food and Aid from Reaching Those in Need." *Global News Canada*, December 31. Available online: https://globalnews.ca/news/4804380/yemen-corruption-famine-food/ (accessed April 20, 2020).

Mounassar, H. (2014), "Qat Cultivation Drains Yemen's Precious Groundwater." *PHYS. ORG*, May 14. Available online: https://phys.org/news/2014-05-qat-cultivation-yemen-precious-groundwater.html (accessed April 20, 2020).

Moyer, J. et al. (2019), *Assessing the Impact of War on Development in Yemen*. Sana´a: UNDP.

Phillips, S. (2011), "Al-Qaeda and the Struggle for Yemen," *Survival* 53: 95–122.

ReliefWeb (2019a), "Yemen: 2019 Humanitarian Needs Overview." February 14, Available online: https://www.humanitarianresponse.info/en/operations/yemen/document/yemen-2019-humanitarian-needs-overview-0 (accessed May 22, 2019).

ReliefWeb (2019b), *Conflict in Yemen: Devastating Toll on Pregnant Women and New Mums Becomes Clear as Malnutrition Admissions Soar – Yemen*. Available online: https://reliefweb.int/report/yemen/conflict-yemen-devastating-toll-pregnant-women-and-new-mums-becomes-clear-malnutrition (accessed May 22, 2019).

ReliefWeb (2019c), "Yemen 2018 Socio-Economic Update," Issue 40 – February 2019 [EN/AR] – Yemen. Available online: https://reliefweb.int/report/yemen/yemen-2018-socio-economic-update-issue-40-february-2019-enar (accessed May 23, 2019).

Salisbury, P. (2018), "Marshalling Order in Yemen: How Reconstruction Will Make or Break the Post-War Order." *The Politics of Post-Conflict Reconstruction*, 56. London: Chatham House.

SIPRI (2019), *SIPRI Military Expenditure Database*. Available online: https://www.sipri.org/databases/milex (accessed May 22, 2019).

Smith, K. and L. Poole (2011). *Yemen Aid Factsheet, 1995–2009: Trends in Overseas Development Assistance*. UK: Development Initiatives.

Stone, Richard (2020), "Yemen Was Facing the World's Worst Humanitarian Crisis. Then the Coronavirus Hit." *Science*, May 28. Available online: https://www.sciencemag.org/news/2020/05/yemen-was-facing-worlds-worst-humanitarian-crisis-then-coronavirus-hit (accessed 19 March, 2021).

Tarsisi, A. (1962), *al-Yaman wa-hadharat al-Arab ma'a dirasa jugrafiya kamila*. Beirut: Manshurat Dar Maktabat al-Hayat.

UNDP 2020, Human Development Report '*The Next Frontier, Human Development and the Anthropocene*', New York.

UNHCR (2019), *Yemen: UNHCR Operational Update*. Available online: https://reliefweb
.int/report/yemen/yemen-unhcr-operational-update-8-march-2019 (accessed May 21,
2019).

USAID (2019), *Yemen*. Available online: https://www.usaid.gov/crisis/yemen (accessed
May 22, 2019).

Varisco, D. (2018), "Agriculture in the Northern Highlands of Yemen: From Subsistence to
Cash Cropping," *Journal of Arabian Studies* 8/2: 171–92.

Varisco, D. (2019), "When the State Becomes a Non-State: Yemen between the Huthis,
Hirak and Al-Qaeda," in P. Sluglett and V. Kattan (eds.), *Violent Radical Movements
in the Arab World: The Ideology and Politics of Non-State Actors*, 137–60. London: I.B.
Tauris.

Varisco, D. and N. Adra (1984), "Affluence and the Concept of the Tribe in the Central
Highlands of the Yemen Arab Republic," in R. F. Salisbury and E. Tooker (eds.),
Affluence and Cultural Survival, 134–59. Washington DC: American Ethnological
Society.

Wang, Herman (2020), "Promising Signs for Yemen's Oil Industry, but Civil War Rages."
S&P Global, January 23. Available online: https://www.spglobal.com/platts/en/market
-insights/latest-news/natural-gas/012320-promising-signs-for-yemens-oil-industry
-but-civil-war-rages (accessed April 20, 2021).

Ward, C. (2014), *The Water Crisis in Yemen: Managing Extreme Water Scarcity in the
Middle East*. London: I.B. Tauris.

World Bank (2017a), *Yemen Policy Note 3: Private Sector Readiness to Contribute to
Reconstruction and Recovery in Yemen*. Washington DC. doi:10.1596/28591.

World Bank (2017b), *Working for the People of Yemen*. Washington DC. Available online:
https://projects.worldbank.org/en/projects-operations/project-detail/P161806
(accessed 19 March, 2021).

Yee, Vivian (2020), "Yemen Aid Falls Short, Threatening Food and Health Programs." *New
York Times*, June 2. Available online: https://www.nytimes.com/2020/06/02/world/
middleeast/yemen-saudi-united-nations-aid.html (accessed 19 March, 2021).

Chapter 9

THE FUTURE OF YEMENI AGRICULTURE AND WATER

Helen Lackner[1]

Introduction

Water is essential to life; therefore, its availability is relevant to 100 percent of Yemen's 29 million people, 70 percent of whom live in rural areas and more than 50 percent depend on agriculture, an essential component of the country's economy. An additional factor contributing to future difficulties is the country's continuing rapidly increasing population, only slightly slowed down by the war and desperate humanitarian situation. Thus, the future of Yemen and Yemenis is intimately linked to water availability for both basic human survival needs, and for agriculture including livestock husbandry. This chapter first examines the current situation and then presents the major constraints and issues which need to be addressed in coming years. It does not discuss the immediate impact of the war on the fundamental features of either of the two sectors.

Yemen's climate is arid: most of the country has less than 50mm rainfall per annum. Some highland areas have more than 250mm, and a few receive more than 800mm, hence this is where most of the population lives. Much rainfall is lost by evaporation: only 6 percent ends up in the spate flows amounting to about 2 billion m³ annually (Taher, T et al, 2012, p 1177). The country has six agro-ecological zones, roughly summarized as (1) the hot humid coastal plains of the Tihama on the Red Sea, (2) the temperate lower highlands forming a belt ranging from Sa´ada to Lawdar, (3) the upper highlands, (4) the Arabian Sea coast, (5) the internal plateau including Wadi Hadhramaut and much of Shabwah governorate, and (6) the desert. The range of crops is vast due to the very great variation in altitudes rising to over 2,200 meters above sea level (masl), water availability, soil quality, and rainfall patterns. The main cereal crops are sorghum and wheat followed by maize, millet and barley; fruit trees range from temperate apricots and apples to tropical mangoes and bananas, and mostly irrigated vegetables. Fodder crops for livestock are also extremely important, usually irrigated.

Regardless of the factors affecting the future, it is important to start with a brief state of affairs. The following is based on prewar data, largely because no new reliable data are available. In addition, readers should note that all figures, whether with respect to water or agriculture should be considered indicative of trends rather than absolute and correct statistical data: with respect to water, actual data are scarce while for agriculture, statistics have often been influenced by political agendas and there are plenty of mutually contradictory figures.

Basic Features of Yemen's Water

Yemen suffers from extreme water scarcity. Since the beginning of the century, Yemen has been using annually one third more water than its renewable supply: in 2010, extraction was 3.5 billion cubic meters (bcm) while renewable supply was 2.1 bcm, the 1.4 bcm shortfall met by water pumped up with modern technology (World Bank, 2014) from non-renewable fossil aquifers. The World Bank estimated in 2010 that the country's groundwater reserves are likely to be depleted by about 2040 (World Bank, 2010, p 21).

Per capita water availability has dropped steadily in past decades as known available resources have remained static, if not diminished while population has increased. In 2018 per capita availability was estimated at 95m^3, this is expected to drop to 55m^3 by 2031. The internationally recognized Falkenmark indicator suggests that there is absolute water scarcity if per capita water availability falls below 500m.^{3} That is more than five times current availability in Yemen! An estimated 90 percent of this water is used in agriculture.

The distribution of aquifers in the country presents major challenges: the western highlands from Saudi Arabia to near the Arabian Sea coast is where aquifers are shallower and most dependent on recharge from annual rainfall. The monsoon rains enable rain fed agriculture thanks to the beautiful and impressive terracing system built over centuries to retain both water and soils. This conjuncture of factors made life and agricultural production possible in the area that became known as "Arabia Felix" in antiquity, allowing the highest population densities in the peninsula for many centuries. Throughout the country prior to the introduction of pump irrigation, water could only be extracted for agriculture through shallow wells and existing technology limited extraction to what could be drawn by hand or with the assistance of draft animals; in many areas the only viable income generating activities were pastoralism and long-distance trade.

There are three main reasons for water scarcity: rapid population growth, averaging 3 percent per annum has increased demand thus reducing per capita water and land availability over generations to well-below self-sufficiency levels. Second, the introduction of diesel-operated pumps and deep-well drilling technology for irrigation has enabled extraction of water significantly above recharge levels, thus causing depletion of the aquifers. Third increasingly violent downpours have further reduced replenishment, as the loss of topsoil prevents absorption of flows, particularly where terraces have deteriorated due to lack of maintenance as people relied on other sources of income during the peak international migration period of last century.

In the 1970s and 1980s, almost all Yemeni families in the former Yemen Arab Republic (YAR) had at least one man working in Saudi Arabia where they both witnessed the use of deep wells and irrigation pumps and earned enough to invest in similar technology at home. They looked forward to improving their families living conditions and returning to enjoy the fruits of their years of hard labour. This strategy resulted in a rapid increase in crops requiring irrigation, whether vegetables, fruit trees or *qat*, thus ensuring short-term economic and financial benefits, but rapidly leading to a series of long-term problems, ranging from depletion of shallow aquifers to increased social differentiation. The latter was due to the fact that wealthier farmers could afford to dig deep wells which increased their irrigation (and income) potential while simultaneously reducing poorer farmers' access to irrigation water. The poorer farmers thus became worse off and were often reduced to selling their lands. The state did not regulate drilling, which was only controlled by customary rules that had no time to adapt to the implications of the new technologies on sustainability of the resource.

The situation in the then People's Democratic Republic of Yemen (PDRY) was different insofar as land management was under state control and drilling of wells only took place within the framework of state sponsored projects which had a greater concern for sustainability. Second, the proportion of migrants to Saudi Arabia was far lower, as citizens of the PDRY did not benefit from the favourable conditions of migration to Saudi Arabia afforded to YAR citizens. Moreover, smallholders were too poor to finance well drilling, though historically pump irrigation had started far earlier than in the north, during the period of British domination. Unregulated drilling, regardless of sustainability or social equity was introduced in the south immediately after unification in 1990, and was an additional factor worsening social tensions in that part of the country. Although significant numbers of landowners involved in wildcat drilling for irrigation were southern returnees from the GCC following the demise of the socialist system, some of them were northerners. This strengthened the perception among southerners of "northern colonialism."

The rise in well-irrigated surfaces in the past three decades has been impressive, increasing from 37,000 ha in the 1970s to more than 400,000 ha in the 2000s, which explains the worsening water crisis. During the same period, as irrigated areas increased by a factor of 15, rain fed agriculture declined by 30 percent (Closas A. and F. Molle 2016, p 76). Among the most striking cases is the situation in the Sana´a basin, which is both an agricultural area for high-value crops such as *qat* and grapes and the source of water for the country's rapidly growing capital city: extraction is estimated at five times recharge (World Bank 2010, p 21, Taher, T. et al 2012). At the current rates of extraction, it is likely that a number of aquifers will be depleted by 2025. In the south this concerns the most important spate irrigated agricultural areas of Wadis Tuban (Lahej Governorate) and Bana (Abyan governorate), while in the north, the most sensitive to this depletion is the Sa´ada aquifer, that is, the area where the Huthi political and military movement started. A further example is of fruit production in the Tihama: in "midstream wadi Zabid, [banana cultivation] increased from 20 ha in 1980 to 3,500 ha in 2000, . . . at the expense of sustainable use of groundwater resources as the number of drilling wells . . . increased by more than five times between 1987 and 2008, from about 2,421 to 12,339 wells" (al-Qubatee, W. et al 2017 p 811).

Impact of Climate Change

Climate change is not a remote and distant prospect in Yemen. It is already part of daily experience although its specific impact in coming decades in different parts of the country is unclear. "Unprecedented" catastrophic climate events have been taking place in recent years at a rate well above what might be expected. Starting in 2015 when two major cyclones hit Yemen within a week, the trend has continued since, with cyclones Sagar and Mekunu in 2018. Overall, the World Bank forecast of 2010 remains valid, with three main scenarios for Yemen, the most likely being "hot and dry" and "warm and wet." Regardless of which actually materializes, "Yemen will be getting warmer, most likely at a faster rate than the global average. . . . there will be more variability of rainfall patterns within years [and] there will probably be an increased frequency of intense rainfall events and therefore possibly an increased risk of floods" (World Bank, 2010, p 20). More recent studies have gone into greater details of likely developments focusing on the expected very different impacts in the six different agro-ecological zones.

Overall, temperatures in Yemen have increased by 1.8° centigrade in the past fifty years and there has been a decrease of 9 percent in total annual precipitation during this period (USAID, 2016, p 2),[2] the latter unevenly distributed to the detriment of the areas which have depended on rain fed agriculture. With a wide range of regional variations, forecast temperature rises average 2.3° with increased durations of heat waves (Kingdom of the Netherlands, 2019, p 4). The expected increase in rainfall and temperatures in the temperate highland zone will not reduce the country's dependence on imports of basic staples (rice, wheat, sugar, tea) regardless of any local increases in production. By contrast significant yield reductions are likely elsewhere, while desertification of existing agricultural land (currently at the annual rate of 3 percent) will persist or worsen. Unsurprisingly both these studies predict more numerous and grave disasters, including floods, land degradation, and destruction of infrastructure.

Although much of the impact of climate change is either not noticeable on a day-by-day basis (such as reduction of arable land, changes in overall rain fall patterns, and the like) or comes in the form of sudden extreme events (floods, cyclones), one feature which dominates daily life for all Yemenis is the water crisis which now affects all aspects of life. Villages have already been evacuated due to complete absence of water. As is all too often the case, the impact of climate change is expected to disproportionately affect the most vulnerable groups in the population, the rural poor and women. They are likely to suffer from increased exposure to its extreme weather events (droughts, floods, loss of agricultural land) and have insufficient financial and technical resources, to recover from climate disasters. A detailed analysis of the impact of climate change on a community in the Tihama provides details of all the different impacts of worsening water scarcity over decades, including desertification, reduced agricultural land and the resulting impoverishment forcing people to migrate (al-Qubatee W. et al, 2017).

The Agricultural Sector

Although agriculture, including livestock, only contributes about 20 percent of Yemen's GDP, it provides about 25 percent of the food consumed in the country and provides significant employment in areas with high concentrations of poverty (MOPIC, 2018), despite the fact that clearly food self-sufficiency is no longer a possibility for rural people.[3] Only about 3 percent of the country's land is suitable for agriculture, including pasture land. Of the 1.6 million ha of agricultural land, prior to the crisis, 405,000 or 25 percent is irrigated by wells, though the data make no distinction between shallow and deep wells, 255,000 or 16 percent by flood or spate irrigation and 105,000 or 7 percent by other means, including springs and dams.[4] Today rain fed crops cover between 50 and 60 percent of cultivated lands, depending on the year's rainfall.

Rain fed agriculture remains the main form of agriculture for smallholders in the mountainous western highlands extending to the southern mountains, that is, all the areas which benefit from sufficient monsoon rains. The main crops are cereals (sorghum, wheat, maize and millet), with traditionally small areas of fruits and vegetables in the best watered areas, as well as coffee and *qat* both of which grow best at altitudes ranging from 700 masl to 1,800 masl.

There are three main types of irrigation in Yemen: the main one is spate irrigation which also includes two models: the traditional model, with structures renewed on an annual basis, or after each major flow episode which usually damage the structures. These are maintained with the use of earth moving equipment, nowadays usually diesel-operated tractors. Modern systems were introduced initially by the British in the 1940s in the cotton growing schemes of Abyan and Tuban. In recent decades they and the main Tihama wadis, have been modernized and updated with major investment loans from the World Bank and other international financiers. However more than half the investments made in rural Yemen last no longer than five years (World Bank, 2014), raising serious questions about the validity of these extremely expensive investments, which increase the Yemeni state's international indebtedness and primarily benefit the wealthier landowners at the expense of the poorer farmers. Smallholders in the catchment areas of these projects complain that their fields are not irrigated, as the water is diverted to the wealthier landowners (Bonzanigo, L. and C. Borgia, 2009, World Bank 2007 section 6, Lackner personal communication re Tuban).

Many crops can be cultivated both rain fed and under irrigation, such as wheat, *qat*, almonds, figs, coffee, though they obviously have higher yields with more water. Therefore, annual production depends on a number of factors, some of them related to the political situation, such as availability of fuel (for irrigation, input acquisition or marketing), financial incentives, competition from food aid, and others on climatic factors (rain fall, drought). While sorghum remains a favoured main staple crop for local consumption, thanks to its drought resistance and ability to grow in difficult environmental conditions, its production has decreased under war conditions, falling from 459,000 metric tons (mt) in 2012 to a mere 164,000 in 2017 (MOPIC, 2018, p 1). Overall national production of cereals dropped by about one third in the period 2012–17, from 910,000 mt to 358,000 mt and the area cultivated with wheat dropped from 9.2 percent to 5.7 percent (MOPIC, 2018, p1). Although the above-mentioned factors partly explain this drop, at the same time the area under *qat* has increased from 11.3 percent in 2013 to 15.4 percent of cultivated land in 2017. The vast differential in income between *qat* and other crops, including coffee, is an issue which is inadequately addressed by the anti-*qat* lobby and promoters of increased production of alternative crops.

Wheat being the main cereal consumed throughout Yemen, and by far the one most imported, it is a good indicator of the country's food crisis. In 2014, representing the prewar situation, the country imported 3.4 million mt, and produced 192,000 mt, that is, 5 percent of what was imported. Self-sufficiency has dropped from 7.8 percent in 2012 to 2.8 percent in 2017 (MOPIC, 2018). While monthly wheat requirements are estimated at 350,000 mt the level of imports since 2015 has been well below that amount, due to foreign exchange and blockade constraints, as well as the increased poverty and lack of income of consumers, thus partly explaining the "near famine" food emergency experienced by Yemenis since the war started.

Despite low agricultural productivity, most rural Yemenis are primarily farmers, and most agricultural work is done by women in crops and animal husbandry. There has been a fundamental change in livelihoods in recent decades: up to the 1990s, the majority of small landowning rural households (up to 1 ha) could survive on the produce of their plots and their livestock; by the beginning of this century, the main source of income for the majority of rural households was the unskilled labour of their (mostly young adult) men in neighbouring towns and cities, except for the minority who still migrated internationally, mostly to Saudi Arabia and other GCC states. This change was due to the following combination of factors: reduction in holding sizes over generations due to population increase, climatic change reducing yields, water scarcity, soil degradation and loss of land from erosion, changes in diet and expectations, need for additional income to finance medical and educational costs.

By the time of the 2002 agricultural census (the only one ever undertaken), of the 1.2 million landholders in the country, 58 percent owned a total of 8 percent of cultivable land in holdings of less than 0.5 ha, a further 15 percent owned another 8 percent in holdings of 0.5 to 1 ha, while 20 percent of owners owned 28 percent in holdings of 1 to 5 ha, and a mere 7 percent of owners controlled 56 percent of the land in holdings of more than 5 ha (Lackner 2017, p 281). These figures ignore the major differences in potential income arising from the varying climatic conditions, quality of soils, or types of access to water. There were also 770,000 landless rural livestock holders. The remaining 2.5 million rural households included sharecroppers, casual agricultural labourers, artisans, shop keepers, as well as government employees such as teachers and medical staff and security/military personnel.

With respect to future prospects, social, economic and political factors suggest that the trends will continue in the same direction, marked by increased fragmentation of holdings as new generations emerge, a concentration of wealth and landowning among the wealthier who can afford to irrigate their land with deeper wells and more powerful pumps and buy land from the poorer, leading worsening poverty and insecurity of those more vulnerable, all factors worsened by the war situation (Ward et al 2007, Morris-Iveson L. and A. Alderwish 2018 p 685). Moreover, climate change is likely to lead to deteriorating yields of the main crops with worst case scenarios at the national level witnessing decreases of 0.1 percent for wheat, 2.7 percent for sorghum,4 percent for millet and 1.4 percent for maize, but with wide regional variations, including notable increases in some agro-ecological zones and far sharper decreases elsewhere (Kingdom of the Netherlands, 2019, p 6).

State Policies in Water Management and Agricultural Development.

Both water and agricultural government policies since 1990 have been characterized by the domination of the convergent neoliberal agendas of the Saleh regime and the main international financiers of development investments. Both focused on strategies remote from the concerns and needs of the majority of Yemenis, let alone the long-term viability of the country whether agro-ecological, climatic or social.

With respect to water, starting with what can be characterized, at best, as "benign neglect," official awareness of the existence of a crisis only translated into policy statements late in the 1990s. During the same period, agricultural development policies focused on increasing production of irrigated cash crops for export, effectively encouraging larger landowners to export water from one of the countries with the greatest scarcity. This strategy ignored the need to reduce the country's dependence on imports for its basic food security (Morris-Iveson L. and Alderwish, 2018, pp 687-8) and favoured larger and more powerful landholders with access to deep wells or the modernized spate schemes, at the expense of the poorer majority dependent on rain fed agriculture or with restricted access to irrigation, regardless of rhetoric calling for poverty reduction (Bonzanigo, L. and C. Borgia, 2009).

A "Water Law" was promulgated in 2002 after years of procrastination, but its by-laws were issued in 2011 demonstrating the intensity of the debate around its implementation. The Law's original defeat took place in early 2003 when the irrigation sector was removed from the authority of the newly created Ministry of Water and Environment and returned to that of the Ministry of Agriculture and Irrigation, the institutional base for large landowners and foreign financed irrigation development projects.

The National Water Resources Authority (NWRA), established in 1995, had previously been formally given full authority on policy development and implementation (Lackner 2014, pp 164-176). In practice it remained a toothless organization, with theoretical authority over policy and sociopolitical issues, while staffed by engineers under a leadership largely composed of individuals which the regime wanted to "kick upstairs." Without the means to enforce decisions, NWRA remained the main interlocutor of the international funding institutions.

In the case of water, these were the World Bank, and the Netherlands and German governments each of which had different approaches and strategies. Their own internal debates were solved by an agreement allowing better cooperation, or simply coordination: the Netherlands took responsibility for rural domestic water, Germany for urban supplies and the World Bank for agriculturally related water issues.

The World Bank in particular, throughout the 1990s and first decade of this century, was deeply involved in drafting a series of strategic documents on water policy, in particular the National Water Sector Strategy and Investment Program (NWSSIP) of 2005 which included massive investment projects, very few of which ever materialized. Although well meaning, official institutions and strategies had minimal impact either on actual implementation or on improving the situation of over abstraction of the limited resource for high-value cash crops by powerful landowners as unregulated drilling continued.

As the state was establishing toothless institutions, water shortages worsened, with increasingly frequent incidents of conflict even around domestic water supplies, and the population became fully aware of the seriousness of the situation. As the main collectors of domestic water, women suffered most from the shortages. Studies demonstrating the severity of the crisis, worsening shortages and poverty alongside political challenges, combined to bring about the January 2011 "Presidential National Conference on Management and Development of Water Resources in Yemen" which produced another worthy statement whose feasibility was never put to the test as it coincided with the national uprisings and later in the year, the political transition. Water issues took a back seat and have remained there since.

Irrigation presents the clearest example of the policy compatibility between the Saleh regime and the international funding agencies. Although both claimed to be working in the interests of the Yemeni population as a whole, in practice these policies privileged the more powerful. The state's heavily subsidized diesel provided cheap credit for the purchase of irrigation equipment (using loans from international funding agencies) and allowed customs free importation of well and drilling equipment. This complemented international funding for major spate irrigation schemes which again favoured the larger landholders. Subsidies were only reduced well into this century when new projects emerged focused on reducing over-extraction of water: claiming "soil and water conservation," their main components supplied subsidized drip and other irrigation technologies to participants. Here again, larger landholders were the main beneficiaries, as poorer ones had neither deep wells, nor the funds needed to finance their share of the costs.

A mainstay of rural water policies, agricultural and domestic alike, supported by the international financiers, was the establishment of Water Users' Associations (WUAs) to improve beneficiary and community participation. These had mixed outcomes: they succeeded where they built upon, or simply renamed, local mechanisms which had operated successfully for long periods and adjusted to changes in technology and local social structures. Where they were perceived as external artificial impositions, they disappeared as soon as funding ended. This demonstrates that participatory mechanisms have to adapt to complex sets of local circumstances, and also that they cannot be used as "social engineering," for example to increase equity in situations where there are strong dominant powerful groups (Taher, T, et al. 2012).

Policies concerning other aspects of agriculture were even slower to change after decades when agricultural research ignored the emerging environmental problems resulting from climate change and the absurdity of Yemen exporting its scarce water. In particular the importance and potential of the rain fed sector finally got some attention, having previously been completely neglected, despite being the main livelihood of poorer agricultural households and having the potential to reduce rural poverty.

To date, the only project focused on rain fed agriculture was the Rainfed Agriculture and Livestock Project (RALP) jointly funded by the World Bank and the International Fund for Agricultural Development (IFAD) completed in 2013 after six years of implementation. Even in this case, only USD 3.4 million of the project's total cost of USD 43 million was devoted to a component for "farmer-based system of seed improvement and management" (World Bank, 2013). Most of the funds went to livestock health and community activities including some which had clear positive environmental value, such as terrace rehabilitation, but did little for the long-term development of rain fed agriculture. This was the only investment directly concerned with improvement and dissemination of local landraces suitable for rain fed conditions. Neither research into new varieties nor new high-value crops was included.

In the current decade, prior to the country being overwhelmed by war, a number of new projects were in the process of design or implementation focused on adaptation to climate change and involving both agricultural activities and domestic water conservation and collection. Most of them have been shelved due to the war since 2015 but, according to their design, none seriously addresses the potential of rain fed agriculture.

Urban and Rural Domestic Water Supplies

Although 90 percent of water is used in agriculture, some of this actually covers domestic use of rural families. Although most discussions of water focus on the issues of piped supply networks for towns and cities, it is worth remembering that most of the 70 percent of the people living in rural areas still obtain their domestic and drinking water from shallow wells, springs, cisterns, and agricultural irrigation pumps. Women and children collect and carry it for significant distances on their heads or by donkeys in 20l jerry cans. While much of this water is now officially described as "improved," this simply means that its level of ambient pollution is controlled, not that it is obtained easily or without significant physical hard labour, or indeed that it is up to WHO standards. Even larger scale sources in rural areas require collection. When water is piped to the houses, there is rarely effective collection of wastewater. The absence of sanitation systems leads to serious risks of water borne diseases through the build-up of pools of stagnant used waters gathering in impermeable ponds.

Urban water supplies have been problematic long before the war started. Sana´a has, for decades, been described as the first world capital likely to run out of water, but only 40 percent of its households are connected to the urban network. Since the beginning of this century, it was decided not to connect some neighbourhoods to the network, including wealthy residential ones (e.g., Attan). Prospects are grim in the Sana´a basin as abstraction already exceeds five times recharge (270 million m³ against 51 million m³) (Closas, A. and F. Molle 2016, p 76). By comparison, the crisis has been far deeper in Taiz since the 1990s, where the 40 percent or so households connected to the state network have been getting water once every thirty to sixty days in the past two decades (Lackner, 2017, p 221).

The worsening water crisis has led to the rise of private sector tanker supplies. Even in areas connected to the network in Sana´a and elsewhere which used to get network water daily, by the first decade of this century, they were only served about twice a week, reduced to once a week since the political crisis worsened, supplemented by private tanker distribution, some of it also collected by women from the tankers in 20l jerry cans, yet a further demand on women's energies and adding to their already heavy daily tasks. The war has led to a vastly worsening crisis in access to water for both urban and rural people. As the public network structures deteriorate, domestic water is increasingly supplied by private operators with a lengthening chain of transfers, and each stage in the transfer provides additional opportunities for pollution. Sanitation services (where they existed) have almost ceased to function, certainly a contributing factor to the cholera epidemics which started in 2017.

Constraints on Future Water and Agricultural Policies

In 2021, neither of the two rival administrations claiming to run the country is giving serious attention either to developing or implementing policies on such fundamental issues as water management or agricultural development, regardless of the very grave long-term consequences of this neglect. It is extremely difficult to predict when the war in Yemen will end or what form the country will take when it does. First, it is unlikely that a unified centralized state such as existed between 1990 and 2015 will be re-established. The nature of the future state or states is particularly relevant when discussing water management and local economic resources, agriculture in particular. Some level of decentralization is probable, though unlikely to take the form of the six regions proposed by the Hadi regime in 2014. To what extent the borders or definitions of future decentralized entities are likely to take into consideration issues such as water basins, aquifers or access to natural resources is unclear.

Second, the worsening social and political disintegration of the country in recent years suggests that future local level leaders will probably obtain far greater control of both existing and potential resources within the territory under their authority. In addition, the level of nationally recognized authority of the entities remains to be agreed. Fragmentation also implies far deeper socioeconomic divergences between entities, which are unlikely to be based on equitable distribution of assets, particularly given the imbalance between population density and availability of natural resources, primarily water but also cultivable land. The current fragmentation of the country is significantly more profound than earlier sociocultural differences within its borders. It cannot be reduced to either Huthi and anti-Huthi controlled areas, northern and southern, or even between Saudi- and Emirati-influenced ones. Even if focusing on nothing other than political control, it would be easy to draw a map including well over ten potential entities. Moreover, many would have to be added if taking into consideration social structure elements such as tribes, *sada* and other social groups or economic features, including availability of resources, water, hydrocarbons, etc.

Third, short of dramatic changes in the dominant world and regional governance philosophies, the current Saudi and Emirati regimes will probably have considerable influence on Yemen's future economic, social, and political development. The policies promoted will likely be firmly neoliberal. It is worth recalling that it is precisely this type of economic policies which has fundamentally contributed to the disintegration of the Yemeni polity and the emergence of the current war (Lackner, 2017: pp 235-286). The policies of the now largely forgotten "Friends of Yemen" of the early 2010s may be revived in their crudest form, with concepts and designs by Western-dominated international financial institutions to be implemented with Gulf capital by consultancy and construction firms belonging to a combination of Gulf and western companies. Thanks to their new political assertiveness, decision makers of the funding GCC states are likely to demand significant influence on the type of investments made. Past experience has shown that the outcome of such approaches is high profits for the implementers and limited benefits for the officially intended "beneficiaries," in this case, the Yemeni people.

The prospect of Yemen being subjected to a GCC development model is disturbing when one considers the future of its social, economic and cultural characteristics. In particular, the cultural and architectural wealth of the country would be seriously threatened. With respect to agriculture, smallholder production and marketing models prevailing in the highlands, with families living in villages and smaller settlements, characterized by traditions and community relations that are specific to Yemeni culture and local topography are unsuitable for mechanized agriculture on large holdings owned by absentee landowners. In the lowlands where the ownership shift has already taken place, it has been accompanied by an impoverishment of the majority of people who have become sharecroppers and labourers; hence the paradox of the Tihama being simultaneously the "bread basket" of Yemen and the area with the highest poverty levels.

However welcome, the achievement of a "peace agreement" ending the external military intervention is insufficient to re-establish actual internal peace and cohesion. Most probably, it will be the first step in a long political and possibly military struggle between a wide range of factions within the country, some seeking local autonomy or independence while others seeking the re-establishment of a more centralized entity. It may be worth adding that the external states involved in such a peace agreement are very likely to also be directly or indirectly involved in these struggles, to a greater or lesser extent.

Conclusion and Future Prospects

What has been made clear in this chapter is that Yemen's future depends on more than political settlements, even medium-term ones. Indeed, the country's very existence as a viable entity will be determined by the policies of its post-war leadership and allies concerning the fundamental issues of water management (affecting 100 percent of the population) and agricultural development (affecting 60 percent of Yemenis). As discussed above, the likelihood of the emergence of a regime prioritizing the well-being of the majority of the population is low. Despite this, it is essential to be explicit about the implications for the future of past and current trends; such a reality check may divert politicians away from their short-term tactics and encourage them to address these problems, if only to avoid disaster.

First water: unless strong policies are rapidly enforced to shift water usage from agriculture to domestic supplies, the most densely populated parts of the country are likely to become uninhabitable within less than a generation. In addition, as the population of Yemen is projected to reach about 50 million by 2040, there will be significant migration to urban areas as well as rural locations with better aquifers. The larger urban populations will need more water, most of which will come from rural aquifers, except on the coast where desalination will have to be a major contributor. With three of Yemen's main cities on the coast, the issue of rising sea levels is another factor which demands urgent attention.

Significant numbers of people will also move to rural areas where ground water is still available, possibly exacerbating social stress. In addition to the additional pressure on the limited natural resources, tensions are likely to emerge as groups with different sociopolitical alignments move in, competing for livelihoods and political space with previously settled socioeconomic groups with some degree of social coherence, if not cohesion. An example which has already emerged in recent decades is the hostility of southern separatists against "northerners," manifested through the forcible expulsion and even attacks on migrant workers from densely populated areas (Taiz, Ibb, and Dhamar governorates in particular) who have been living and working for many decades throughout the country, including Aden and other southern areas. While this is publicly presented as a political objection, the underlying element is competition over access to the few jobs available. Such trends are likely to worsen as more people leave areas as a result of water shortage and other climatic factors, let alone political ones.

If the water crisis becomes severe enough, thousands of families will become "climate" refugees and be forced to migrate out of Yemen, heading in desperation for the neighbouring countries, primarily Saudi Arabia and Oman, regardless of fences and other physical barriers. Policies giving priority to domestic water supplies can prevent such disasters from taking place. To provide adequate water for domestic purposes to both rural and urban areas will in future require a highly sophisticated approach which takes into consideration a range of different factors: topography, nature and capacity of the water source, per capita availability, most appropriate distribution mechanism to ensure sustainability (which may well be very different from the desires of the people dependent on the source), and suitable sanitation infrastructure.

With respect to urban supplies straightforward technical solutions can be combined with location specific approaches to financing and management ensuring that supply and costs are distributed equitably, and that the poor are not burdened with disproportionately high costs. Individual urban management mechanisms will be larger scale and cover populations ranging from 10,000 to millions, similar models may be appropriate to multiple sites, but no single system should be imposed nationally, and flexibility will be essential to ensure effectiveness.

The most important and difficult issue will be the establishment of equitable mechanisms to supply urban networks from the surrounding rural areas where the aquifers are located. This will involve a transfer of water use from rural agricultural households to urban ones, and therefore a loss of agricultural income. Unless satisfactory mechanisms are identified, firm resistance must be expected. In the highlands, the Sana'a basin is a prime example of an area where powerful landholders cultivating the highly profitable *qat* and grape crops will have to give up some of their water (and thus cultivated areas) to provide domestic water for the city. As the Taiz pilot project in the mid-1990s demonstrated, this cannot be successfully done without providing long-term compensation to the rural areas that are losing this resource essential to life. Sophisticated negotiations and compensation mechanisms must be developed to succeed.

In rural areas, on the other hand, and readers must remember that this concerns about 70 percent of the population, domestic supplies must be designed on a case by case basis, with deep beneficiary participation, taking into consideration the source (shallow well, deep well, cistern, spring, irrigation pump, seasonal or permanent surface flow), timing (rainy season when flood flows are available and also where there are permanent flows), the size of population dependent on the source, the social structure and power relations within the community served, types of settlements (dispersed or compact), conflict history and more. Community-based management systems should be encouraged but must ensure equitable access to all. The size and scope of each individual project must be adapted to the multiple factors listed above. Here again ensuring linked sanitation system must be included to prevent new water supply systems from being sources of further water borne diseases.

Widespread awareness of the water crisis and the long history of sophisticated community-based mechanisms to regulate the use of water are major assets in addressing the problem of scarcity. Traditional laws and regulations, Islamic precepts prioritizing drinking water for people and livestock over other uses, alongside a multiplicity of traditional regulations must be used to form the basis of a solution, alongside strong, firm, and equitable enforcement by the state (Ward, C. 2015 pp 257 +, Taher, T. et al, 2012, World Bank 2007 etc.). Neither state enforcement nor community-based systems is sufficient on its own; they have to operate in synergy. In addition, further awareness raising is essential given the complexities and invisibility of groundwater aquifers.

Agriculture will remain an important economic resource for Yemen, even if the prospect for nationally produced food security is illusory. Despite rural emigration resulting from water shortage and the increased numbers of households, millions will stay in their rural homes, and therefore it is essential to develop effective agricultural policies enabling them to achieve acceptable living standards. Appropriate policies will differ from one area to the other according to the type and availability of water source, existing land tenure systems, and agro-ecological factors such as the optimal crop combination for any given area.

Where sustainable irrigation is feasible, that is, where there is sufficient water for domestic supplies and agriculture, and the water is not needed to supply more remote towns and cities, new approaches to irrigation will enable farmers to use less water, fulfilling the slogan "more crop per drop" so widely mentioned but rarely applied. This should also include an emphasis on higher value crops, primarily for local consumption, thus ensuring greater availability of fruit and vegetables for the national market. Given overall scarcity, another important point will be to improve equity in access to irrigation water by controlling well depth and preventing the drilling of deep wells which deprive the smaller farmers from access to the shallow aquifers.

Most importantly, priority in agricultural development must be given to the development of rain fed agriculture as this will have a major impact on poverty reduction. This is crucial given that the smallholders involved cannot, in current circumstances (even in the absence of war) earn sufficient income from their holdings to feed their families. Research and dissemination of drought-resistant and fast-maturing varieties of traditional cereal crops is a first step, particularly given the preference of Yemenis for local cereals for which, income permitting, they are willing to pay higher prices. In addition to this, which would also contribute to reducing the need for imports, households living in rain fed areas also need cash crops, therefore research and dissemination of new high-value rain fed crops must also be top priorities.

Regardless of effective water management and improved agricultural incomes, Yemen's increased population will need additional economic activities. Rural incomes could in future be supplemented by a well-managed ethical rural tourism, focusing on hiking, bird watching, landscape and photography. Other forms of cultural tourism focused on the country's archaeology, history, Islamic culture, and architecture also have significant potential. These must be established in a manner which is respectful both of the country's natural constraints (water scarcity and topography) and its culture, avoiding the worst features of international tourism (sex tourism, construction of large soulless hotel chains) and other elements which undermine local culture.

At the national level, the development of a wide range of new economic activities appropriate to the twenty-first century is necessary to reduce the very high levels of unemployment. A first indispensable step in this direction is a rapid and fundamental transformation of the country's education system, to prepare future generations for the new opportunities emerging in the post-industrial world. Given the country's population and limited resources, major innovative policies will be essential to enable Yemenis to achieve reasonable living standards, including the opening of the GCC to Yemeni workers from lowest to highest skill levels, long called for by Yemenis and rejected by the GCC. Remittances have for centuries been major contributors to Yemen's economic development and the survival of its population. They will remain essential to allowing thousands of families to stay at home and enjoy the positive features of their beautiful country. Such labour migration can contribute to solving many problems in Yemen's labour hungry neighbours. All these development strategies must be combined to provide coming generations with better means of earning a living than joining militias, smuggling networks or worse.

For the GCC states, the alternative may well be to see the arrival of thousands, even millions, of climate and poverty refugees across their borders, should the basic measures discussed above not be taken. This would not only jeopardize Yemen's future but also become a real threat to the GCC states, Saudi Arabia in particular. The synergy of population growth, the collapse of the water supply, rising seas levels, poverty and desperation will not only lead to a migration flood but also to increasing security risks from frustrated and angry youth facing desperation at home and seeing the wealth and comfort of their Gulf neighbours, supposedly their Arab brothers.

Notes

1   Many thanks to Emeritus Professor Linden Vincent at Wageningen University for detailed and helpful advice and help on water issues and structure. Any and all remaining errors are entirely my own responsibility.
2   It is worth noting that this and the following document mentioned in the text provide very different estimates on rainfall prediction.
3   Although not discussed further here, the fisheries sector employs a further 5 percent of the population and, in recent years, provided a better standard of living for its practitioners than other rural economic activities.
4   These figures are for 2012; the debatable nature of all figures is illustrated by the fact that for 2004, FAO website gives 540 000 ha irrigated with ground water and 254 000 with surface water (FAO Aquasat website, accessed 05 06 2019).

References

al-Qubatee, W., H. Ritzema, A. al Weshali, F. van Steenbergen and P. Hellegers (2017), "Participatory Rural Appraisal to assess groundwater resources in Al Mujaylis, Tihama Coastal Plain, Yemen," *Water International* 42(7): 810–30.

Bonzanigo, L. and C. Borgia (2010), *Tracing Evolutions of Water Control in Wadi Siham*. Yemen: Lambert Academic Publishing.

Closas, A. and F. Molle (2016), *Groundwater Governance in the Middle East and North Africa*, IWMI project report no 1.

Kingdom of the Netherlands, Ministry of Foreign Affairs (2019), *Climate Change Profile Yemen*. Available online: https://www.government.nl/documents/publications/2019/02/05/climate-change-profiles (accessed April 20, 2020).

Lackner, H. (2014), "Water Scarcity: Why Doesn't It Get the Attention It Deserves? Chapter 8," in H. Lackner (ed.), *Why Yemen Matters*. London: Saqi.

Lackner, H. (2017), *Yemen in Crisis, Autocracy, Neo-liberalism and the Disintegration of a State*. London: Saqi.

Morris-Iveson, L. and A. Alderwish, (2018), "Experiences with local water governance and outcomes for vulnerable communities in the Tihama region of Yemen," *Water Alternatives* 11 (3): 684–98.

Republic of Yemen, Ministry of Planning and International Cooperation, Economic Studies and Forecasting sector (2018), *Yemen socio-economic update*, issue 38, November.

Taher, T., B. Bruns, O. Bamaga, A. al-Weshali and F. van Steenbergen (2012), "Local Groundwater Governance in Yemen: Building on Traditions and Enabling Communities to Craft New Rules," *Hydrogeology Journal* 20: 1177–88.

USAID (2016), https://www.climatelinks.org/resources/climate-change-risk-profile -yemen.

Ward, C. (2015), *The Water Crisis in Yemen, Managing Extreme Water Scarcity in the Middle East*. London: I.B. Tauris.

Ward, C., S. Beddies, K, Hariri, S. Yaffei, A. Sahooly and B. Gerhager (2007), *Yemen's Water Sector Reform Programme: A |Poverty and Social Impact analysis (PSIA)*, Washington: The World Bank.

World Bank (2010), *Yemen, Assessing the Impacts of climate Change and variability on the Water and Agricultural Sectors and the Policy Implications*, 2010 report no 54196-YE.

World Bank (2013), *Rainfed Agriculture and Livestock Project: Implementation Status and Results*, Washington DC.

World Bank (2014), *Future Impact of Climate Change Visible Now in Yemen*. Washington: World Bank. Available online: http://www.worldbank.org/en/news/feature/2014/11/24/future-impact-of-climate-change-visible-now-in-yemen (accessed April 20, 2020).

Chapter 10

GETTING YEMEN WORKING

RETHINKING ECONOMIC PRIORITIES TO DELIVER LONG-TERM PEACE AND STABILITY

James Firebrace, with Alia Eshaq[1]

Introduction

In this chapter we make three interrelated points. Firstly, in the opening sections, we review Yemen's economic development and its legacy of grievances and regional imbalances[2] and argue for viable regional economies as both an incentive and condition for sustainable peace. Secondly, in the middle section of the chapter, we outline the significant economic opportunities ahead and the role of business, aid and civil society in their realization. Thirdly, in the final section, we argue for a longer-term perspective looking beyond the bleakness of Yemen's current situation to the (often interlinked) dimensions of a post-war economic rebound. The four maps seek to reinforce these points, by illustrating the current distribution of Yemen's key assets and the most significant areas of potential.

Little academic work has been done on Yemen's potential post-war trajectories, and this work relies on extensive discussions held with a range of Yemeni and international commentators, large and small businesses and development practitioners. We have drawn on our personal experience of advising and designing the practicalities of successful development in fragile and post-conflict situations to focus on what Yemen could realistically achieve.

The future shape of post-conflict Yemen is likely to reflect the high degree of political fragmentation that has taken place particularly over these last six years of war. Arriving at an agreed intent between the parties to enable Yemen's regions to develop as viable economic entities overseen by well-resourced regional administrations, would provide an important incentive toward the sustainable settlement of the current conflict. It would support the resolution of past conflicts over resources and of the regional neglect that has undermined Yemen's economy and political stability for many decades. A key theme therefore is to make the case for *"leave no region behind,"* while being aware of the security fears and other forces that drive centralization and the neglect of less aligned regions or those without the political clout.

The current civil war has reduced much of Yemen to a state of extreme vulnerability. But even before the war Yemen faced multiple challenges—inequalities between regions, a terrorist threat, a poor investment climate constrained by political corruption and the shaky application of the rule of law, huge military spending, gender inequality, rudimentary public services, population growth, limited local capacity and massive water scarcity, to highlight the most pressing. These constraints must be addressed, and some solutions are offered here, but we have also sought to look beyond them. For Yemen has the potential not only to recover from the current war but in time to generate significant and widespread prosperity.

A clearer understanding of opportunities ahead can help develop the ideas and provide the energy needed to solve more immediate problems, as well as support the compromises necessary to transcend current political differences and build a lasting peace. This chapter should be read in this spirit. It is neither a prediction nor a roadmap, but an attempt to highlight the potential that lies ahead once sustainable peace is achieved, building on the recognition that economies do rebound, often dramatically, after civil war.

Relationship between Yemen's Economic Sectors and National and Regional Revenues

Yemen's key economic sectors can be grouped by their relationship to national or local revenue generation into three categories. The productive sectors are those which potentially generate revenue for national or local government through licensing and taxes on profits generated. These include oil and gas production, agriculture, fisheries, manufacturing and trading, electricity generation including from renewables, ports, information technology, and tourism.

The utility sectors, such as water, sanitation and electricity distribution, are revenue neutral or rely on government support. They form a crucial part of the value chain for the productive sectors. Utility sectors in Yemen face widely differing regional challenges and a variety of limitations, depending on population density, local resource depletion and administrative capacities.

Finally, the service sectors, such as health and education, require funding through national or local government. Along with the utility services, these are crucial to public perceptions of "development." They are therefore often a priority plank of donor programming and, in the current context, of regional power play and influence seeking. The service sectors tend to be employment intensive, including providing skilled jobs for graduates.

Prewar Constraints on Yemen's Economy and the Impact of the Civil War

Earlier chapters in this volume have discussed some of the main constraints of the prewar period. Despite the many difficulties, the private sector did enjoy growth and had become a significant employer of skilled labor. In Ta'izz, for example, most families were financially dependent on the extensive local industrial production, largely of food and drink products but also construction items and household goods.

Yemen's multifaceted civil war has led to a high degree of political fragmentation and the emergence of war economies that have empowered local and regional actors with varying degrees of influence which will have to be taken into account in building a new Yemen. Three key political groups—the Huthis, the Internationally Recognized Yemeni Government (IRG), and the STC—control major sections of Yemen's economic assets and resources. Both the IRG and the Huthis pursued entirely separate policies as they put their economies on to a war footing, creating virtually two separate economies (as discussed in Chapters 6 and 7). New mechanisms for revenue collection have been adopted, increasingly ad hoc and at a local level, often driven by the location of checkpoints, in contrast to the strong centralization of the past.

The Huthis have used foreign military intervention and the impact of coalition blockades of sea and airports to rally support. They now govern 65–70 percent of the Yemeni population (see Chapters 3 and 6) and have consolidated control over several areas. particularly ports and road junctions, of strategic significance for generating revenue. One major source of revenue is tax on imports through Hodeida, which with nearby Salif receives around 70 percent of all imports. Salif's primary function has been the reception of grain shipments discharging into silos at the port and feeding local flour mills, although no cranes and other port facilities are as yet available here. Ras Isa, also under Huthi control, was traditionally a terminal for exporting crude from Marib's oil wells in but ceased operations after the conflict started.

The IRG key strategic asset is the oil and gas sites around Marib, although the governor there operates largely independently and retains local control over oil revenues. Beyond this the IRG lacks clear control over the port of Mocha, which is in the hands of the National Resistance Force led by Tariq Saleh. Saudi efforts to cajole the IRG and the STC into implementing the Riyadh Agreement may have led to the formation of a new coalition government but in early 2021 it was the STC that controlled Aden and the surrounding areas including the ports of Aden and Balhaf. The STC can divert local sources of revenue to maintain its control but lacks the capacity to provide the full range of essential services in Aden.

Though northern Hadramaut is under IRG control, the coastal area is influenced by the STC and is led by an independent-minded local governor. Hadramis now demand a high level of control over Hadramaut's natural resources, mainly the oil fields in Wadi Masila, and seek special status as a region with a high degree of autonomy regardless of the future status of the south. Al-Mahrah (and Soqotra) have since 2015 successfully kept out of the intense fighting and gained a degree of independence from Yemeni political forces (Kendall 2018). However, regional players have begun to fill the space. Saudi Arabia now has a military presence in Al-Mahrah and has launched development plans in the governorate. In Soqotra, the UAE installed military forces setting the scene for the recent STC takeover of the island.

Addressing Geographic Imbalances by Developing Regional Economic Opportunities

Yemen's economic resources are widely distributed across the country, but some areas are relatively disadvantaged while others have a concentration of wealth-producing assets. (Maps 2–5) Yemen's regions have suffered very differently from the current war, depending on the level of ground fighting and bombardment experienced, the extent of loss of livelihoods and the magnitude of population displacements. With past centralization, there was only limited correlation between location of an asset and local prosperity unless it generated significant employment, such as was the case at ports and industrial sites. This has changed radically with the war. Looking ahead, the location of assets and the allocation of revenues from licensing and taxation, including the overall national-regional split, will be key to maintaining a sustainable peace.

Geographical imbalances are pronounced for some key sectors. Oil and gas are concentrated in the eastern and southern governorates, while industry is clustered in Ta'izz, Hodeida and Sana'a. On the other hand, Yemen's major ports are relatively well distributed, with two on the Red Sea coast and two in the Gulf of Aden. Fisheries, albeit depleted in some areas, are well dispersed along both of Yemen's two coasts. Agriculture is found throughout the highlands with spate irrigation in the Tihama plain. The areas of greatest rainfall, around Ibb and Ta'izz, have the greatest economic security and support the highest density of population.

These variations highlight the centre-periphery dilemmas and the political and economic choices ahead. For lasting peace and stability, there will be a need to deliver across the country basic services, jobs and at least a rudimentary level of prosperity, as well as sufficient income for both central and regional administrations. Viable economic opportunities will be needed in the regions to create alternative sources of income to attract young men away from the militias and give them a future in a stable Yemen.

Central Government and the Regions, the Allocation of Revenues

It is difficult to see a full reversion to the prewar centralization, and strategies for the empowerment and efficient delegation of powers to local authorities will be essential. But how can that be achieved given the geographical distribution of assets and the reality of de facto local control?

Prewar models have lost much of their relevance. Under the existing Yemeni constitution, the state has the sole monopoly over natural resources and their use. The draft constitution of 2014 did, however, part from this and instead stated, albeit somewhat nebulously, that "the people" are the owners of natural resources. Under the Saleh regime fiscal management of revenue was centralized, limiting the role of authorities at the governorate and district levels. The wealth generated by oil and gas trickled down only to a limited degree, and vast sums were made by those in positions to benefit from the issuing of licenses and contracts.

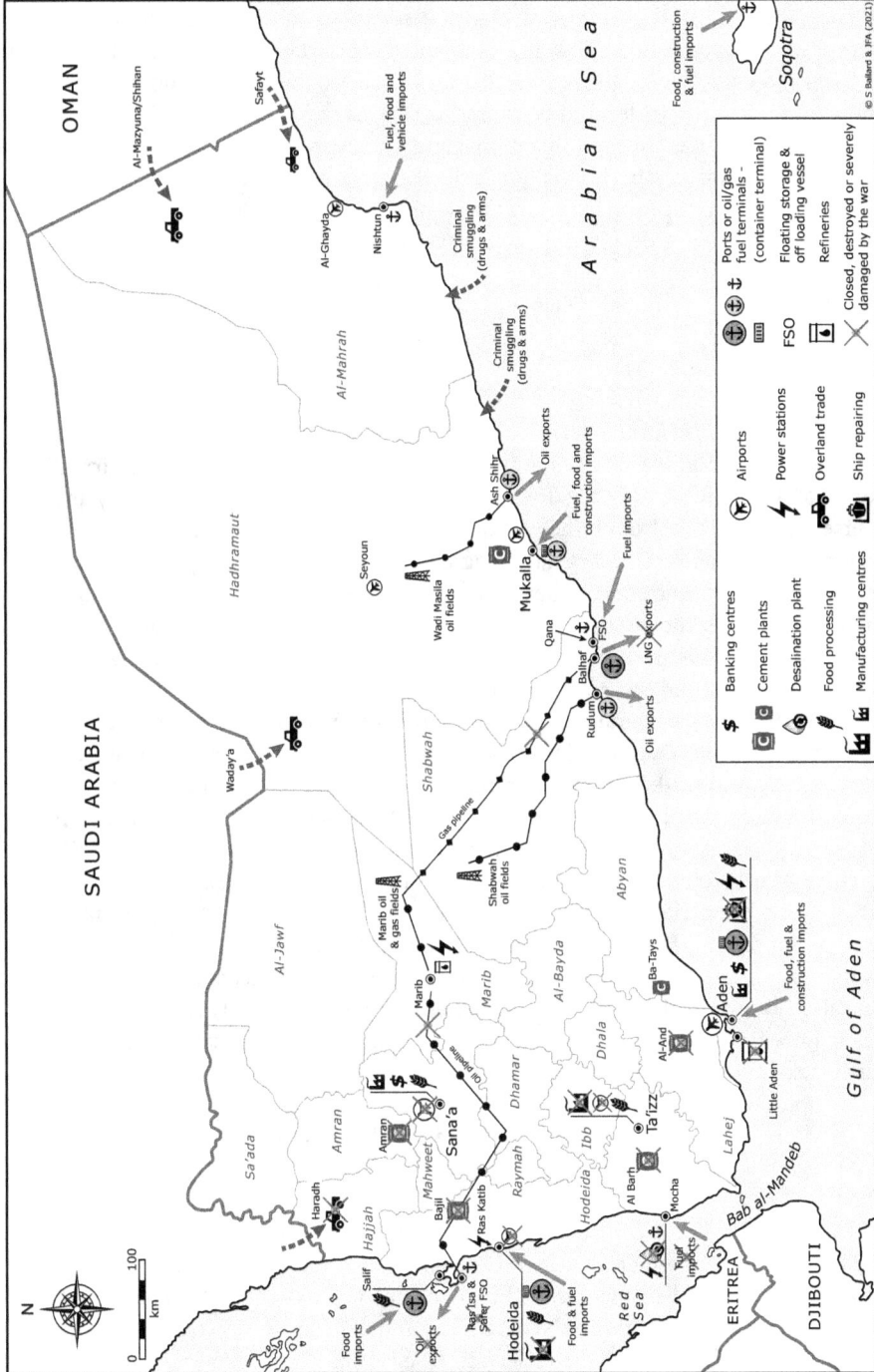

Map 2 Current Economic Activity, including elements of the war economy and assets closed or destroyed by the war. See.[28] for details.

Legend:

Symbol	Description
⊕ ⊥	Ports or oil/gas fuel terminals - (container terminal)
▥	FSO
▣	Floating storage & off loading vessel
◨	Refineries
✕	Closed, destroyed or severely damaged by the war
✈	Airports
⚡	Power stations
🚚	Overland trade
⚓	Ship repairing
$	Banking centres
C	Cement plants
◉	Desalination plant
🌾	Food processing
🏭	Manufacturing centres

Place labels:

OMAN, SAUDI ARABIA, Arabian Sea, Gulf of Aden, Red Sea, Bab al-Mandeb, ERITREA, DJIBOUTI, Soqotra

Al-Mazyuna/Shihan, Safayt, Al-Ghayda, Nishtun, Fuel, food and vehicle imports, Criminal smuggling (drugs & arms), Al-Mahrah, Hadhramaut, Seyoun, Wadi Masila oil fields, Oil exports, Ash Shihr, Fuel, food and construction imports, Mukalla, Qana, FSO, Balhaf, LNG exports, Fuel imports, Rudum, Oil exports, Shabwah, Gas pipeline, Marib oil & gas fields, Shabwah oil fields, Al-Bayda, Abyan, Ba-Tays, Al-Jawf, Marib, Dhamar, Dhala, Al-Anad, Aden, Food, fuel and construction imports, Little Aden, Lahej, Sa'ada, Amran, Sana'a, Raymah, Ibb, Ta'izz, Al Barh, Hodeida, Mahweet, Bajil, Ras Katib, Mocha, Fuel imports, Salif, Ragʻlsa & Safer FSO, Food & fuel imports, Food imports, exports, Haradh, Hajjah, Waday'a, Amran

Food, construction & fuel imports

© S Ballard & IFA (2021)

Until the war the main source—to the tune of over 90 percent—of local revenue was a central government grant. Three other sources of local funding were envisaged by Law 4/2000: independent district revenue, collected by the district authorities and utilized at the district level; local common revenue, collected by the district level to be shared at the governorate level; and common public revenue, collected by both national and local authorities. At the same time, the central authorities traditionally allocated only a minimal percentage of the national budget to the local level, less than 1 percent in 2014 (Berghof Foundation 2018). This created a deeply centralized system and poorly functioning under-resourced local authorities.

Following the National Dialogue Conference (NDC) in 2013 and prior to the current conflict, Yemeni parties reached a consensus on a new form of decentralization reflected in both the NDC outcomes and the 2014 draft constitution. The latter referred to the devolution of authority within four layers of governance: the central federal authority, the regions (federations), the *wilayat* (sub-units of the regions, seen as similar in their authority and borders to the current governorates) and the districts. The regions would enjoy a level of autonomy and oversee some key functions hitherto assumed by the central authority, for instance regarding international cooperation agreements, development plans for the regions and the appointment of key executive figures. The authorities delegated to the *wilayat* and to the districts would follow the current local governance system with few alterations. How much of this will still be relevant or acceptable post conflict is unclear and the constitution will have to be revised.

Since 2011 the weakening of Yemeni central government has led to a chaotic "de facto" decentralization. Some of these decentralizing developments are positive, suggesting that moves toward an effective local governance structure would be of great value for overall stability and post-conflict recovery. Marib is one example. Early in the war, its governor reached an agreement with the IRG to share Marib's oil revenues, giving the governorate a 20 percent share (Baron 2018). Soon after, Hadhramaut and Shabwah were also allocated 20 percent of local oil revenues. Marib has thrived from the additional income including from its light crude which can be used directly as a diesel substitute, and from bottled gas sales, both smuggled across the frontlines into Sana'a. A local economic boom has followed, as many businesses relocated to Marib, allowing local authorities to further expand their revenue from taxing trade and enterprise.

During the war other governorates, Aden, Hadhramaut, Shabwah, Al-Mahrah and Soqotra, have to varying degrees commanded high levels of external support from regional players, particularly Saudi Arabia and UAE, and to a lesser extent Oman.

Lands under Huthi control have limited resources, and due to the lack of a public budget for these areas it is unclear how much local authorities receive. A large proportion of their income is likely to be devoted to fighting the coalition. It is estimated that the Huthis now generate an annual income over a trillion Yemeni Riyals (c.$1.8 billion) from the collection of customs dues, corporate taxes and licensing fees (UNPoE 2021). Customs dues are imposed at the ports of Hodeida and Salif as well as at an additional customs collection point in Dhamar for goods crossing from ports such as Aden outside their control. Further income derives from fuel imports and from taxing smuggled goods.

The Huthis have inherited the strong centralizing policies of previous regimes in Sana´a and have imposed tight control. through their network of political supervisors (*mushrifin*) established by the Huthis in parallel to state structures (see Chapters 3 and 6) but Huthi-appointed governors tend to be from that region to build and maintain local trust (Nevola 2019).

The relocation of the Yemen Central Bank from Sana´a to Aden in 2016 along with continued warfare, corruption and mismanagement crippled the links between the IRG in Aden and the local authorities under its jurisdiction. From 2014 to 2018, there was no IRG public budget and no clear basis for revenues to be allocated to the local level. The UAE bypassed and undermined the local authorities in supporting parallel local entities such as the Security Belt and the Elite Forces and for a time paying the salaries of local officials in parts of the south and in 2021 was still financially supporting the STC. The IRG finally issued a public budget in 2018 with revenue allocated for local authorities intended to cover half of their operational expenses as well as public servants' salaries.

A post-conflict government may seek to maintain tight central authority but will be faced with new local assertiveness and will need to devolve project decisions to regional governors and councils and work out new arrangements for the allocation of centrally and locally generated revenues to ensure well-functioning regional administrations. The need for balanced regional solutions cannot be understated. Far-sighted policies from the centre will be necessary so that benefits are shared in a way acceptable to people both in the regions where assets are located and in other regions without those resources. This will not be easy especially when dealing with oil and gas and their refined or bottled products, electricity generation and (further ahead) the transfer of water to areas of high population density. However, businesses will continue to prioritize investments in their home areas where they have most familiarity and contacts and a supportive local business environment, including measures to deter corruption and rent seeking, will influence those investment choices.

Yemen Now Faces a New Set of Key Economic Drivers

An Uncertain Future for Migration and Remittances

Prospects for Yemen's future economic growth will still rely to a great extent on its vital asset, the mobility of its labor force. Remittances, while currently facing challenges[3], will continue to play a powerful role in economic recovery and will support investment, particularly in smaller local projects. The current conflict has displaced more than three million Yemenis (UNHCR 2020), many of whom have relocated to neighbouring countries. Of those who have left Yemen, many have settled in Saudi Arabia and the UAE, but also in Ethiopia, Djibouti, Egypt, Jordan,

Somalia, Sudan and Oman. For example, Oman witnessed a Yemen influx of 50,000 refugees in 2017 alone. Estimates of the numbers of diaspora Yemenis range between six and seven million in total[4]. Those fleeing the current war include a large component of professionals—business families, political activists, journalists, judges, and intellectuals. While this group of "exiles" constitutes a significant brain drain, it makes an important contribution to the overall remittances to Yemen. This workforce if successfully harnessed could prove invaluable for post-conflict recovery in bringing back skills to the Yemeni labor market.

The Overarching Challenge of Population Growth

With growth rates of over 3 percent per annum, Yemen's population doubles every twenty-five years, a rate that is unsustainable—not least for water use. The first step is to reduce family size especially in rural areas which still make up some 70 percent of the population and where women play more traditional roles. Yemen can learn from other countries that have launched policies targeting the education and empowerment of women. Growth of GDP per capita measuring average individual prosperity should be the key indicator, replacing GDP growth.

Scarce Urban Water and Its Wider Implications

Water scarcity is the most fundamental constraint to Yemen's development (Ward 2015; Varisco 2019). Estimates regarding opportunities from future higher rainfall should not lessen the urgency of addressing water issues. Rural water has been seriously depleted by irrigation pumping, including for the cultivation of *qat*. Large falls in the water table have greatly increased pumping costs, while also affecting urban supply. Two major cities, Ta'izz (Handley 2001) and Sana'a, already face a critical situation and are now dependent year by year on sufficient annual recharge of ground water. In Ta'izz the pumped groundwater is heavily contaminated, high in salts content and generally undrinkable. The city now relies on a network of mini-desalination plants, known as *kawther*. There are some twenty of these around Ta'izz processing the polluted water into a drinkable product, but lacking economies of scale, they add greatly to costs and the burden on family expenditure.

Coastal desalination combined with pumping from the coast is likely to be the only longer-term solution and recent studies on Ta'izz (Firebrace 2015) have shown this would result in a reduction in the family water bill. Before the current war, efforts had concentrated on upgrading the limited desalination facilities at Mocha on the Red Sea. Technological innovation is leading to significant reductions in desalination unit costs, and cheap energy (or heat supply) will make desalinated water and its transfer even cheaper.

This raises the possibility of a solution for the high costs of transferring water to Sana'a, a much larger city than Ta'izz and at a higher altitude, where the likely route of any pipeline from the sea would have to cross two mountain ranges. The option of transferring cities to the coast has been raised. Businesses are increasingly likely to start new operations in coastal areas, with better access to overseas markets and closer to desalination plants. But large-scale relocation of populations is not only politically fraught and faces the problem that coastal living involves significantly higher energy use (Firebrace 2015). Other unexplored sources of fresh water in Yemen need further investigation. These include the large underground reserves in the Empty Quarter at Umm Al-Rudhuma in the Hadhramaut, but excessive depth and isolation may mean these are uneconomic for extraction.

Cheap Renewable Energy Will Help Address Water Scarcity

Low energy costs are a major driver of a healthy economy and of standards of living. Figure 10.1 highlights the interlinkages between energy costs and selected major sectors. Cheap energy greatly benefits a wide range of sectors from the competitiveness of manufacturing and the affordability of desalinization. Yemen has a range of valuable renewable sources. The high intensity and seasonal continuity of sunlight can provide cheap solar power. Many areas, especially on the coast, experience the high wind speeds for efficient wind turbines, although seasonable variation is a constraint. There is considerable biomass potential from the major cities, which would also address public health issues from existing rubbish dumps.

Each of these renewables, with sufficient economies of scale and access to low interest capital, could produce electricity at around a third of the prewar price of fossil-fuel driven generation. Potentially even greater savings could be realized if the benefits offered by international carbon schemes are well utilized. Future international climate change treaties are likely to give further impetus for such schemes. There has been little development of large-scale renewables in Yemen to date, while the war and power disruptions have provided a major boost for small private solar installations. Local informants estimate that three-quarters of urban dwellings and half of rural dwellings now use solar energy.

Geothermal energy has particular attractions in Yemen. Unlike solar and wind, it is produced continuously all day and throughout all seasons, thereby requiring no back-up. The extraction of geothermal energy takes little land and can be used to produce direct heat, as well as electricity. This is important for cement production and for desalination, potentially radically cutting the unit cost of desalinated water. Discussions with geothermal developers in Ethiopia, indicate that Yemen, with geothermal projects of sufficient scale, could also achieve similar low prices. With robust local power purchase agreements[5], unit costs can be reduced further. Studies have consistently pointed to Dhamar governorate as the most promising high temperature source, but there is also potential in the north eastern area of Amran, as well as lower temperature potential on the Red Sea coast south of Hodeida (Minissale 2006).

Such low-cost energy sources would act as a major spur to local industry and would greatly reduce the otherwise prohibitive cost of transferring water to regions with limited local supplies. National electricity distribution depends on a functioning grid of sufficient capacity, which will require the achievement

Effect of changes to sectors (below) on other sectors (to right)	Oil and Gas ⋔ $$$	Renewable Energy ⋔⋔ $$$ R	Ports and Trade ⋔⋔ $$ R	Manufacturing ⋔⋔ $$$ RR	Agriculture ⋔⋔⋔ $ RRR	Fisheries ⋔⋔⋔ $ RR	Water ⋔	Minerals ⋔ $$$	Hospitality ⋔⋔⋔ $$ RR
Oil and gas declining reserves		**Spurs diversified energy**		Spurs switch to renewables			Spurs switch to renewables		
Renewables development: cheaper electricity than fossil fuel generation; attract international grants	**More oil and gas available for export**		Cheaper port movements	**Greater competitiveness due to lower production costs**	Cheaper pumping (*but potential threat to water levels if unregulated*)	Cheaper power for cooling, freezing and canneries	Lower costs of pumping and desalination. Geothermal by-product	Lower extraction costs, increased competitiveness. Use in remote locations	**Small scale solar enables accommodation in remote locations**
Ports: expansion of existing ports				Supports export potential	Supports export potential	Supports export potential		**Supports export potential**	Enable visitors arriving by sea
Manufacturing: more competitive supporting greater import substitution and regional exports		Potential local businesses eg solar panels, businesses in value chain	**Utilisation of ports through increased exports**		Greater local production of agricultural inputs	Local boat production finetuned to local conditions	Potential local production of water meters etc	Potential for some processing, eg gold and silver	**Local food products attractive to visitors**
Agriculture: shift to rainfed / new varieties / new crops			Supports export potential (for cash crops)	**Inputs for food processing or packaging: coffee, fruit, almonds**					**Local food varieties attractive to visitors**
Fisheries: more secure production, community mgt, regulation of. IUU and overfishing	Diesel needed for engines	Increased demand off grid	**Greater port utilisation with increased fish exports**	Revitalisation of tuna canneries		(*But need for measures to address potential over-fishing*)			Fish products attractive to visitors –lobster, shrimp, cuttlefish
Urban water: secure provision of clean water in cities		Spurs growth of renewables sector	Secure provision of water for port operations	**Cheaper reliable water key for industrial development**	**Reduced conflict with agricultural users**	Clean water needed for fish cleaning; also salt production	**Less conflict with urban water**	Water needed for mineral extraction and refining processes	**Necessary for visitors to urban areas**
Minerals: development of extraction sites			Supports export potential	Potential raw materials for industry	Potential mineral fertiliser products	Potential salt inputs	(*Can use large quantities of water*)		Local sales eg gold and silver attractive to visitors
Tourism: security and investment allows successful development	**Spurs solar in off grid locations Potential link with geothermal**	**High energy needs spurs renewables growth**	Greater utilisation of ports	Supports local processing of local food products	**Potential revenue stream for agriculturalists**	**Market for high-value products**	**Spur for provision cleaner water**		(*Care needed not to damage views etc*)

This table shows the many positive impacts of developments in one sector on other sectors. **Bold text** indicates a highly positive relationship. But not all these linkages are positive. (*Italic text in brackets*) indicates some caveats. Job creation potential in the sector is indicated by the symbol ⋔. The potential for government revenue is indicated by $ signs, while the potential for the investment of remittances is indicated by Rs.

Figure 10.1 Interlinkages between key economic sectors—many positive interactions.

of sustainable peace and an end to attacks on power lines. For rural areas, away from the main population centres, off-grid options such as solar have the most potential, as is already being witnessed, but use for pumping groundwater will need regulation.

Economic Opportunities Ahead by Sector

An Oil and Gas Sector Long past Its Peak (Map 2)

By 2003, Yemen had reached the peak of its oil production and barring unexpected major discoveries Yemen can no longer rely on these revenues as the major source of future income. With the return of a secure investment environment, it is possible that Yemeni hydrocarbon production will enjoy a long "tail"[6] particularly for gas whose export potential is now facilitated by the major LNG terminal at Balhaf in Shabwah (YLNG 2005). This remains undamaged and can resume full operations once circumstances allow.

Oil and gas reserves are concentrated in Marib, Hadhramaut and to a lesser extent in Shabwah. Export is through Al-Shihr in Hadhramaut for the Masila heavy crude fields, and until the war Ras Isa on the Red Sea for Marib's light crude. The Ras Isa export terminal is now inactive and the offshore cargo remaining on the aging FSO SAFER storage vessel threatens serious environmental damage (Ralby 2019) and constitutes a severe risk to local fisheries. The Marib to Ras Isa pipeline is now being bypassed by a pipeline to Rudum in Shabwah. Yemen's main refining capacity near Aden, an aging plant dating back to 1954, is currently out of action due to lack of maintenance. There is some secondary refining capacity in Marib.

Agriculture, Rural Water, and the Impact of Climate Change (Map 4)

Agriculture has traditionally been the main employer in Yemen but faces increasing challenges.[7] Poverty is most acute in Yemen's rural areas and rural families often only survive because male family members work in the cities usually in temporary construction jobs. Women undertake the bulk of the agricultural labor and have done so since migration became a major alternative source of income. Over recent decades Yemeni agriculture has shifted from rainfed to irrigated, which now faces sharply increased pumping costs with declining water tables due to over-extraction.

Agriculture has been severely affected by the war (Mundy 2017) so peace and security will revive this sector relatively quickly. In Ethiopia in the post-war period after 1990, offers of small holdings and micro loans proved to be the key component of its disarmament, demobilization and reintegration (DDR) programme (Mulugeta 2019). In Yemen, this labor-intensive sector could also provide employment for demobilized young men.

There is much potential for the revitalization of rain-fed agriculture on highland terraces[8]. Rainfall can if necessary be supplemented by small-scale irrigation during dry periods. Abandoned terraces can potentially be brought back into production with new designs requiring little maintenance such as gabion construction using stone-filled wire baskets. Road water harvesting practices (RWHP) have great potential to capture scarce water in highland areas (Gebru 2020) and reduce erosion of cultivatable land.[9] These could be major components of "food for work" schemes or their cash equivalent.

Such schemes proved to be a successful component of major post-war terrace building programmes in Tigray, northern Ethiopia[10]. In Yemen they could encourage ex-fighters "back to the bilaad" providing important benefits in the populated highland areas, which have suffered high levels of food insecurity during the war. Yemenis, even in the cities, keep their links to the rural villages of their parents and grandparents. The revival of the terraces would also fit with Huthi ideology (Nevola 2020). There is also the potential for agricultural improvements to be supported by diaspora remittances, as has been the case in earlier phases of Yemen's history.

Research needs to be directed at new plant varieties suited to local highland conditions and soils, helping Yemen to cope with future challenges from climate change. To date, only limited seed trials have taken place, focused narrowly on irrigated agriculture. Over time, the spread of new better-adapted varieties will lead to a decrease in costs, further spurring dissemination and replicating the agricultural revival enjoyed by many African countries.

There is much potential for rain-fed cash crops such as almonds, which have traditionally carried a high price premium in Yemeni and Arab markets. Yemen claims to be the origin of coffee, but with the growth and profitability of *qat* in recent decades, much coffee production has been displaced and trees uprooted. However, there is now evidence of a reverse shift spurred by more effective branding and international marketing of Yemeni coffee. Honey production is another example where effective international marketing can massively increase profitability. Such developments will require considerable initial support but are likely to take off rapidly once farmers see the financial benefits. As elsewhere (Nir 2019) agriculture can revitalize its image as an "old sector" and benefit from Yemen's strong entrepreneurial culture to slow or even reverse the drift of the rural young to the cities.

Climate change, in bringing greater weather variability and extreme events such as flooding, will pose significant challenges. Nevertheless, the two detailed studies undertaken (Netherlands MoFA 2018; USAID 2016) agree that a high proportion of Yemen's agricultural areas could benefit from greater rainfall and higher temperatures. These studies do not always share identical conclusions, but they concur on the mixed impact on agriculture, with "*production increases in the highlands (from Sa'ada to Ta'izz) due to higher temperatures*" (Netherlands MoFA 2018), whereas "*significant decreases in crop yields are expected in the south*" (USAID 2016). Likewise, a recent global report (McKinsey 2020) puts Yemen into the category of becoming "significantly hotter and more humid" and (along with the Horn of Africa) predicts *less* water stress. Heavier rainfall in the highlands could also play an important role in the replenishment of water tables, but only if floods are managed and population growth flattens. On the coast rising sea levels

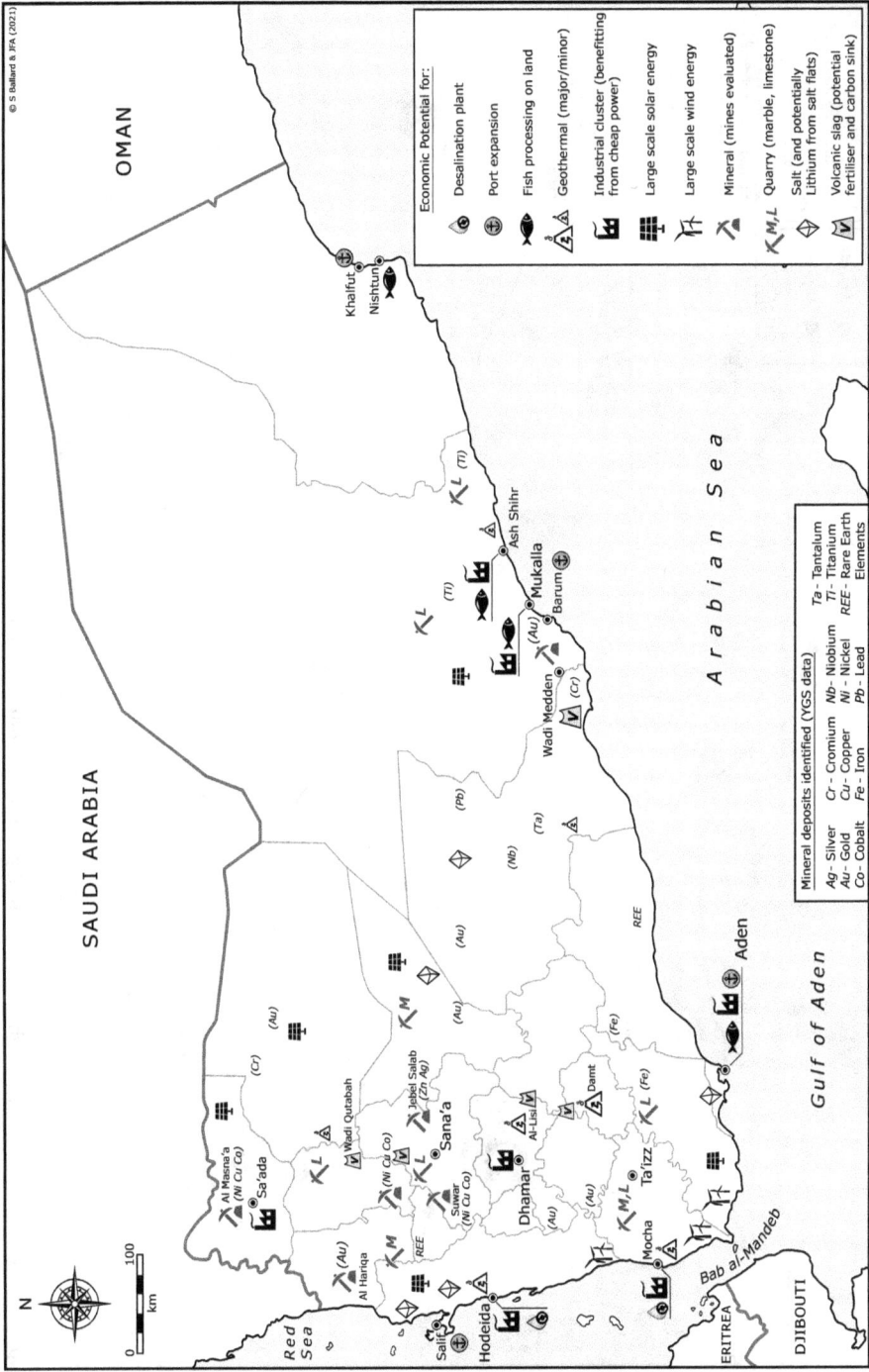

Map 3 Areas of Economic Potential, showing some pointers for the future, including increasingly valuable minerals deposits.[29] for details.

Legend:

Economic Potential for:
- Desalination plant
- Port expansion
- Fish processing on land
- Geothermal (major/minor)
- Industrial cluster (benefitting from cheap power)
- Large scale solar energy
- Large scale wind energy
- Mineral (mines evaluated)
- Quarry (marble, limestone)
- Salt (and potentially Lithium from salt flats)
- Volcanic slag (potential fertiliser and carbon sink)

Mineral deposits identified (YGS data)

Ag - Silver	Cr - Cromium	Nb - Niobium	Ta - Tantalum
Au - Gold	Cu - Copper	Ni - Nickel	Ti - Titanium
Co - Cobalt	Fe - Iron	Pb - Lead	REE - Rare Earth Elements

© S Ballard & JFA (2021)

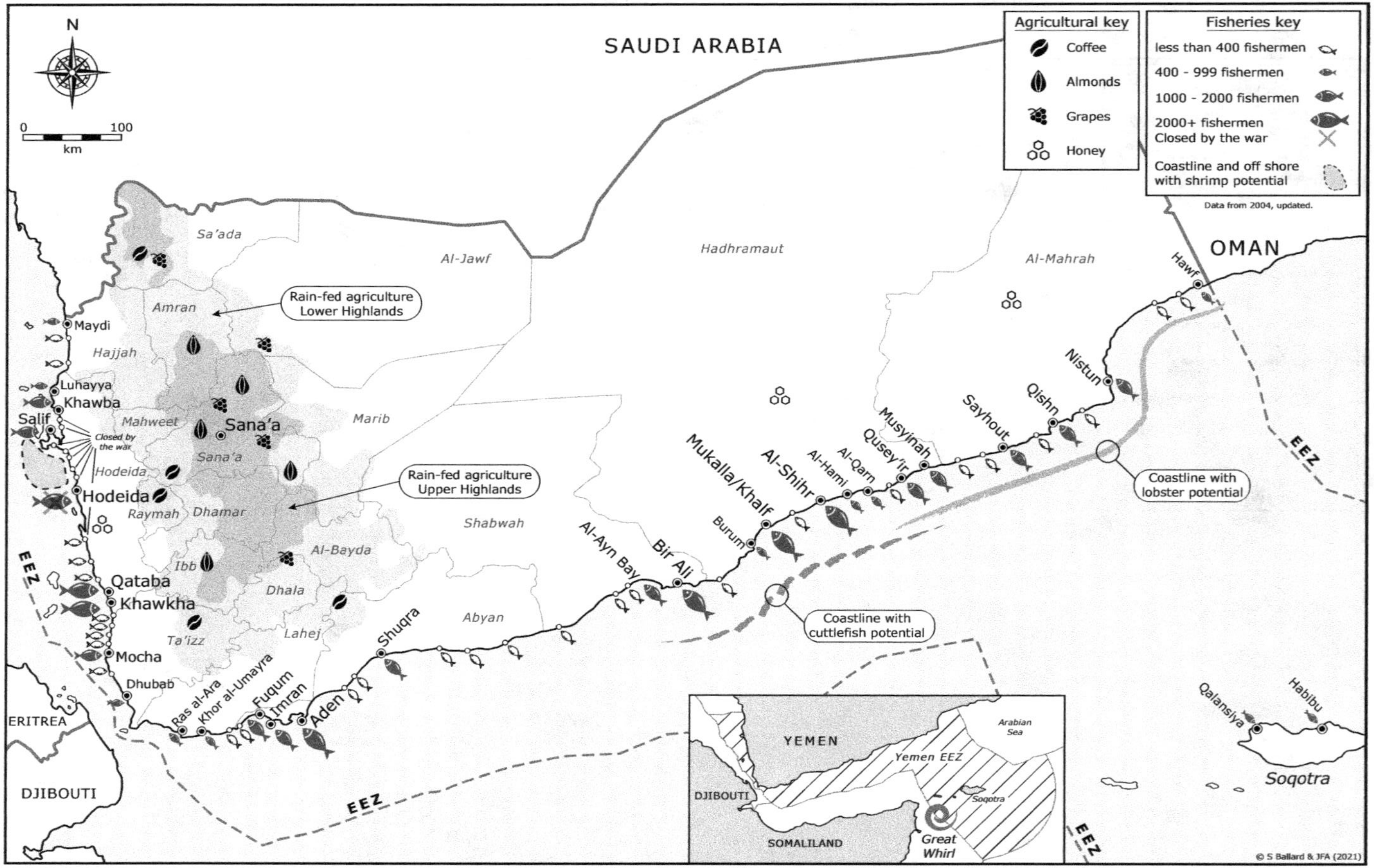

Map 4 Agriculture and Fisheries, highlighting areas of potential in both highland agriculture and high-value fishing exports. See.[30] for details.

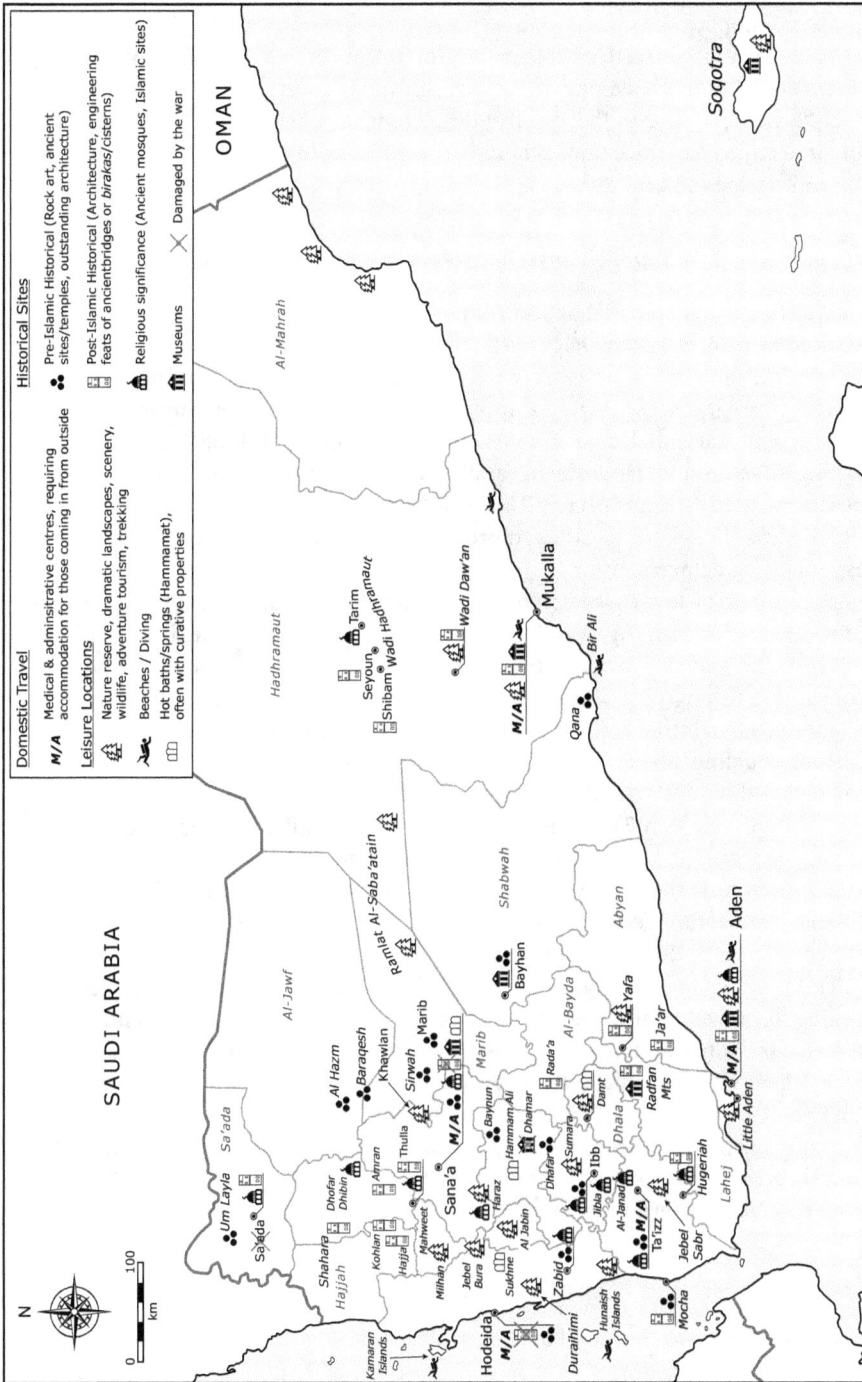

Map 5 Hospitality Sector, with high potential for job creation throughout Yemen including in rural areas. See[31] for details.

will increase sea water intrusion in low-lying areas and affect agricultural water and local supplies.

Sadly, there is a dearth of continuous historical climate data. The collection of recent statistics has been one of the casualties of the war. Further climate related analysis is imperative to the effective development of Yemen's agricultural sector, and it needs to prioritize understanding the differing impact of climate change on Yemen's varied eco-regions.

Fisheries and the Restitution of Yemen's Marine Economic Zone (Map 4)

Fishing has much potential but only if managed carefully, with local communities allowed to protect and manage their own stock[11]. By 2011, coastal fisheries had approached and in many cases exceeded the limits of sustainability for most species through overfishing and unrestricted fishing in nursery areas. However, the current war has led to a substantial reduction in fishing—the numerous fishing sites around Hodeida have all closed for example—and an immediate peace dividend can be expected. This sector needs to learn from the past and from experiences elsewhere to adopt more sustainable community-driven practices, especially for demersal fishing.

A number of low-cost technological innovations could help the sector. The introduction of Fish Aggregation Devices (FADs) and handheld GPS devices for instance, could provide more certainty to fishing sorties and reduce fuel-consuming fishing time. These devices transformed local fishing in Jela'a Bay in Shabwah, when introduced as part of the company's compensation scheme during the construction of the Balhaf LNG Terminal. There is considerable potential for high-value lobster and cuttlefish fishing[12], particularly in Hadhramaut and Al-Mahrah (see Map 3) and for shrimp off Hodeida if the latter waters can be reclaimed from the Egyptian vessels currently taking the bulk of this catch.

However, it is the offshore deep-water fisheries in the Gulf of Aden that have the most potential. Yemen's Exclusive Economic Zone (EEZ) covers a vast area which extends to the seas east and south of Soqotra. But a high proportion of the catch from this area now goes to foreign fisheries, especially Iranian gill-netters fishing illegally, but also French and Spanish boats. Yemen must urgently bring this under control and halt the devastating impact on valuable stocks to the point now where few tuna make it to full adulthood. The Great Whirl (see Map 4) combined with a northerly jet stream currently benefits Gulf of Aden fishing by bringing nutrients up from the deep, although its effects are very variable. In the longer-term climate change warming will negatively affect Yemeni fish stocks, but the expected northern movement of the Great Whirl may largely offset this.

Industrial Recovery and Expansion (Maps 2 & 3)

Yemen's indigenous industry has suffered badly during the war. In Ta'izz, Yemen's industrial centre, factories were initially hard hit and running at much reduced capacity. But once the fighting moved to city areas further west, production resumed, in some cases exceeding prewar levels, an indication of Yemeni adaptability in the face of war.[13] Other industrial centres have fared less well. Much Adeni industry was damaged at the beginning of the war and has not yet recovered. Generators for the Aden refinery are no longer functioning putting the whole facility out of action. In Hodeida, the cluster of factories in the eastern suburbs suffered extensive destruction in 2019.

A number of factors will support industrial recovery—the return of prewar demand levels as the humanitarian crisis subsides, an increased labor pool following the demobilization of militia, less punitive taxation, and, in the longer term the promise of cheap renewable energy (fuel represents a significant cost for Yemeni manufacturing), further opportunities for import substitution and market expansion into the Gulf and the Horn of Africa potentially based around the processing of Yemen's agricultural and natural resources[14]. Underlying this recovery will be a return of investor confidence (discussed below).

Ports and Trade (Maps 2 & 3)

Well-functioning ports have been crucial to addressing the war time humanitarian situation. This will continue in the post-conflict Yemen, which will still import some 90 percent of food staples. Over two-thirds of these imports enter through Hodeida and Salif, with Aden and Mukalla making up the bulk of the rest. Land routes from Saudi Arabia and Oman are relatively insignificant. Post war, regions without easy access to the sea will face particular challenges, and it will be essential to repair roads and bridges, while improving low-cost transport corridors from Yemen's ports into the hinterland.

Salif, with water depths of more than 20 metres in its approaches, could become a promising deep-water port. A container quay built on the south west side of Salif is likely to be an attractive investment. In contrast, deepening the 22 km long approach channel at Hodeida may prove prohibitively expensive. The revival of Aden port will be central to strengthening the economy of Yemen's south. However, Aden is one of the top 20 cities in the world facing major climate change-induced sea level rise and storm surges (Netherlands MoFA 2018), and this must be addressed in good time.

Minerals, Tourism, and Financial Technology (Maps 3 & 5)

Mineral exploitation is likely to be a vital sector in the long term, with the potential to offset Yemen's earlier dependence on its increasingly depleted hydrocarbon reserves. Discussions with senior mining executives with knowledge of Yemen indicate that Yemen holds much promise. Of the metals, gold, zinc, nickel, cobalt and copper were all being investigated in the prewar period and numerous other sites have been identified in Yemeni geological surveys (see Map 3). Industrial minerals can be exploited by smaller companies, with mining sites close to Yemen's main ports. Natural stone is already quarried in large quantities for the local market, and there is a major opportunity to produce for the growing international market (World Bank 2009). All this will require full collaboration with local tribes and long-term investment in extraction and transport infrastructure for which a peaceful stable Yemen is a precondition.[15].

For many decades, tourism and the closely related hospitality sector (comprising accommodation and restaurants) has been repeatedly judged a "promising sector," important in generating employment of guides, drivers and hotel and restaurant staff. Yemen is rich in architecture and archaeological heritage, and its mountains and deserts hold a unique beauty[16]. However, due to insecurity and lack of infrastructure the economic potential of tourism has never been realized, beyond limited niche "adventure tourism." Confidence will take time to return and will always be vulnerable to isolated violent incidents[17].

This sector is by no means limited to Western tourists, increasingly tourists come from Asia[18]. There is the longer-term possibility to link tourism with other sectors, for example with geothermal sites and highland agriculture. There is also considerable promise for Arab-world tourism, with specific interests in Yemen's important religious sites and numerous (but hitherto basic) hammams based around hot springs with curative properties. Internal travel and accommodation enabling medical visits to the cities with the necessary facilities is already an important market for city providers of accommodation.

Financial technology is another promising sector in Yemen. Emerging markets and countries with less established financial institutions have proved highly receptive. The widespread use of mobile banking in several African countries was driven by the demand for quick and less regulated solutions, especially where banks are crippled by financial crises and economic stagnation. In Somaliland, the Zaad mobile payments system has displaced the bulk of cash transactions, even for scarcely literate nomadic populations. The challenges facing traditional banks in Yemen, exacerbated by the division and relocation of the central bank, opens the door for this sector which could take off with the speed that social media have been adopted by Yemeni youth.

The Role of Business, International Aid and Civil Society in Yemen's Recovery

A Central Role for Yemeni Businesses Post-conflict

Yemen has a long history of entrepreneurialism dating from the early days of international trade from the Hadhramaut and later Aden, to East Africa and the Far East. A small number of highly effective Yemeni business groups have emerged with a range of international contacts particularly in neighbouring countries. Nevertheless, there are challenges. Under the Saleh system of patronage (Alley 2010), imports were controlled by state-issued import licenses given to members of the president's inner circle who sold them on to merchants for profit. This eroded the role and influence of official state institutions and damaged what had been a growing independent private sector, as merchants and business families became dependent on their alliances with Saleh's close circle. The result was reduced levels of investment and a move toward a rentier economy with oil wealth concentrated in the hands of the well-connected. While large sums of money were made, little was reinvested in Yemen (Salisbury 2015).

Nevertheless, a number of older and well-established businesses took a different approach, diversifying outside Yemen while continuing to invest in what they saw as their "home areas." These businesses often identified with particular cities. Indeed Ta'izz, Aden, Hodeida and Salif all have a single dominant business group, and this pattern reaches down even to smaller population centres like Yafa.[19]

Yemen's private sector will have a pivotal role to play in post-conflict economic recovery. Government institutions are likely to remain fragile for some considerable time and will require support to effectively deliver basic services and rebuild infrastructure. Yemen's established businesses are well placed to make major contributions to reconstruction efforts whether undertaken as sole ventures or through public private partnerships with donors. Foreign direct investment is unlikely to flow into the country in substantial amounts for some years as international investors will remain wary of instability, although for major projects international financial agencies can do much to reduce risk. Historically foreign investors have tended to follow the strategies of domestic investors and will invest when Yemeni entrepreneurs do and will seek partnerships with them.

The Yemeni private sector will thus have a particular responsibility to be at the forefront of the immense task of rebuilding the Yemeni economy. Investment in reconstruction is potentially highly attractive for Yemeni business with positive secondary benefits. Financing infrastructure, such as increasing the capacity of ports or rebuilding road networks, will have a long-term positive impact on the economy. New areas for investment in renewable energy and mobile banking could emerge as highly profitable as has been the case in numerous economically fragile contexts in Africa.

However, an enabling business environment will underpin the private sector's ability to deliver its full potential. A minimum level of security and judicial reform, ensuring the enforceability of contracts, for instance, will be required to provide necessary guarantees to external investors. Transparency and accountability are the best defence against government corruption at all levels. Such measures will also help create the conditions for a rise in entrepreneurship and SMEs across Yemen. For manufacturing, labor, energy, raw materials and water are judged (in that order) to be the most significant components of business costs[20]. Addressing the twin challenges of water and energy will thus be key to profitable business ahead.

International Aid After the War—Following Whose Agenda?

Yemen will need considerable international support to recover from its current low point. We have argued that the best scenario is an overview role for central government (or two if the south breaks away), with considerable authority resting in the regions, including potentially an ability to independently pursue bilateral relations with donors. There is much work to be done to reassure Yemen's centralist politicians that this would enhance rather than undermine security.

With peace, Yemen's economy will emerge from its existing dysfunctional "war economy." But it also needs to build on the important shift that has occurred from prewar centralization toward regions acting and using local resources independently.[21] Prewar problems in the relationship with donors must be addressed: ineffective practices, poor capacity of those in charge of absorption procedures, complex procedures and excessive bureaucracy (Executive Bureau 2015).

Gulf donors, who enjoy great wealth and influence in Yemen, will be critical to the future. It remains to be seen how this power asymmetry will play out in the post-conflict period. Across the Gulf of Aden, in the Horn of Africa, aid and know-how have been used to secure political alliances, playing a central role in intra-Gulf competition, both between Arab states, and wider rivalries with Iran and to a lesser extent Turkey (International Crisis Group 2019). Regional power struggles and the dissemination of imported ideologies are central to these donors' motivations, taking precedence over local development concerns.

At the same time, these regional actors, especially those nearest or bordering Yemen, have a mutual longer-term interest in a politically stable Yemen, with secure shipping lanes and effective cooperation against terrorism, piracy and the drugs trade. They seem ready to offer such support and to encourage their private sectors to invest but will want to see evidence that Yemenis are ready to reconcile their differences and build new governance arrangements[22]. Yemen's neighbours in practice have a vital interest in a well-functioning Yemen[23], with both national and regional authorities adequately resourced to deliver essential services of health, education and water provision, and with jobs available to lift Yemen's wider population out of extreme poverty. Historically disadvantaged regions, such as the Tihama and the far north, can no longer be ignored. It is here (and in the IDP camps) that poverty and ill health are most severe. Such measures are also crucial to prevent the revival of long-held grievances that play into the hands of terrorist groups.

International players and traditional donors with a less sectarian interest in Yemen need to ensure that post-conflict aid and investment into Yemen follows the over-riding principles outlined in this chapter: that the choice of priority projects reflects a commitment to Yemen as a whole and that all regions benefit from the recovery effort and are able to run viable sub-economies. Aid and investment based on the aspirations of Yemenis will go a long way to supporting a sustainable peace and the internal transfer of resources necessary for an efficiently functioning economy.

Civil Society Organizations, a Major Local Resource to Complement Local Government

CSOs have been playing an increasingly important role in Yemen. The first CSOs were established to do charitable work in the aftermath of the 1990 Iraqi occupation of Kuwait supporting the million Yemenis who had to leave their jobs and businesses in Saudi Arabia at short notice. In time the emphasis of CSOs shifted toward development work. In the period after 2005, CSOs started to appeal to Western funders, who had become disillusioned with the corruption of government and were attracted by a focus on mobilizing local communities, local engagement, human rights and women's empowerment. Some of the most respected of these CSOs, such as the Social Fund for Development (SFD) and its subsidiary the Small and Micro Enterprise Promotion Service (SMEPS), have grown into major organizations with active branches across Yemen, employing a well skilled and committed workforce.

The onset of the Arab Spring in 2011 gave a major impetus to this sector, with many new organizations springing up. By late 2013 there were over 8,000 registered CSOs[24] with a young and energetic leadership but needing to strengthen capacity and improve coordination (World Bank 2013). Since the start of the war, a lack of funds has seen the collapse of many organizations not aligned closely with specific political groups, and a growth in religiously affiliated groups funded by external powers. Nevertheless, considerable space still exists, even in areas where official mistrust is high. In Sana'a, for example, CSOs seen to be aligned with anti-Huthi sentiment have been closed, but those operating transparently and without a political affiliation are allowed to operate, albeit closely monitored and facing delays over project approval.

After the war and the relaxation of political tensions, this sector will find its operating space improved and have the opportunity to regain its essential role helping channel local energies, particularly of women and youth. In focusing on smaller community-level initiatives, it will complement the activities of larger business and aid-funded government projects which lack local contacts. But it will need support to build capacity from a low base.

A Longer-Term Perspective

Countering the Current Short-Termism

In the current war political leadership has prioritized the immediacy of battle and territorial control while ordinary Yemenis have focused on survival and coping strategies in this tough environment of food insecurity, displacement and loss of livelihood. Inevitably this means that a "scarcity mindset" of short-termism and firefighting dominates. Political and security issues need to be addressed before any longer-term plans can be implemented, although there is some scope for earlier action in areas of stability distant from the fighting. The fundamental prerequisites of successful development include property rights, government transparency and essential regulatory frameworks (Wittes 2020). But difficult though it is, consideration of the long term is more important than ever, with serious debate needed beyond the current dramas of Yemen. Opportunities come into focus and paths forward become clearer when illuminated by a vision and sense of purpose—even when faced with lack of data and the uncertainties of hard prediction.

Futures thinking offers a way to think about intractable and complex social challenges and provides insights into how best to navigate the uncertain path ahead. It is most powerful when a wide range of actors are involved—not just sectoral "experts," where academic silos can inhibit cross communication and the understanding of interdependencies—but voices bringing perspective from wider society and a consideration of the interests of future generations. Futures thinking has the potential to stretch thinking, shift mindsets, challenge assumptions, make unseen connections and imagine new possibilities rather than linear prediction (Shallowe 2020).

Many of the recent examples of successful futures planning have emerged from the most developed, better educated, industrialized societies, including some important examples from the Middle East[25]. Such thinking needs to be adapted to the distinct context of Yemen debilitated by war, with only a recent tradition of governmental planning and a heavy reliance on external aid professionals. Yemen also has had limited experience of formal engagement with stakeholders, but the NDC successfully involved representatives from across Yemen and covered a wide range of issues.

Megatrends and Discontinuities

The proliferation of "shocks" or crises with enduring impacts underlines the necessity for such a longer-term mindset. Just ten years ago, many of the central issues of today were not on Yemen's radar or were still only weak signals. Some, such as COVID-19, the overthrow of President Saleh and the flaring up of a nationwide civil war were "black swan" events—having major impacts but relatively unforeseen and only rationalized with the benefit of hindsight.

Many of these shocks have global origins but with far-reaching country-level implications. Climate change is already having major impacts on Yemen from cyclones, floods and droughts, while potentially offering opportunities for highland agriculture benefiting from wetter and warmer growing seasons. COVID-19 swept through Yemen's urban areas with little to curb it. The death toll was extensive until the virus peaked, although lack of data, limited health infrastructure and personnel, and a stigma associated with the illness have meant numbers are impossible to quantify with accuracy. The long-term impact on those infected but who survived is still largely unknown. In contrast, the massive impact of malnutrition on children's health and cognitive abilities is better understood—a major and little discussed long-term impact of the war.

Other shocks specific to Yemen have been well debated, including critically the urgent need for diversification to introduce new revenue streams and as a side-effect of the war economy, the removal of crippling subsidies. Yemen's economic fragility has been apparent for many years, albeit masked during periods of relatively stability, economic growth and (largely unrecorded) levels of remittances. But few foresaw the sheer magnitude of Yemen's recent wartime collapse. The long-term impact of an under-educated generation, due to wartime school closures from bombing of premises, unpaid teacher salaries, forced displacement and loss of livelihoods, will have immense implications. Yemen's water crisis, long foreseen, every year takes another turn for the worse, yet there is still no agreed strategy to address it. Likewise, more effective plans are needed to check Yemen's high population growth and its impact on limited resources.

Highlighting the Connections: Sectoral Interlinkages and Circular Economies

The extreme low point that the war has inflicted on Yemen's economy offers the opportunity for a different way forward, jettisoning the constraints of the past. Figure 10.1 highlights the way that developments in one Yemeni sector can influence others. The table also highlights areas of high job creation (a critical issue in the context of militia demobilization, high poverty levels and local grievances), and impacts on Yemen's macro-economy, specifically on the trade balance, and the potential for making use of local popular investment from remittances.

A number of the interlinkages shown in the table have been highlighted in this chapter. Yemeni manufacturing will benefit from cheaper and more reliable energy and water, opening opportunities for further import substitution and exports within Arabia and to the Horn of Africa, benefiting in turn Yemen's balance of payments. Renewable energy could drive cheaper desalination and lower water transfer costs, potentially offering a lifeline to the water-stressed cities of Sana´a and Ta´izz.

Furthermore, Yemen's future economy at local level can rebuild on "circular economy" principles, where waste from one production system is reused in another. Geothermal power production could be combined with rare mineral extraction and spa tourism based on a modern application of the traditional Arab *hammam*. The Blue Lagoon tourist resort in Iceland combined with the sale of spa

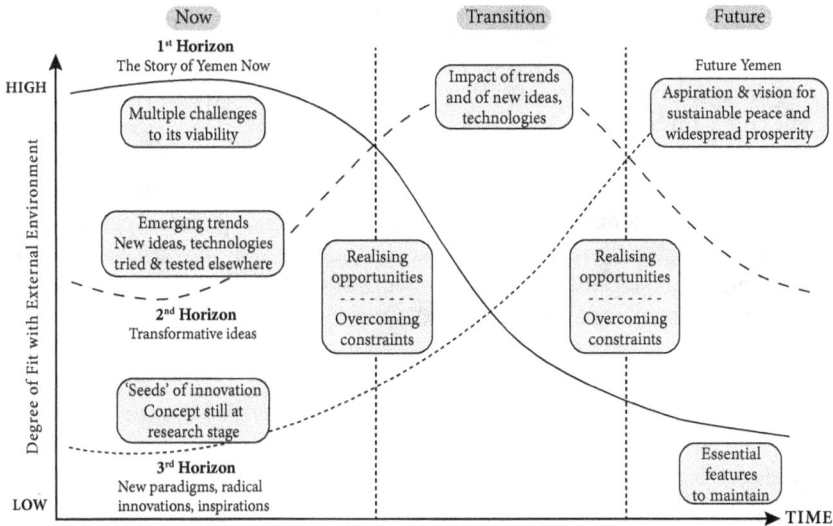

Figure 10.2 The Three Horizons model applied to Yemen. Adapted from "Three Horizons" thinking, first developed by the International Futures Forum (www. internationalfuturesforum.com/three-horizons).

health products and scarce mineral extraction from waste streams yields more income than the geothermal power station around which these side-industries are built[26]. Such a project would also ensure future usage of existing drilling and other equipment from the oil and gas sector, thereby guaranteeing a future for a raft of Yemeni service companies. Industrial parks, such as already effectively exist in the Howban area of Ta'izz, can build on the advantages of co-location of manufacturing and suppliers, creating economies of scale and skill hotspots.

Turning around Yemen's Economy, Realizing a More Prosperous Future

Yemen faces many constraints and barriers to change but also major opportunities. These can be seen on different timeframes with different degrees of certainty. The Three Horizons model seeks to capture these dimensions of change—see Figure 2. The first Horizon, what can be seen now, is "business as usual." The second Horizon brings in innovations and opportunities that are already advanced elsewhere.

Many of the ideas floated in this chapter sit on this second Horizon, as they have been "tried and tested" in other countries. One major opportunity is to promote a "green recovery," not because Yemen bears any significant responsibility for global climate change, but because such an approach leads to solutions better adapted for the future, while also attracting considerable external support, on which Yemen can capitalize. Ethiopia did so with great success after its own lengthy civil war in the 1980s, attracting substantial donor funds for green energy linked into an ambitious industrial strategy. This enabled it to achieve consistent growth rates of around 8 percent over two decades.

Nevertheless, the importance of the third Horizon, the less visible and even less certain emerging opportunities, must be emphasized. It creates an aspiration and a direction. The twenty-first century will not unfold as simply a linear progression of trends or build only on current technologies and innovations[27]. The impact of major disruptions must be considered, with some assessment as to where these might come from. This is important in generating greater preparedness and a more future-oriented mindset among all those able to influence the path forward for Yemen. Areas distantly visible on this third Horizon would include the use of Yemen's deserts for concentrated solar power; using crushed volcanic rock, plentiful in Yemen, on agricultural terraces, both to increase crop growth and remove atmospheric carbon (James 2020); and the use of fungi in the bioremediation and recycling of polluted water (Sheldrake 2020).

Integrating Longer-Term Thinking into Yemen Planning

There is an urgent need for more far sighted thinking to be applied to Yemen's situation. Future political arrangements will largely be determined by the outcome of the war and the details of the peace agreement reached, but there is great scope to rethink the economy on which long-term prosperity and political stability will depend.

Such longer-term thinking complements more traditional policy making and needs to be integrated into strategic planning and visioning for the future. This is currently coordinated centrally by Yemen's Ministry of Planning and International Cooperation (MOPIC), which should open a department focused on the longer term and tasked with extensive external dialogue. We have argued that local planning should be prioritized, and in all cases there must be an engagement with the perspectives of aid, business, and civil society. Looking ahead international aid is likely to face constraints as traditional donors in both the Gulf and the West, post-COVID, confront major financial challenges of their own. Business and civil society will play a more central role in Yemen's future, and both require conducive environments to thrive. Both also provide new opportunities to engage locally, especially with those hitherto more marginalized, including youth and women.

Conclusions

A major strand of Yemen's current conflict lies in deep-seated local grievances stemming from political and economic marginalization, underdevelopment, and lack of basic services of water provision, electricity, and health care. Well over half of Yemen's working age population is unemployed or has enrolled in military forces or militias to survive. Five years of war have destroyed much infrastructure, closed over a third of businesses and severely eroded irrigated agriculture and fisheries. Large parts of Yemen now face a high degree of political and economic fracturing. This is a radical change from the centralized politics and resource allocation of the prewar period.

It is unlikely that post-conflict Yemen will have a single dominant centre. Its future stability will depend as much on the fair distribution of economic benefits as on the political compromises between the multiple parties involved in the conflict. Yemen's regions will need increased capacity to manage services and attract investments, and this in turn will require ensuring adequate regional budgets and revenues. The key "Track 1" external players in the current drive for peace in Yemen, from the UN Special Envoy to well-placed diplomats, have to date paid insufficient attention to this sub-national dimension of Yemen's economy.

We have identified a number of opportunity sectors and have highlighted renewable energy, rain-fed agriculture, and fisheries as most worthy of support and investment. There are major challenges ahead, not least the impact of climate change, but well-managed these could be turned to advantage and yield significant benefits for employment and local prosperity. In emphasizing the opportunities and how these can mutually reinforce each other, we have highlighted a positive scenario for Yemen's long-term future. We have resisted the temptation to portray Yemen as a basket case of multiple crises, too problematic for anything but emergency aid. There is a sad dynamic at work here—international aid stresses economic fragility and vulnerability to attract funding, while business and enterprise require stability, manageable risk and less uncertainty to attract investment.

Yemen is increasingly being described in apocalyptic terms, as a "failed state" facing political, economic, and environmental collapse and massive food insecurity. But countries do recover from civil war, sometimes dramatically. Indeed, much needed changes are sometimes only possible under high pressure or when a major crisis has to be confronted. We have seen this nearby in both Ethiopia and Somaliland. Back in 1970, Yemen itself rebounded quickly from eight years of civil war.

While we have emphasized the centrality of employment, addressing water scarcity and low-cost energy sources will be equally important, and we have stressed the role of local businesses, large and small, in Yemen's recovery. We advise against an over-reliance on international aid which follows donors' priorities, political interests, and development "fashions," while often lacking the business discipline where the sustainability of an investment is hard-wired into the assessment of future returns. Import substitution businesses as well as a greater export orientation to Middle Eastern markets and the growing economies of the Horn and East Africa will provide major support to Yemen's national and regional economies. The opportunities ahead can be realized by both local manufacturing and agricultural ventures, from large enterprises down to family farms on a few terraces.

Oil and gas production is well past its peak in Yemen, but with new drilling and extraction technology gas could continue to provide significant revenues for some time. Minerals, increasingly in demand for the new technologies of the twenty-first century, such as in electric cars and mobile phones, may in time replace the dwindling hydrocarbon income stream. Remittances, although currently under threat, will remain important and could evolve from their current role of enabling family wartime survival toward providing investment for small ventures, whether for innovations in agriculture and fishing or the new opportunities of financial technology.

Profound changes will be needed to fully capitalize on the resourcefulness and entrepreneurialism that have characterized Yemenis throughout recorded history. Longer-term thinking is necessary to see the opportunities and threats ahead more clearly and to allow better, more far sighted decision-making. With these in place, Yemen's innovative culture and international outlook are well-positioned to attract both the local and international investment essential for a revitalized economy and deliver the promise of a transformed future for Yemen.

Notes

1   I am particularly grateful to Alia Eshaq for her analysis of regional revenues in Yemen and for her insights in looking beyond the present.
2   This chapter is a reduced version of an earlier text which also covered the details of Yemen's political fragmentation and the multiple constraints on Yemen's economy. Many of these issues are covered elsewhere in this publication and references are made at the appropriate points.
3   Migration levels are driven by fluctuating demand dependent on the oil price and on host government policies such as moves to indigenise the workforce.

4   Discussion with the officials at the Yemeni Ministry of Expatriates.

5   Geothermal will require either connection to a well-functioning grid or guaranteed demand locally.

6   This has been the case in other basins in decline such as the North Sea.

7   Chapter 9 gives details on the evolution of the sector.

8   See also data published by the ACLED *https://acleddata.com/tag/yemen/*

9   Much land was lost during the early phases of rural road construction due to poor construction techniques. RWHP can be retrofitted on such roads.

10 Discussions with Relief Society of Tigray and local development workers.

11 Discussions with Stephen Akester of MEP and others.

12 These will require efficient routes to foreign markets to achieve full potential.

13 Discussions with HSA Group senior management in December 2019.

14 A route taken by many African countries, with Ghana and Ethiopia standing out as successful examples.

15 Discussions with former Minister for Oil and Minerals, and with mining company executives

16 Jordan, Ethiopia, and Nepal are examples of poorer countries that have successfully built this sector from low beginnings.

17 Both Rwanda and Ethiopia have built major tourism sectors following their respective civil wars. The sector in Egypt has been vulnerable to terrorist attacks but has always bounced back.

18 Discussions Cushman and Wakefield, Hospitality Consultants, in February 2019.

19 Discussion with range of Yemeni business groups 2018–20, including on investment criteria.

20 Discussions with HSA senior management in 2012–14.

21 Discussions with former senior officials in Ministry of Planning.

22 Discussions with senior Saudis working on Yemen relations in 2019.

23 Many Yemenis believe that Saudi Arabia wishes to keep Yemen in a state of dependent poverty or will only assist to exert influence. The reality is more nuanced. The repercussions on Saudi Arabia from the impoverishment of Yemen during the current war is likely to lead to a revised strategy.

24 This figure excludes the purely humanitarian CSOs.

25 The UAE has a "Ministry of Possibilities" and has founded both a "Future Energy Lab" and a "Museum of the Future," while Saudi Arabia's "Vision 2030" drives its economic diversification agenda. But it must be stressed the context here is hugely different from that of the Yemen.

26 See www.resourcepark.is

27 Nevertheless, longer-term thinking is often resisted even in stable conditions. Politicians, civil servants and businesspeople tend to be comfortable in Horizon 1, entrepreneurs in Horizon 2 and visionaries in Horizon 3, but they all have their part to play, with a vision of longer-term possibilities driving short term actions.

28 This map shows key locations for current Yemen economic activity (early 2021), including all-important food-import ports and key processing sites. Many assets have been closed or severely damaged by the war—airports and ports, factories, refineries, and cement plants (shown by an X), while there have been new developments in response to changing areas of control, such as new pipelines, oil terminals, and fuel imports points. The map also shows other elements of the war economy such as smuggling routes on the southeast coast. Agriculture, fisheries, and the hospitality sector are not shown here, but are covered in Maps 4 and 5.

29   This map shows a range of pointers for the future, in the renewable energy sector
     (including the considerable geothermal potential) with associated desalination and
     industrial clusters, port development, fish processing, minerals, and quarrying.
     Mineral deposits have been progressed commercially in only a few cases, shown here
     as "mines evaluated," but there are many other sites identified by Yemen's Geological
     Survey including for nickel, cobalt, titanium, copper, zinc, gold, rare earth elements,
     and lithium (potentially from salt flats). All these are important for the emerging
     technologies of electric cars and electronic devices. Opportunities in agriculture,
     fishing, and hospitality are covered in Maps 4 and 5.
30   Rain-fed agriculture in the highlands (shown here) has long been neglected in favour
     of irrigated farming, now facing constraints due to over-pumping. Highland terraces,
     many now abandoned, can benefit from new varieties suited to the changing climate
     and from new techniques to strengthen the stone wall terraces and capture water
     run-off from roads. This will be a key area for the employment of demobilized militia.
     The map also shows traditional crops (from coffee to honey) whose economics can
     be much improved with more effective international marketing. Fishing is well
     distributed along both the Gulf of Aden and the Red Sea. There is much potential
     to reclaim the lucrative tuna and shrimp fishing from foreign vessels. More effective
     marketing and cold chains can deliver the high-value exports of lobster and cuttlefish.
31   This is an important sector for Yemen given its wide potential for job-creation
     including outside Yemen's main cities—generating jobs in construction, hotels and
     restaurants, and as drivers and guides. Currently the accommodation sector is dominated
     by travellers into the major cities for visits to hospitals and administrative offices.
     Both domestic and international tourism has been limited by lack of infrastructure
     and security. In the shorter-term Yemen's range of sites from ancient mosques dating
     from the dawn of Islam to steam baths with curative properties will appeal to Arab
     visitors. In the longer-term, locations of interest to Western and increasingly Asian
     visitors include Yemen's many outstanding sites of ancient civilizations and its unique
     architecture, but also its landscapes and nature reserves.

References

Alley, A. (2010), "The Rules of the Game: Unpacking Patronage Politics in Yemen," *Middle
     East Journal* 64(3): pp. 385–409.
Baron, A. (2018), *The Marib Paradox: how one province succeeds in the midst of Yemen's
     war*, London: European Council for Foreign Relations.
Berghof Foundation (2018), *Local Governance in Yemen: Challenges and Opportunities*,
     Berlin.
Executive Bureau (2015), for the Acceleration of Aid Absorption, Report Jan 2014 to Jan
     2015, Republic of Yemen Executive Bureau, Sana'a
Firebrace, J. (2015), "Yemen Urban Water: Extreme Challenges, Practical Solutions in
     N. Brehony and Alsarhan S," in *Rebuilding Yemen, Political, Economic and Social
     Challenges*, 123–48, Berlin, Gerlach Press
Gebru, K. et al (2020), "Adoption of Road Water Harvesting Practices and Their Impacts:
     Evidence from a Semi-Arid Region of Ethiopia," *Sustainability* 12(8914): 1–25.
Handley, C. (2001), *Water Stress, Some Symptoms and Causes; a Case Study of Ta'izz*,
     London: SOAS.

International Crisis Group (2019), *Intra-Gulf Competition in Africa's Horn: lessening the impact*, Washington. Available online: Intra-Gulf Competition in Africa's Horn: Lessening the Impact (d2071andvip0wj.cloudfront.net (accessed January 29, 2021).

James, R. (2020), *Presentation to the Royal Geographic Society on Negative Carbon Emissions*, University of Southampton.

Kendall, E. (2018), "The Mobilisation of Yemen's Eastern Tribes: Al-Mahra's Self-organisation Model," in Marie Christine Heinze (ed.), *Yemen and the Search for Stability; Power, Politics and the Search for Stability after the Arab Spring*, 71–92, London and New York: IB Tauris.

McKinsey Global Institute (2020), *Climate Risk and Response; Physical Hazards and Socioeconomic Impacts.* Available online: Climate risk and response: Physical hazards and socioeconomic impacts (mckinsey.com) (January 29, 2021).

Minissale, A. et al. (2006), "Thermal Springs, Fumaroles and Gas Vents of Continental Yemen," *Applied Geochemistry* 22: 799–820.

Mulugeta, G. (2019), *Transitions from War to Peace*, Massachusetts: World Peace Foundation.

Mundy, M. (2017), *The war on Yemen and its Agricultural Sector*, Institute of Social Studies. Available online: Empire of Information: The War on Yemen and its Agricultural Sector | Middle East Centre (accessed on January 29, 2021).

Netherlands Ministry of Foreign Affairs (2018), *Climate Change Profile for Yemen.* Available online: Yemen (4).pdf (accessed 29/ January 2021).

Nevola, L. (2019), *From Periphery to Core: a Social Network Analysis of the Huthi Local Governance System*, University of Sussex Conference paper.

Nevola, L. (2020), *Huthis in the Making: Nostalgia, Populism and the Pollicisation of Hashemite Descent*, Unpublished paper

Nir, S. 2019, "Millennials make farming sexy in Africa, where tilling the soil once meant shame," *New York Times*, May 2019. Available online: "Millennials 'Make Farming Sexy' in Africa, Where Tilling the Soil Once Meant Shame"—*The New York Times* (nytimes.com) (accessed January 29, 2021).

Okruhlik, G. and P. Conge (1997), "National Autonomy, Labor Migration and Political Crisis: Yemen and Saudi Arabia." *Middle East Journal*, 51(4): 554–65.

Ralby, R. et al (2019), *Onboard the FSO Safer: A Preview*, Washington DC: Atlantic Council.

Salisbury, P. et al. (2015), *Yemen: Corruption, Capital Flight and Global Drivers of Conflict*, London: Chatham House.

Shallowe, A. et al. (2020), *A Stitch in Time? Realising the Value of Futures and Foresight*, London: Royal Society of Arts, Manufacture and Commerce.

Sheldrake, M. (2020), *Entangled Life: How Fungi Make Our Worlds, Change Our Minds and Shape Our Futures*, London: Vintage.

UNPoE, Yemen Report (2021), United Nations Security Council, Document S/2021/79, January 22, 2021.

UNHCR (2020), "Updates on Yemen's Humanitarian Crisis." Available online: Yemen | Global Focus (unhcr.org) (accessed January 29, 2021).

USAID (2016), *Yemen Climate Change Risk Profile*, USAID.

Varisco, D. (2019), Pumping Yemen Dry: A History of Yemen's Water Crisis, *Human Ecology* 47: 317–29.

Ward, C. (2015), *The Water Crisis in Yemen, Managing Extreme Water Scarcity in the Middle East*, New York: IB Tauris.

Wittes, T. et al. (2020), *Stabilization and Human Development in a Disordered Middle East and North Africa*, Brookings. Available on line: https://www.brookings.edu/research/stabilization-and-development-in-a-disordered-middle-east-and-north-africa/ (accessed 20 March, 2021).

World Bank (2009), *Mineral Sector Review*, June 2009. Available on line: documents1.worldbank.org/curated/en/303111468183283295/pdf/479850ESW0YE0P1C0Disclosed061251091.pdf (accessed January 29, 2021).

World Bank (2013), *Yemen Civil Society Organisations in Transition*, June 2013. Available online: World Bank Document (accessed January 29, 2021).

YLNG (2005), *Overview of the Balhaf LNG Project*, Sana´a, Yemen Liquefied Natural Gas Company.

INDEX